I AM
THE BODY, THE MIND
AND
THE SOUL

SAMI S. JARROUSH

authorHOUSE

AuthorHouse™
1663 Liberty Drive
Bloomington, IN 47403
www.authorhouse.com
Phone: 833-262-8899

Published by AuthorHouse 10/13/2021

ISBN: 978-1-6655-4130-5 (sc)
ISBN: 978-1-6655-4135-0 (e)

Library of Congress Control Number: 2021921360

Print information available on the last page.

DEDICATION

I dedicate this book to Agnes Jarroush who is my soul mate, my wife and my best friend in this world. Since the day I met Agnes, she has stood by me and supported me without question. We continue to fly together from one cloud to another, through the sun and the rain, in the light of day and in the darkness of night. Thank you, Agnes, for all your help which made it possible for this book to see the light.

CONTENTS

ACKNOWLEDGEMENTS

A big thank you to my two sons, George and Joey, and to my beautiful daughter, Maia, for the effort they put into accepting the new me. Life is always beautiful and you three are the best gift that this life has given me. I also thank my brother, Suhail, who taught me Reiki, through which I found the real Me.

INTRODUCTION

I am writing this book, but I am not the author. This book was narrated to me by James, my guardian angel. Since the year 2008, I have been having a continuous dialogue with my soul guide, James, whose presence I am now aware of every second of my life. James and I are in continuous conversation about every subject under the sun; from heaven to hell, from death to living. Do not be overwhelmed by this. I am an ordinary person like you.

Like everyone else, in my life I had my ups and downs and my share of winning and losing. I had many good experiences and many bad ones. I have known happiness and I have known confusion. I have been a source of happiness for some people and I have also terrified more than a few. I judged and blamed others for my bad experiences and took credit for the good ones; at the same time, others judged and blamed me for occurrences in their lives, if I was at fault or not. This routine led me to feel stressed and lost. My solution at that time was to seek help from doctors who prescribed pain and stress medications. Life went on and I remained in misery.

During all this chaos, I walked through the door of my brother's healing and learning center. This is where my journey to self–awareness began. I attended two of his self–awareness classes which started to change the way I looked at life, although I was still in a state of fear and confusion most of the time. Two years later, an angel walked through the same door. She needed help too. This person who I called an angel, I later discovered, is actually my soul mate. Since we met, she has had a huge effect on the direction that my life has taken. As we learned and grew through our dear friendship, my awareness of Who I Am started to grow.

I have come to understand that many incidents and experiences that happened to me and those that continue to take place since I met Agnes, depended on, and still depend on her presence in my life. As a matter of fact, our souls continue to travel together to many places around the world and far out into the universe for knowledge and experience. Some people call this kind of travel out–of–body experiences…well, yes.

At the same time, a light of great hope appeared unexpectedly through the face of my guide, James. He appeared to me one day as I was looking in the mirror, washing my hands in the men's room of a local restaurant. I could not believe my eyes! There I was taking care of business and this handsome older man with soft white hair and a trim white beard, wearing a white flowing robe, was standing next to me. I have to say this was one of the scariest moments of my life. I quickly left the men's room and went back to the table where my brother and my soul mate were sitting. I tried to act normal but James was now sitting with us at the table! I told them about what I was seeing, and my brother simply told me, "Why don't you talk to him?" There and then and to my greatest joy, I discovered myself. James became the mirror through which I could understand me. He is always with me, leading me on my path to freedom and awareness; that path which is taking me to my higher self – the place of total awareness where fear, blame and judgment do not exist.

This brings me to the main reasons why I am writing this book about my journey to self–awareness. First, it is to tell every human being who reads it that life on Earth is always beautiful and it is up to each one of us to accept or reject this beauty. We all have the great gift of free will, and it is up to each one of us to choose to make our life a happy one or a miserable one.

The second intention of this book is to help people understand that death on Earth is an illusion. Life has no end. Really! While there is physical death, the honest truth is there is no real death in our universe. Death, as it has been explained to us throughout our lives, does not exist. It is not a horrible event as it has been described through the ages. Death is simply total freedom from the weight of the physical. Death is going back to where we were before being born. In simple terms, the physical body dies but the soul comes back in a new physical body to finish its mission; and this happens again and again.

In this book, through my dialogues with James, you will read about what Spirit is, what a soul is and especially who and what a soul mate is. We will also discuss metaphysical entities and angels that exist in this universe. We will answer essential questions that have been asked since the beginning of time. Where does a human come from? What is the reason for humans on Earth? But, the heart of this book is to answer the most important question humans ask which is: what is death really all about?

It is my hope that anyone who reads this book will have answers to many unknown questions. These answers will be different from the answers that your guesses, beliefs and traditions usually provide for you; now you will have more choices to consider. It is my hope that every reader will find peace in knowing the beauty of our journey on Earth… and of our death.

The format is written true to the way I received the information through my constant communication with James. I asked questions and

James answered me. We spent days and nights discussing many subjects. I was given a lot of information that I needed to learn. This information was the tool that would open my eyes to see the beauty of my earthly journey without fear, blame or judgment in my life anymore. In fact, my friends, James and I are still together and we will stay together until the end of my current life and my future lifetimes on Earth. My dialogue with James continues, twenty–four hours a day, seven days a week. I still ask questions and he still answers me. He even teaches me through my dreams when my physical body is asleep at night.

For now, James and I chose the best words – words that are full of wisdom – to create a book that we hope will be helpful to every human that chooses to hold it and read it. This book is meant to communicate to the readers the way *I* now understand life and death. I believe that I have finally found the God that is within me. This is a very humbling discovery of hope and infinite love. I have found my way. For me, this is the right way. This is the way I see life and the way I believe life should be. This is why my soul mate and I decided to open a Reiki healing center to help others understand the power that is within them to heal their lives.

Many people will believe in what I say and many will disagree. But, as James always whispers in my ears, "In this life on this Earth, there is no right and there is no wrong. There is just belief and faith; and whatever you believe in and whatever your faith tells you, will always be the right way for you."

So, dear friends, enjoy the glory of the words in this book and let James be your guide too. I assure you that you have not taken this book in your hands by accident.

FOREWORD

I am Agnes, Sami's soul mate. Our journey together began with a dear friendship that led to partnership and then marriage. I give my deepest gratitude to Life for this beautiful gift.

The first day I met Sami, we were both at a Reiki Share event at the center where I was enrolled in a self–awareness class that taught me Reiki energy healing. This was a monthly event where people came together at the center to give and receive Reiki. At the time, Sami was somewhat involved in marketing at the center, but I had never met him before. On this particular evening, I showed up for Reiki Share feeling excited to practice and receive Reiki. It was customary at the end of a Reiki Share event for Reiki practitioners to offer Reiki to each other. So at the end of the evening, I went over to the left side of the room where I saw Sami lying down on one of the Reiki tables waiting for his turn. I walked over to him and put my hands on his head to start the Reiki session. I moved my hands over his third eye and throat chakras and then I put my hands on his heart. As I lay my hands on his heart, I was stunned by the tears that flooded my eyes and rolled down my cheeks. I asked him, "Why am I crying over your heart?!" He did not have an answer for me. No one did. All I knew was that I felt a strange closeness to this man that I had just met and I could not understand why. I felt the strangest and most beautiful feeling of closeness and oneness that I had ever experienced. I felt like I had reconnected with the oldest and dearest friend I had ever known. I felt confused but elated.

Very soon after our meeting, Sami and I began working together at the center and our friendship grew and grew. We became inseparable. We both confided in each other our deepest pain, our most hopeful dreams, and our greatest desires for a truly happy life. We knew more about each other in the first week of our meeting than most people know about another person in a lifetime. There was absolute freedom between us! No judgment, no holding our tongues, no obligation to satisfy the other.

When Sami started hearing and seeing James, we learned that Sami and I are soul mates. Our souls had planned to meet in this lifetime to help each other finish experiences in our present earthly journey. We also came to know that our souls have met many times before in previous earthly journeys. All of this made perfect sense! We've actually known each other for ages and ages, and that's exactly how we felt!

As Sami began writing what James was telling him, he shared all of it with me. He told me that he will be sharing his dialogues with James with the world by writing a book, and that this book would help many people to understand the reason for their earthly existence and their physical death. I agreed to hold his hand, walk beside him and help him in any way I could. At that time, I had no idea how my involvement would change my life.

Helping Sami with this book has been an extraordinary experience for me personally, as I learned to open my heart to hear James' words and my own voice of wisdom. "Am I going crazy?" was a question that Sami asked me many times as we experienced the love and wisdom of his guardian angel who continues to speak to, and through, Sami every day. I often teased him and answered, "yes". We laughed and cried and learned to truly love ourselves, as we continued to hear beautiful words of love and wisdom from James.

We went through many experiences together that have shown us the beauty of life. We know that "Sami" and "Agnes" are simply shells that our souls are using this time around. This knowledge, by itself, is tremendously liberating. We are enjoying every day, having fun while "adding more and more knowledge and wisdom in the bank, to let us control these humans that our souls are residing in for now." These wise words are not my own. James used these words one of the many times that he spoke to me, through Sami, about how I have the power and the gift to control my Subconscious; and being so, happiness is my choice. Astounding epiphany! Keep reading.

Chapter 1

LIFE

Tell me a little bit about life on Earth. Also, is it possible that there is life somewhere else on other planets?

Life started billions and billions of years ago in this universe. Life has always been, and it will exist for eternity. There were many planets that once existed that had life, but no longer exist due to geologic/energy effects. They are gone, but new life is here.

Every life entity on any planet that exists now or has ever existed has a soul. All these souls belong to the same Source, but a soul that lives on one planet will not live on any other. The body, or shell, that a soul occupies in a lifetime will live for its purpose and it will die when its time comes. The same soul will come back again and again to experience life in a new shell, or body, only on the same planet. When the soul is done experiencing, it will have mastered itself; then it will become united with Source, for Source to gain all the wisdom that it was looking for through that soul.

For now, let me tell you a little bit about the planet Earth. Earth was a hot rock planet that cooled down with the passing of billions of years. The atmosphere was created by a combination of natural gases produced by the vapor of boiling rocks combining with oxygen. Earth used to be covered with boiling water and over many, many years it started to cool. The water created steam that turned into rain. The rain that fell formed boiling seas above cooling crystal rocks. Large comets then hit Earth and made it boil again. With the boiling of Earth, volcanoes were formed and erupted, which formed mountains and valleys. Over time, Earth cooled. This process created microbes that created more oxygen, changing the atmosphere of the planet. Then it was easy for more life to exist on Earth.

Soon after land was formed, life began when energy sparked chemical reactions that created DNA. Through this DNA, life began to exist on Earth. The residue that comets left behind mixed with water and became the soil that supported this new life. On land, first there were small plants then trees. The roots of all these plants and trees helped to condense the soil. Very soon, plant–eating animals from the sea began to live on land and in fresh water. These animals began adapting to life in water and on land. The bones of land animals hardened over time, so these animals became bigger and bigger. With more microbes and bacteria forming all the time, more and more oxygen was created, which allowed for oxygen–breathing life to take root on Earth. Eventually, humans inhabited Earth.

Life itself is a very complicated subject so I gave you a general idea. Many assumptions were made and stories told about the creation of life on Earth, which became legends that humans believed. The important thing to understand is that life is here to stay and souls will continue to reside in humans on Earth.

Chapter 2

SOULS AND SOUL MATES

James looked at me with a smile on his face and said:

Let me show you a nice way to start writing your book. This might be the best way to include all that we have talked about during the past year, so that the readers of your book will know what the soul is and what a soul mate is. First, we will talk about what a soul is, then soul mates. When readers follow all that is written they will understand that soul mates play a big role in a human's day–to–day life on Earth. This will help your readers understand how this book is going to give them the help and knowledge they have been seeking. Later on, we will discuss the soul some more, but it is important that we introduce the reader to some facts about it now.

The soul is a flicker of brightness like what a human observes out of the corner of his eye on occasion. Spirit or Source, which is also called God, is the energy that created the world; the soul is a part of Spirit. Spirit and the soul are the same, where the soul is a very small fraction of Spirit. Spirit's desire is to experience its absolute knowledge through the soul. Spirit condenses all the wisdom that is gained from all experiences that the soul goes through when it experiences in the form of a human body. When the soul finishes its job on Earth, it will go back to its Source. Spirit will send the same soul or a part of that soul back again, to reside in a physical body from birth, to get more information and knowledge through experiencing again. All souls come from the same Source.

Now let's talk about soul mates. The important thing for a human to understand is that there is such a thing as soul mates. Basically, soul mates are humans who have had experiences with each other, sharing the good and the bad in a past lifetime, who have come back together again to help each other through a new experience. It makes no difference if a human discovers or recognizes his or her soul mate or not. A soul mate will play an important role in that human's life either way. Most of what you and I discuss on a daily basis, most of the experiences that have happened to you lately and most of what is written in this book involves experiences you had with your soul mate – no matter how rough or smooth they were.

A soul mate could be a human that lives with you, or not; someone who is in your life for a short time or a long time, depending on the need of the experience. Soul mates could also be a part of the same soul inhabiting different humans in the same lifetime. The second they meet or glance at each other, soul mates will locate, link, and click very easily with each other. Soul mates are attracted to each other through their feelings that can include love, sexual attraction, spiritual connection or all their opposites. The important thing to understand is that soul mates may experience a variety of different relationships without any sexual or romantic love.

A soul mate could be a spouse or any family member, a friend that is already in a human's life, or someone he has yet to meet. Soul mates could be of the same or opposite sex and their relationship has nothing to do with the gender or relationship that they had in a different lifetime. They might both accept every part of the other's personality and feel at ease dealing with each other; or they might hate each other and interact with each other only to give the other a hard time and agony. A soul mate can bring out the best or the worst in the other human, keeping in mind that the purpose of a soul mate is to teach a spiritual lesson. A soul mate exists to provide you with an experience, so that you can find the best *you* in that experience.

A soul mate makes existence come to life. A soul mate is that other human that is trusted and loved or resented and despised, according to the result of the experience. Remember what we said before: a soul mate can bring out the greatest part or the most awful in the other human; it always depends on the experience that the human is going through.

Very often, when a human meets and gets very close to his soul mate, he tries very hard to hold on to this person. He feels that his life is now beautiful only because his soul mate exists in it. This human must balance his need with his wisdom for the soul mate experience to accomplish its purpose. The wiser he becomes and the more experiences he finishes with the help of his soul mate, the more he will realize that life is even more beautiful when he depends on and believes in himself first. He will then be able to continue to experience with the help of his soul mate but without being dependent on that human. He will understand the message that he can do miracles on his own if he has faith and believes that he can. He will drop his dependency without dropping the beautiful friendship between them. He will then go through a lot of experiences using the help of his soul mate, but now he will be depending only on himself and his beliefs to get him through it.

You and your soul mate both felt like you knew each other for ages and ages, ever since the first flicker of light in this universe. The relationship between your soul mate and you became stronger by the day when you started to work together and understand each other. In this life, the more soul mates get to know each other and the closer they become, the more they find the power that unites them. Your soul mate is a big reason why you changed your life, and she will continue to have an important effect on the way you are going to run your life from now on.

When soul mates love themselves, they will love each other, and they will know how to help each other. Love is *pure* love when two soul mates can connect with each other in a lifetime without wanting or needing anything from each other. I want you to always remember these words: love is not love, and it could not be taken for real and felt, until it becomes pure love. Pure love starts by loving you, and soul mates will help each other to learn how to love themselves. When they have the knowledge of helping and loving themselves and each other, then they can love and help the world without obligations or reservations, which is what you and your soul mate are doing.

A human can live his lifetime asking and wondering who his soul mate is, and even though he may be living in the consciousness of pure love, he might not determine who this other human is. But there are times when it comes on a golden platter without asking or wondering, as it happened with you. In this case, the humans feel purity in the heart, which leads them to act as it was planned by their souls. When their soul mate experience for a lifetime is over and they both leave through physical death, they will not have to find each other anymore because both souls are parts of the same energy we label Spirit.

Is it possible for a soul to exchange physical bodies?

When a soul decides to occupy a human body, it will occupy one human body at a time. It will plan and create the body that it wants to experience in for that lifetime. Now pay attention. The only time there could be an exchange of souls is while the fetus is still in the womb. There are times when a fetus dies inside the womb and there will be another soul waiting to take over that fetus – but this does not always happen. It will occur only when the first soul planned for an experience inside the womb only and then exits the experience; and when the second soul planned for a shorter time in the womb and then a birth and full human experience to follow. It is very important to understand that this kind of body exchange does not happen between souls after physical birth occurs. It all depends on what the souls planned on before they decided to occupy a fetus or a human body. Again, the human body is the shell for one soul, and only that one soul. Two souls cannot occupy the same human body.

When the body dies, the soul leaves and goes back to Spirit where it will start planning and selecting a new fetus and a new human body to come back with. The soul will come back again to experience with other souls that are also part of Spirit. All these souls will reside in different humans to help the main soul finish its experience the right way. Keep in mind that the other souls are also finishing their experiences through the help of the main soul. This happens because the soul still needs to finish all kinds of experiences that it had planned but were not finished yet. It needs to go through them so it could gain knowledge and wisdom from them.

All souls have a path that they follow attempting to start from a physical body; but the soul is not ruled by the body. The soul is free in where and how it experiences. The object of the soul controlling a physical body is to experience through it; and then to find its way back to Spirit after it is satisfied with what it accomplished; and to become one with Spirit again.

What is the best way to take care of my soul? Is there a special procedure to follow?

The most common challenge for a human is to connect with his higher self, or his soul. When a human is aware of his connection with his soul he could master himself very easily. Let me say it this way: you already know that for a human body to grow, it has to eat and drink; for the mind to grow, a human has to nourish it with the special exercise of continuously providing it with information. For the soul to grow, it also needs to be fed. Very often the soul is deserted and neglected. When a human neglects to take care of his soul, he puts himself in a loop that will keep him away from being happy and purified.

If a human knows and understands that the soul comes from Spirit and that it comes to Earth to experience for knowledge, then he should also know that the soul chooses what life method it wants to run. It will decide if it wants to be poor or rich, healthy or handicapped, male or female, and so on. It will also decide when to start this life and when to end it. The soul matures as the human grows through experiencing. This means that the human will grow in wisdom as he achieves completion through the experiences he goes through. Achieving completion depends on the methods that the human uses to handle his experiences, as well as the enjoyment that he accomplishes in his life. The human's completion comes from happiness and love. The soul's completion comes from *all* experiences – it does not matter if they are good or bad, as long as the human learned and gained knowledge from them.

Sometimes the experience will be very pleasant and it will pass without any complications, and the human will gain a lot from it. Other times, the experience will be very tough and the human will pray for it to pass quickly and finish. But I tell you, good ones and bad ones, are all needed for wisdom to be gained. Nothing improves the soul's completion more than gaining knowledge from a bad experience. A human needs to learn to forgive himself and others, and not to blame or judge himself or others when a bad experience happens, knowing that it was meant and planned to happen.

An important factor for the soul's growth is for the human to never desire what he does not have. Material things are good for the ego but they are the worst enemy of the soul. So when a human starts loving and attaching himself to the material things of this Earth and if he becomes a slave for the material and nothing else, he will never find satisfaction. He will have everything he needs, desires and wants but he will still be dissatisfied with his life. What he will be missing is the satisfaction of the soul, because loving earthly things will take him away from what his soul planned on doing. Instead, he should be thankful and appreciate everything that he has, and he should live with the belief that his stay on this Earth is temporary and it is for the purpose of gaining knowledge.

This knowledge of life is earned by experiencing other people and by experiencing different situations. Knowledge will feed the soul and the soul will then finish more of these experiences using the knowledge it gained from previous ones. Unless a human understands the real purpose of his creation, he will always be afraid to create new things. He will be afraid that he might be re–creating a physically or mentally painful experience similar to a past experience he had; this assumption will lead him to do his best to try to avoid that pain, which will stifle his progress.

Sometimes this human will have the courage to go through the same experience again but he will start looking for help from other people, especially if he has a best friend he can rely on. Humans meet other humans for a reason in this life; mostly so they could assist each other through hard times. But, this kind of help does not only come from a best friend. It could even come from a stranger. The help could be spiritual, emotional, mental or physical. It could be that after this help is given, these humans will disappear from each other's lives. This disappearance will be what was planned by the souls before they came to reside in human bodies. They had decided to help each other in the coming life in a specific way. This help could come for a few seconds, a few years or even a lifetime. They will stay in each other's lives for as long as they are needed to push each other to accomplish what they needed each other for.

Always remember, every human will give help and advice according to his *own* understanding of the problem that the other human is experiencing, according to the experiences that *he* went through in his own life, not from the other human's perspective – and this is exactly how it was planned!

In this life, a human should always look for answers so that he can keep moving forward towards his soul's satisfaction. He should know that whatever is considered a problem is something that the human asked to experience. Life is full of tests and surprises only for the soul to learn and gain more knowledge. Sometimes humans try to ignore a problem and do their best not to deal with it. If they succeed in ignoring the problem, their soul will try again in a different lifetime in a different human, to experience what this human did not finish.

To take care of his soul, a human has to heal himself first. He has to clear himself from all his pain, free himself from any stress, get rid of heavy loads from his shoulders – which he has created – and always be happy in whatever he is doing. He can start doing this by searching his Subconscious for a happy time or event from his past and concentrating on the feeling he had then. This simple exercise will make him happy and worry–free most of the time. If the human chooses to go the opposite way choosing to only live his life according to the negative fear–based data in his Subconscious, he will then accept his misery and believe that this is the way his life should run. Believe me when I tell you that the second a human changes the data he is living by, and the second he can make himself believe in what his heart is telling him, all his worries will vanish. This is the only way he can be a happy human. When he reaches this stage of happiness, the better the soul will deal with the way it planned its experiences in this lifetime.

I tell you, the best therapy for the mind is to connect to the soul. To do this is very easy if a human can feel unconditional love for himself, unconditional kindness toward others, and have this same belief toward all forms of earthly creation. This will keep a human in a higher spiritual stage all the time, where meditation will no longer be a must because he will be living in that calmness.

Now remember, most humans cannot reach that stage unless they meditate, so they should. It is best to meditate next to running water, like on the edge of a river or a stream or by the seashore. The sound of the water will let a human calm his mind so that images and visions with the answers he is seeking will come to mind much easier. Another good way to calm the mind is to focus on only one thing, which will clear the mind of everything except the object of focus. While doing this, the human should control his breathing by inhaling very slowly, pausing his breath for a few seconds, and then exhaling very slowly. This routine should be repeated until the mind is clear of all distracting activity. This is when beautiful answers and solutions will be heard.

Humans generally do not realize the power that is within them that lets them create alone, or co–create with other humans. This lack of faith leads a human to judge other humans' creations if they do not match his own beliefs. Let me tell you, when a human can create without judging and blaming himself for the result of his own creation, he will be able to stop himself from criticizing others. He will then believe that every creation and experience is always perfect because everything occurs as it was planned. This will put him in a higher stage of consciousness where he will be powerful enough to master himself. He will believe that everything that happens is valuable, whatever the experience is and no matter the result that comes out of that experience.

Again, always keep in mind that every human on Earth has soul mates to help him go through and finish his experience creations with. When two humans feel very close to each other, they are attracted to each other on the same level to work on a certain experience together. They each play a part in the other soul's experience. This will benefit all souls involved. It could be one or one–hundred soul mates; the number does not matter. These soul mates could live in the same neighborhood or in different countries. Take you and your soul mate as an example. You were both born and grew up in different countries, then in different states within the same country until you met in New Jersey. There is nothing more exciting than two humans who meet each other and feel a connection spark between them, even though they have never met before. These humans should know and understand that this kind of connection is the soul mate connection and they can be sure that this meeting was planned and meant to be.

Now let me explain something for you first, and for your readers second, so that your readers and you understand the purpose that you and your soul mate came together to finish this book. You each came to this life and lived your own good and bad experiences. It took years for you to meet each other, and it was meant and planned by both of your souls to come to an earthly life to experience together. On Earth, this meeting is said to be by chance, but I tell you this meeting was not by chance. You and your soul mate lived lives together before, and now you are living this life – and there are more lifetimes to come – helping each other. Your souls are from the same Source and you are two souls that have always decided to help each other when you come to an earthly life. When your souls decided to work together, it did not mean that you had to be born together and it did not mean that you had to belong to the same family or be the same age or sex. It meant that in a period in this lifetime, you and your soul mate – as humans – would meet and be together to have many experiences together. It does not matter how good or how bad these experiences are; it only means that you will be with each other to help each other finish them. Writing this book is one of these experiences.

Explain more to me. Are humans that are born twins, soul mates?

Twins are the most common soul mates ever known. Twin soul mates decide to come to Earth as twins sharing the same womb. Now keep in mind that when more than one fetus occupies the same womb at the same time, all the fetuses are being controlled by a part of the same soul. Pay attention for a minute and try to follow me. Imagine a pyramid shape. At the top is the main soul. This soul then splits into a few or even many different parts. These parts are called soul mates. When one of these parts splits, these are twin souls that will be in the same womb at the same time and they are also soul mates. The same is true for triplets, quadruplets and so on. Most twins share the same life, sharing the same experience, but each one is seeing it from a different angle.

For humans it has become very common to have two or more babies at the same birth time. Twins come either identical or fraternal, but three or more can only be fraternal. The difference between them is that identical twins come from the same egg where, after it is fertilized, it splits in half before it starts to develop. Identical twins have the same DNA and are the same sex. They look the same and act in a similar way too. Fraternal twins come from two different eggs that have been fertilized from the same sperm at the same time and they share 50 percent of their DNA. They do not always look alike and they are not always the same sex. Sometimes the way they act will be similar and sometimes it will not. Most of the time, twins are born with the same abilities and are conditioned to the same routine, but the way each one communicates is different, depending on the data that each is provided with by the humans that are raising them.

Sometimes it is planned that one of the twins will be perfect and the other will have problems growing, even inside the womb. The weak one might not experience life outside the womb because he will die in the womb; or he may only experience the birth procedure and then die. For the strong twin that survives, this will be very disturbing. This infant will feel that he lived for a few months with a brother or sister, even if it was in water inside the womb, and suddenly the brother or sister died and left him all alone, before or after seeing the light. This infant will have this feeling until he becomes familiar with life, which is about five or six months of age. He will slowly forget about his twin until the parents start telling him about it. This will be a reminder that will create fear and a sense of guilt in the surviving twin. This feeling of guilt and responsibility for killing his brother or sister will develop either consciously or subconsciously, which means he may or may not be aware of it. His guilt might go far enough to cause depression, especially because as this child grows up he will have no recollection of what happened in the womb. His only reference at that time will be what his parents tell him. Parents usually deliver the story full of their own guilt and insecurity, doubting if they are capable of raising and protecting the surviving twin. The parents' insecurity will only feed the guilt and blame that the surviving twin feels. He will then, little by little, fill his mind with negative thoughts about himself, only because he was the one who survived.

As you know very well, not all twins die in the womb. A lot of them survive and live a life full of experiences. Each of the twin soul mates discovers their own power very slowly, as they notice their individual strengths and abilities through their own experiences. This power is basically created spiritually and completed physically.

For twin soul mates to meet in a lifetime it means that they have been through many lifetimes together; and after this life is completed, they will reunite again in a strong bond that could not be broken. I remind you again to always look at every human situation with the understanding that it was all planned way before any human was conceived.

Chapter 3
ANGELS

Tell me about angels and tell me more about you.

Since the universe came to existence, creatures and humans were created and so were angels. Angels go back to the beginning of life in this universe. Life is and has always been all over the universe – not only on Earth and in your known world. Life is of all shapes and kinds and so are angels. Angels float all over the universe, very close to you and also very, very far. They are spiritual beings without bodies of flesh and bones, though apparently, they have the ability to appear in human form.

On Earth, angels and angel stories go back to the Sumerians who lived even before the existence of Egyptian society. They were the first to use human figures and sculptures with wings. They were also the first known by your society to have left stories behind about messengers who would communicate between gods and humans. These angels were always made in the image of a human with wings and it was said that they were healers, killers, defenders and messengers. Other societies believed that angels were flying spirits. All religious books, from ancient to modern, talk about generous angels that cooperate with humans.

There are different kinds of angels with different personalities and tasks. They could be in the shape of a male or female; or they may not be seen, only felt. Children, in their purity, can see their angels because they are always connected to their higher self. As an adult, it is harder to open up to see angels or your guardian angel unless another human, a book or an incident shows you the way to see. These angels are usually seen as humans providing assistance to other humans. It does not matter what kind of help is provided. It could be physical, emotional or mental help. The best-known assistance is when a human sees another human, connects into his life, gives him the help that he is asking for and then disappears without any wants or needs.

Every human has angels, all the archangels, and his guardian angels to ask for help anytime he feels that he needs it. All it takes is to have faith and believe that they do exist. These angels have always been with every human since the beginning of humanity when souls decided to reside in humans on Earth. But you have to understand that these angels are not problem–removers. Their job is to help the human go through any experience that is considered a problem in the easiest way possible – and the help comes in many different and unexpected ways. Sometimes the human will not recognize the help that he has been waiting for, only because that help might not fully satisfy his need. But I tell you, a human should always accept the help that is given, and then the help will help itself in becoming a full understanding. Countless life changes have happened on this Earth through the help offered by these angels.

Now let me tell you more about me. I am your guardian angel. I have never been a human. I am an un–earthly being whom you now feel and see all the time. I have been with you from one lifetime to another and I am going to stay with you until your soul decides to go back to Spirit for good. My job is to be with you always, to grab you from the edge of tragedy and to give you clever advice. I was assigned to you by your soul – to guard and guide the shell it decided to reside in regardless of how you choose to run your life. I only see the good in you, whether you believe in me or not, and I watch over you while you go about your everyday actions. I have always given you, and still give you, protection and wisdom without any judgment. I can guide you and show you the right way to finish your journey as your soul planned it, without interfering with your free will.

You are on Earth. I reside in a place of Existence. I am on Earth; I am in the Universe. I could be seen only if a human chooses to see me. I whisper in the ears of humans, and they hear me only if they choose to. You can only see me, hear me and feel me through your heart. You are now able to do this very easily because you have discovered a great power: love. My existence to you is simply a matter of faith without the need for me to prove to you that I exist. You can call on me anytime you want and I am here for you like an open book ready to be read.

You thought you knew yourself before you found me, but you had some experiences that – to tell you the truth – put you over the limit of what you were able to handle. You confused yourself when you did not see solutions that would satisfy your needs. But believe me when I say that now you exist in the stage of your higher self, where it does not matter to you anymore if you have a good or a bad experience.

You already know that I am not with you to change the way you choose to run your life. I am here to help you go through your experiences as comfortable as possible. I will help you to be the greatest or the worst you can be, according to what you choose. I love you with a love that is greater than any love that is available on Earth. Do understand that my love for you does not have any needs or conditions. I have always had unconditional love for you, and now you have unconditional love for me; so this makes us both one–in– love.

When you discovered who you are, you discovered your higher self. When you discovered your higher self, you discovered the *real* me. Also know that *all* the people that have existed in your life were there for a reason and they were also angels that helped you change the way you chose to run your life. It does not matter if they did it consciously or unconsciously. They were angels in human shape or form; and there is still a place for more of them to come. Some of these angels are going to be healing angels like you and your soul mate. You both talk to other humans or put your hands on them and they feel different very quickly. With your touch or hug these humans feel stress free and relaxed. This makes you both their healing angels in human bodies.

Where were you before in my life? Why couldn't I see you or hear you?

When you ask me where I was before, I will tell you again that since the second your soul decided to come to this Earth, I have always been with you. Before, your eyes were closed. You could not see me until you cried your eyes out. This crying, in fact, washed your eyes and let you see much better. Before you heard me, you received all my messages indirectly, not knowing how. You did not know how to communicate with me until you started feeling me and listening to my words. Now, because you can see, hear and feel me directly with a better understanding of who I am, we communicate with no difficulties at all. You always see me in a human figure. Sometimes you touch me and you can feel me. Sometimes you feel me touching you without seeing me, but still hear and feel me around you. You see me the same way you have seen yourself – floating like a cloud in a human figure, flying in the air.

Now, I want you to listen to me well because what I am going to tell you is going to affect you. I tell you and assure you, the way you see me is actually the way I look, only because it is your view and perception that has created the way you see me, or let's say that you are experiencing *your seeing reality*. What you are seeing is the real me. I am floating energy coming from the same Source that you came from. The difference between us is that I have never been a human before; and my job here is to love you, protect you and give you all the knowledge that I can give you to help you finish this journey.

Before, you did not know that I existed in your life, so I was always hiding within you, waiting for you to uncover me. When you saw me, heard me, and felt me you decided to recognize me. Because you are one of these humans that does not believe until you see, hear or feel something, the direct communication between us is what is making you believe in me. There is nothing at all wrong with that as long as you have opened your eyes, your ears and your heart to find the new you.

Anytime you and I talk together, you write what we talk about. You somehow understand the idea behind what we are discussing; but believe me when I tell you, the real understanding and the full absorption of an idea will happen only when it becomes an experience on the physical level of your existence. The more the physical touches, sees and experiences feelings, the more the human will understand. But the important thing is not to doubt what you hear from me. You can sometimes hear something coming directly from my mouth when we are talking together; sometimes you are all alone and an idea or thought crosses your mind; other times you have a dream or a daydream that you remember very well. But know and believe that it does not matter how or from where the idea or thought or wisdom comes to you. However it comes to you, it is always me that is feeding it to you.

One of the main reasons that we communicate with each other is for you to understand the way the human ego works. In this life on Earth, according to human–created rules and according to what society dictates, there is wrong and right. It is usual for a human's ego to always tell him that whatever he is doing is the right thing, without showing him a way to evaluate his action. These kinds of humans will never admit they are wrong. You are one of these humans that always thought he was right, period. But I tell you, the more we talk and the more we communicate, the more you open your eyes to the idea that your ego is not always right, and *you* are not always right. Between now and then, you see that you are wrong. It is good that now you admit you are wrong here and there, according to what your society considers wrong. But, since you and I know that there is really no right or wrong, let's just say that there is nothing wrong with you being right and other humans also being right!

Think about how your life has been going so far. If everything that you ever chose was *right*, and the way you handled all your experiences was never *wrong*, then there would be no reason for me to be communicating with you. Understand that one of the most important reasons why we communicate with each other now is for you to believe that good and bad – or right and wrong – are all experiences that your soul decided on, and that you are the main actor in your soul's journey. I am here to make it easy for you to accept the right and the wrong and to help you not get stuck in any of your experiences. Whatever your creation is, if you always think that you know it all and that you are always right, then there will be no more willingness to create within that experience. You will have already condemned the experience and convinced yourself that your way is the only right way, no question about it. You will then be stuck in your ideas and thoughts and you will be killing any chance you might have for a change in your life.

You and I talk all the time now, and we discuss your ideas and experiences. This will help you to be on the right track according to what your soul decided on, and it will help you to see clearly and change *you* to a better *you*. You can now work on reprogramming yourself and your thoughts to create a happier you. Wipe out all the old data that was told to you by other humans about how to run your life and only listen to your higher self. Follow your heart, and all your experiences will go in the direction that they are supposed to go so they could finish according to your soul's plan.

Now I want you to think back to the time when you used to pray. You were taught that when you want something you should talk to God. Open the Book and read a prayer – even if you do not know what you are saying – and God will hear you. So this is what you did. You prayed and prayed and when you did not get what you prayed for, you got pissed. You were upset that you had spent time praying and got nothing. But there were other times when you sat by yourself and talked to someone who was a part of you, even though you did not know who you were talking to. You expressed yourself coming from the heart, and that was when your request came true. Now, your thoughts, feelings and love for you make all your prayers start with being thankful. You are satisfied with what you have and you are thankful for what is yet to come, with no want or need as a basic condition.

In the stage that you are in now, you cannot make yourself believe what your thoughts create for you if your heart does not agree. If your words to me or to you are not from your heart, then your mind will correct it for you. You have to understand that as a human, you can trick other humans by telling them anything you want and they will believe you if you seem sincere enough – but you cannot trick yourself. You have reached a stage where *you* can now catch *yourself* when you go off track. You now make sure to remind yourself to be thankful, and you know that you will receive what is meant to be; so you are satisfied all the time. Being in this stage of awareness will keep you at peace, without any fear of the unknown or of what the future might bring. You are now beyond all these things and you understand that in this life, there is nothing to fear – not even death – so most of the time you run your life with no worries, no blame, and no judgment for yourself or others.

I tell you that writing this book is an experience that your soul planned on, and it is going as it was planned so far. You are sharing your discussions between you and your guardian angel with the world. Keep in mind that many words have been spoken and written by many different masters. People gathered around them to listen to their words and their wisdom, and these listeners wrote what they heard according to what they understood. So think with me now. The real meaning of the words heard was absorbed by these writers in the way *they* understood them. For the people that will read your writings, it is going to be the same. Some will follow their hearts, and others will follow their emotions. A human's perception of what is meant by what he reads ignites his feelings, to make him understand in his own way. If an experience happens to him according to what the human understood from what he read, his understanding will be validated, as it relates to him. This validation can only happen if a human has a physical experience to translate his real understanding. Let me make it easier for you and your readers to understand. It means that a human can read all he wants and gather all the knowledge that he can, but unless he has an experience on the physical, where he applies what he understood from what he read, then all that he reads will just be for general information, only to increase his common knowledge.

Accept and live every day the way it comes. Live it with love, faith, and no fear; and always remember that now you and I are One working together to finish this journey.

When my soul mate and I visited a senior rehab center I saw a lot of entities, figures, and energy. Why am I seeing all this? What is the best way for me to communicate with the spirit world now?

Know, believe and understand that you are now reaching a very high, powerful stage in your life. Some of the things you see and feel will confuse you for now. Do not keep anything to yourself. This will only make you feel lost and scared, especially since you will be discovering new things every day. Keep on talking to me. Do not wait a few days trying to guess on your own. The more you wait, the more confused you will get. I know that you have trust in me and in every word I say, and you know that I love to tell you as much as I can – to educate you and help you understand what is going on. So now listen to what I am going to say and ask me whatever you want as we are talking.

What you saw a few days ago at the senior citizens' rehab facility was very beautiful. As you stood in the physical therapy room looking around and admiring every person there, the idea of death occurred to you. You decided to study each human – some were scared to be there; others were trying to convince themselves not to care but they were also worried about death. You knew their life stories, you knew that most of them were there as a last stop before leaving this Earth and this life. You were wondering if they finished all the experiences that their souls came here for, or if there were still parts of these experiences that were not accomplished. You were thinking if there was anything you could do to help them understand and accept the situation they were in.

You noticed an old woman looking at you from the minute you walked into that room. Your soul mate was giving her Reiki with all her love and you felt that you also wanted to give. You hesitated at first because you wondered if you, as a man, were allowed to touch people at this place, especially women. You decided to put your hands on her hands, and within a few seconds she stared at your eyes, her look was full of love and a peaceful smile was on her face. You touched her on the head, shoulder and hands; and you even kissed her hands. You told her what a beautiful soul she is, and you comforted her by telling her not to worry too much because she is going to be o.k., no matter what her soul decides to do. She could not answer you because she had no voice. The only answer she gave you was a look of love and a big smile. You felt great satisfaction doing what you did because you knew that your touch and your words made her feel comfortable and relaxed.

You started noticing all kinds of energy, entities and figures filling the room. A lot of them looked like old people and some looked young; some were male and others female. Let me tell you, what you saw is what all humans go through when the time comes for them to leave this life. You were seeing the seniors' guardian angels and their other angels surrounding them. These angels always come down to help the soul to let go and go back easily when it decides to leave the mind and body of the human it occupies. These angels will not interfere with what the soul wants to do; they will not lead the soul into anything not planned. All they do is make it easy and smooth for the soul to finish what it wants to do. Seeing these angels around these old people does not mean that they are going to die today or tomorrow. They might go very quickly, or their soul might stay for a while longer.

You also saw energy – from dark to white – floating like a cloud in the room and you recognized the difference between the demons and real angels. You saw how they were both attached to these humans, trying to grab their attention. The demons you saw are here on Earth to make humans change their souls' plans, even at the last minute, to make it rough for these humans to leave this life. White angels are here alert and on guard. Their job is to give help and love to whoever wants it and asks for it, directly or indirectly. White angels help humans finish what their souls planned on, preparing them for a smooth return to their Source when the time comes.

All the seniors that you saw in that room are religious people; some of them are very religious. Their religions never taught them, or helped them to understand anything about death, so they do not even speak the word "death." They will say that someone "passed away" instead of saying he "died", only because that's what they were taught. Believe me when I say that they do not even know what the words "passed away" mean. They do not believe that they will be coming back for another life on this Earth, so they are worried and concerned about what is next. Others will be happy to face the end of their life just to end their pain and misery. They still do not know where they are going, but they rather take the exit route rather than staying here in misery.

Their holy book, regardless of their religion, has also taught them not to talk to anyone who has a psychic ability and can communicate with souls. It tells them that their God is the only leader that should be consulted throughout their lives, and that when they die, they will go back to this God; but they have no idea what this means. Their holy book taught them that what is said by their God is always true, and that reading the word of God will help them understand what life on Earth is all about. These people will believe in all that is said, even though they do not understand what is really *meant* by what is said. This is not for you to judge – it is only for you to learn from.

So what you saw is very beautiful. As I always tell you, you can now see and do way more than most humans can see and do, only because you want to, not because you are better than any other human. You now go to your higher self, and you can stay there most of the time; and because you can do this, you are going to see more and more angels around people that you know, and around others that you do not know. You are going to see and feel good and bad energy surrounding you every minute of your life from now. Listen to your soul mate when she reminds you to cut the dark energy off you, to protect yourself at all times. I know you are doing great on your own, but a reminder here and there does not hurt. Take care of yourself and do not hesitate to help anyone. Remember, you are here to give and to help humans heal.

Look at how many people you are helping because you chose to follow your heart. See how many humans you have affected so far. See how you answer them and give them wisdom, leading them to find the right way to accept the situation they are in. Pay attention to yourself when you talk to people, and see how they are affected by your words and your love. First, look at what you are doing for your soul mate. Every day you are helping her directly and indirectly. You are teaching her and learning from her. She is learning a lot by what she sees and hears from you, and by you sharing your writings with her every morning. You are helping her to accomplish her soul's plan and she is helping you to do the same. You are helping many people only because you love to give; not because you want or need anything from these humans. You are getting there, my friend. Do not stop it; and never again doubt what you can do.

Believe me when I tell you that a lot of people would love to see and feel angels, energy and entities like you can – yet you are not exceptional; every human can do what you do. They only need to believe that they can. All a human has to do is to calm his mind by meditating and focusing on only one thing, relaxing the body and the mind at the same time. I suggest the best time to do this is around dusk, when it is not too dark in the room, until the human gets used to it. Once he can do this easily, he will be able to do it at any time of the day. It is always better to have a mirror facing him to focus on. The human will feel his body parts starting to relax up to the point of tingling, and suddenly he will start seeing the mirror getting foggy and cloudy; then images and figures will appear in the mirror. At this time, he could talk to them and listen to them, or he might just see them without audio. The figures will last from one second to however long this human chooses to keep seeing them. As long as he is connected and concentrating, the human will always see and feel; but the second he loses the connection, he will lose the scene also. You do not have to be a unique person to distinguish what most cannot. The human that cannot see angels cannot do so only because he will not allow himself to see.

Now to answer your question directly, yes you are now communicating with the spirit world if that's what you want to call it – and stop asking me why you are seeing energy. I hope after our long talk today, you understand the reason. You are going to do miracles; you are going to help heal a lot of people before you leave this Earth because this is what you are here to do. Keep on doing whatever you are doing. Stay with me all the time, and please, for the sake of the love that we carry for each other, do not doubt and do not worry. I promise you that you will finish what your soul came to accomplish the way it is meant to be done.

Chapter 4

ARCHANGELS

Since you are leaving the office early today and you have a little bit of extra time, why don't you stop by the metaphysical store in your neighborhood and buy yourself a deck of tarot cards?

Are you for real? Why are you asking me to buy tarot cards? Is there something I could learn from them?

Later on, you will know the answer to your question. Believe me, you are not going to be a fortune teller.

I stopped at the store to buy some tarot cards as James told me to do. I did not know what I was looking for, so I used my pendulum,[1] and it chose Archangel Oracle cards for me. I bought the deck, went home, I unwrapped it, put it in my briefcase, and forgot about it for the night. The next day

---

[1.] A pendulum is a tool activated by energy. It is a stone or a piece of metal or glass that is attached to a chain or string. It is activated by energy and directed by the human's Subconscious, which is led by his heart. It is used to find an answer to a question or to help the human choose the correct answer among multiple options.

I opened the box, took out the cards and started looking at them. I looked at the Archangel Michael card first. I read what was written under the picture and I stared at it for a few seconds. That was when I saw James and Archangel Michael sitting next to me. Michael did not look like the rest of the angels and figures that I was seeing. He had a blue/purple halo around him and he was sitting, staring at me with a big smile on his face. I could see him and hear him very well. James stared into my eyes and these words came flowing out of his mouth:

You are clearing a lot of dark energy lately. You cut dark energy and you take it far out to the universe, but you always do it with your soul mate and me. You never thought of asking for Archangel Michael's help. Michael is the one that is always helping you in clearing all this energy, even though you haven't noticed yet. We are with you to observe and to help you if and when you need it – but you are doing it with Michael's help.

Then Archangel Michael looked at me and said:

You are doing a good job in clearing energy and you feel great about doing it. Now let me tell you something very important. No human can clear energy from another human or other humans unless he, himself, is clear. You can see energy all over, you can see the colors of energy, you can tell what is dark and what is not; you can tell what is good and what is bad, if you want to use earthly labels. You know how to protect yourself from allowing all the dark ones to attach to you; and if they do attach to you, you know how to cut them off. That's great. I want you also to know that I am always with you protecting you, cutting the energy off you and protecting your household. Indirectly, you ask for me all the time, so keep on doing what you are doing, and if you ask for me or not, I will still be with you.

Your soul mate is always with you to see and do what you are doing, which is exactly what was planned by your souls, that you would provide her with this help. I tell you, she will start seeing by herself very soon and she will start realizing how beautiful what you are doing really is. She comes to you and asks you a lot of questions that she does not have an answer for, and you do your best to answer her; and if you do not know, you come to us, and then you both have the answer. But I tell you, she knows how to cut and clear energy and very soon, she will be able to see and heal like you do. I suggest that both of you continue to do what you are doing together. You cannot imagine what beauty lies ahead for you.

Another figure with a green halo showed up and I was introduced to Archangel Raphael.

I am Raphael, the healing angel, and I am here to help you finish healing yourself. I want you to understand that a great healer is one who is pure himself; and fear is an obstacle to purity and balance. Fear is one of the tools that a human adopts from all the teachings and data that is fed to him since he is born, so it is normal in every human. Pretty soon, you will get over all your fears. Nothing should scare you in what you are accomplishing; remember, the minute you have fear, it will create doubt in you which will lead to an unbalanced you. This fear will stop you from healing. You started healing with the understanding that healing does not mean healing the physical; it means healing the whole, which in the end will help heal the physical if requested. You are doing a great job. Keep on doing what you are doing.

You know that you can ask your guardian angel for any help that you want. Most of the time, he can provide it to you by himself, and a lot of times he will look to us. You should also know that you can always ask for our help as individuals or as a group. When you ask for our help, tell us what kind of help you need. We will provide you the help as a thought, a dream, or an actual physical incident. We all put our hands together to provide you with the help you request; all you have to do is accept it. Take a deep breath, look for us, and ask.

Every human can ask for the same help and we will provide it to them. Sometimes the help they ask for will be right in front of their eyes, but because of the stress and fear in their heart, they will not be able to see it. They are blinding themselves from seeing the help when all they have to do is just grab it. In that case, a human can also seek help through another human. This other human might give him a hint or make a gesture that will help him get over the fear that is preventing him from connecting to us; which basically means that we will be helping him through another human.

James then looked at me and said:

Pretty soon, you will be meeting a lot more archangels. Each one of them has a specialty. They can all do miracles individually or they can combine their powers and provide a greater miracle if needed. I just want you to know and understand that if you meet them all or not, they are all here, like me. We are all with you always to help you finish the great task that you have started. Hang in there; keep the faith and belief in you. Believe me – everything will finish the way it was planned.

On the following morning, James, Michael and Rafael were sitting with me when James introduced me to Gabriel.

This is the angel that will help you and your soul mate finish the project that you are working on.

I looked at Gabriel and saw a very beautiful light bronze halo around her. She looked at me, smiled, and in a soft voice she began speaking to me.

Every human still has a kid in him. It is up to the human to bring that kid out. When he does, it is great for this human to love the kid in him and take good care of him. The kid that is in you will make you smile, play, jump, act silly and be merry all the time. I am the angel that will protect that kid in you, all the kids in this world, and the kids that are inside all other adults. I also protect parents and show them how to deal with their kids by providing them with the wisdom to raise them.

I am here to tell you not to be scared of anything. You have a kid in you who always loves to come out and play. You have a soul mate who is a great partner who always has you come out and play; you dance together, you laugh together, and you do things together that for ages you did not even attempt to do. The kid in you was hidden for a while. Lately, you are releasing him to come out and see the light; let him be. This is a very important step in letting you love every part of you, so that you can love every other human with the pure heart of a child. I promise you that I will always protect the kid that is in you, and in your soul mate.

I am always helping you and protecting you. It does not matter if you ask me or not. I am here to look over you and remind you daily that the power you have discovered in you is very beautiful. You should love every second of your life now, and you should hold close to your heart what you have discovered.

You are here to learn and to teach. Your soul mate is learning from you, and she is also helping to guide you for now. I will guide her way and your way in dealing with and teaching others. I will show you what to do and how to do it in a very easy and accurate way so that you both will not be misunderstood. Anytime you are stuck and not listening to me, you can listen to your soul mate. She is guided by me also. Remember, you teach what you learn and these teachings are going to stay even after you leave this Earth.

I also want you to know and understand that I am here to help you finish writing your book. I know that you are confused now and do not know how and where to start; but we will work together, and I will lead you and provide you with all the help you need. I assure you that the help you need will always be in front of your eyes. Your soul mate will be involved in this book because she will provide necessary help that you will need later. For the time being, you and I will work on the base; then your soul mate will start correcting whatever is needed. Finally, the three of us will do the last touches. All you need to do is trust you and believe that you can do it – and it will be done. Just stay relaxed and be yourself. Everything is going to go the right way and everything will be great until you finish this life as your soul already planned it to be.

Then Michael looked at me again and said:

There is something very important that I want you to do from now on. Before doing anything that is new to you that you are unsure of, I want you to ask for guidance. The right guidance is the best weapon that you could have. You are now in a stage that you can do miracles; but remember, the miracles do not happen by themselves and they also happen for a reason. Following the right guidance will lead you to a path where you can see very clearly, to absorb the right understanding of the purpose and effect of the miracle.

James is with you all the time. You can come to him at any time. He speaks and understands your language better than anyone else. I am also here and I will always be with you; so with the help of your soul mate, with my guidance and support, with James' guidance and support, and with all the archangels' support, you are going to finish what your soul planned for you before you came to this life.

Then James said:

Now that we reached a higher stage of awareness, as I told you before, you are going to be faced with many new experiences and surprises. I say "we reached" because you and I are one, and with my help you have reached where you are. I will remind you again and again that I love you, and I will always be your guide and your connection to the archangels, if you forget one of these days to ask them directly.

James, tell me a little bit more about Gabriel. Since I saw her last, I have been trying to contact her, and somehow, I am out of luck. What am I doing wrong?

You have been trying to contact her for days, and she has been answering you. The reason that you have not been hearing her is because you get too excited when you are asking for help for yourself. You are trying very hard to hear, and this is what is preventing you from hearing her. She has been with you all the time. But before I tell you anymore about Gabriel, we are going to take a trip[2] to Egypt to see the biggest monastery ever made for an archangel. Follow me, and when we come back, I will tell you a few things that you do not know about Archangel Gabriel.

My soul mate and I followed James all the way to the desert in Egypt, to a region called Fayoum. From a far distance we could see a huge, high border wall made of stone standing at the bottom of a mountain. We also noticed a small town a few miles away. Behind the wall there were very

---

2. My soul mate, James, and I take many trips through astral travel. Any human can astral travel through deep meditation.

old–looking towers of different shapes and forms, and building attachments, all within one structure. It looked like a fort that was protected by a mountain on one side and open to the desert on the other three sides. We looked down to the inside and we saw small, empty prison–like cells next to each other. We started walking through what looked like ancient ruins of courts next to the cells. It seemed like it was a place where people used to be tried and jailed. We went through a big door, which was the entrance to a church. We looked inside and at first sight we noticed that the inside did not match the outside. The outside looked like a place that had aged quite a bit, but the inside looked like it had been modernized.

The first thing we noticed was the beautiful aroma inside the church. For all the ages that this church has been in existence, the burning of incense has left a very pleasant residue. Looking straight ahead we saw three altars; the middle had a semicircle entrance with columns on each side with Archangel Gabriel's image on the background wall; so we assumed it was dedicated to her. The altar on the right had the Virgin Mary's image and we assumed it was her altar. The altar on the left had an image of a saint, *whom I thought was Saint George, and my soul mate agreed, so we assumed it was an altar for him. The church itself was divided into four sections. The altars were separated by wooden dividers and they were in one section at the front of the church; while in the back center was another section that had benches for the people to sit. On the right and left were two other smaller sections, and if I am guessing right, these sections were for the choir and chanters. There were many massive columns in the church full of icons and decorations. Our thought was that these columns were to support the roof and the top of the church from collapsing; it looked like the bases were there for centuries and they are still being used for support. On top of them, it looks like all new posts were added to keep the church structurally safe so that it can survive from generation to generation. Huge murals and icons of saints, angels and archangels covered the walls. Wherever we walked we could smell and feel the purity of this holy place. To our surprise, we did not see an image of Jesus anywhere.*

Outside the church we saw the monastery and a good number of monks. There were different shapes and sizes of rooms where these monks lived. On the other side of the church, there were apartments that were occupied by people. James told me that these are for the pilgrims that come to visit and spend a few days here. We tried to talk to the monks and spend some time with them, but they refused to speak with us. They had very mean looks on their faces and it seemed like they did not want to deal with us at all. We asked James why these monks were behaving this way.

These monks are refusing to talk to us because they believe that they are the only purified people on Earth. They do not communicate with any human unless he is a monk like them. Now let's go back to earthly reality and we will discuss what we saw.

I hope you both loved what you saw, and I hope you enjoyed the beauty of what you felt and touched. I wanted you to visit and see it only because if you see, it will help you believe. When you tell other humans about it, it will make a big difference when you tell it as a fact that you saw and experienced, rather than something you heard from someone else that you are just repeating. So now, after you saw what you saw and you felt what you felt, I want you to relax and listen to me. Let me enlighten you with more information about Gabriel's monastery so you can understand who she is and what she can do for human beings.

What you just saw was a monastery dedicated to Gabriel. The name Gabriel means *God is my strength*. Archangel Gabriel is the third on the list of archangels. You always see a bronze or copper halo surrounding this angel who wears a beautiful blue dress. This angel has been known for ages and ages. Many written and spoken stories and legends about this beautiful archangel have been passed down from generation to generation of humanity. Every human on Earth has heard, learned from and used this angel's help. Many monasteries and churches were built in the name of this angel and still exist to this day. The most famous and well–known monastery is the one that you just toured. It was founded in the fifth century in the Fayoum region of Egypt.

Archangel Gabriel is the angel of knowledge, the angel of love, and the angel that protects kids and brings families together. This archangel has been known as a male figure in the Arab and Jewish part of the world but, in fact, this angel can be seen as a male or a female figure. The form in which she reveals herself to each human depends on the human himself. Humans will see her as a male or female depending on the culture, beliefs and traditions that the human's community has taught him. When this angel is seen in the Middle East, some people actually see her as a female figure, but because the traditions and the culture always told them that this angel is a man, they will be embarrassed to say that they saw this archangel as a female. The truth is that it does not matter if this angel is seen as a male or a female; what matters is what the human gains by his experience dealing with this archangel. You see this angel in female form. It is your belief that makes you see and feel her the way you do.

Gabriel is the angel of love, knowledge and truth. She is also the guardian of paradise. She always reminds humans that love is not something to fight for; that love comes from within. She guides humans to see that love is sharing feelings with others whether you care about them or not; it is finding forgiveness for the self and others for whatever was done – regardless of the situation – without any judgment or blame. Her powers are very strong and effective and she answers everyone that asks for her help.

The way a human should ask for her help is to be clear with his question and his request. The human should go straight to the point, without going left and right with his words, and without trying to figure out how to ask. A human who asks for her help should always be prepared and ready to receive her answers and to accept her energy. When answering a request for help, most of the time she reveals herself. She wants to make sure that humans see her for real, to give them the confidence to believe in the answer they receive.

Keep on asking for her. She is hearing you. Ask her directly and stop trying too hard. She is answering you every time; listen to her voice when she talks to you, and make no extra effort to try to see her. I assure you that you are able to see and hear her the same way you see and hear all the others.

Keep on doing what you are doing. You two are almost there. Keep on trying and do not give up on anything. You are a beautiful team full of love. All that you are now trying to do is to help heal others. You are doing great but with the archangels help you will do even better. Never doubt for a second what you both can do.

Now that we talked a little bit about Gabriel, would you tell me more about Archangel Michael? What kind of powers does he have and how does he help humans?

Archangel Michael is with you all the time now. Michael is with you when you use power and energy; every time you put your hands on any human; when you cut energy and relax people. Michael is the most powerful one of all the archangels and he is the eldest.

The word Michael means *he who is as God*. Michael is also called the father of eternity. Michael is seen and known as the commander of all angels and his name is the war cry of all white angels who fight the devil and his dark angels. He has been known as the angel of the wind, lightning, thunder, rain, snow, hail, and fire; he is considered the defender of heaven, Earth and the universe. He is the greatest help against evil on Earth and against dark energy on Earth and all over the universe. Michael is the protector from physical and spiritual enemies; he is the protector for heaven and Earth against the endless hate of the challengers. He is the archangel that revealed a way to make humans eternal by keeping the same memory active forever. Michael is known by every religion on Earth. He is mentioned in religious books, and religious leaders all over the world preach about him. Cultures across this planet consider him the messenger from heaven that has supernatural power; through him the legend of angels was born.

For a human to see Archangel Michael, he should always look to the south. He should concentrate and look to see a glowing figure of fire. Looking through this brilliant shine, a human can see a beautiful glowing figure that has a blue–purple halo around him, holding a burning sword in his hand that represents courage. This sword will help the human that sees it to face the threats that life presents him with. When a human sees Archangel Michael, he will feel as if he had been in a closed, dark room and has suddenly come out to take comfort from the sun's rays, which energize and give power to his body and soul.

Other times, this archangel will be seen wearing a steel shield over his chest with a lion or dragon engraved on it in gold. The lion signifies the defeating power, the existing energy, bravery and desire in all life on Earth; while the dragon signifies human fear, which is simply exterminated when supported by belief and bravery. A human should always call on Archangel Michael when seeking bravery, courage and power; he will shield the human and convert his fear into peace, happiness and self-confidence.

When a human sees and talks to Archangel Michael, the archangel will look at the human with a very joyous expression; with eyes full of love and with the brightness of the burning red flame coming out of his hair. Then, very quickly, he will swing his beautiful sword of fire to cut all the dark energy that is on that human to make him ready for the battle he will be facing soon after.

When a human feels stressed or depressed where this feeling is causing him bodily and/or emotional pain, he should make sure to call on Archangel Michael. Michael will help him to get rid of the fear that is produced by whatever experience he is going through, no matter what it is. When a human calls on this archangel, he should make the specific request to be cleared of all dark energy, or negative power, and for this dark energy to be taken far away, deep into the universe. This will help the human get rid of the fear, sadness and stress that has been living inside him.

When a human is asking Michael for help, he should start by taking a deep breath and slowly letting it out. By breathing in, he will be inhaling healing energy, peace, and calm. By exhaling, he will be releasing the stress and sad feelings that are inside him. He should then take another deep breath, this time inhaling all the knowledge that he needs to go through his experience; and exhaling to let go of all blame, judgment and fear from within him. Then with a third and last deep breath, inhaling will let the human see his guardian angel and all his angels joining hands with him, to guide him toward the easiest way to reach his higher self. With the last exhale, he will be able to communicate with these angels to ask them to join together and stay within his body chakras. The energy of all these angels will then be within him, spreading pure love energy to every part of him, which will put him at peace with himself and with every other human on Earth.

I am happy I had the chance tell you about Archangel Michael. It will be important for your book, so that your readers can understand the importance of archangels and angels in a human's life; and how angels could help them to live a balanced life.

We've talked about Archangels Michael and Gabriel. Can we now talk about Archangel Raphael?

Archangel Raphael is also known to all religions on this Earth and by people on all the continents of this planet. The name Raphael means *the God who heals.* Archangel Raphael is one of the three most popular and well–known archangels. For a human to see him, he should seek to the east, close his eyes and focus his mind. He will then see this archangel, who is the master of light and the angel of physical and emotional wound healing. Archangel Raphael is seen with a green halo surrounding him. He wears a golden silk robe with the Aquarius Symbol on his chest. This symbol is a representation for humans on Earth to know that around the corner of this life, there is a reality that leads to an eternal life, and to the belief in lasting humankind.

A human will see Archangel Raphael standing upright, his hair glittering like the rays of a beautiful sunrise. He will be holding a sword in his hand that sparks sharp slivers of diamond light, which mirror the sun rays of his hair. He will raise his sword to greet every human that looks for him and finds him. This sword symbolizes the belief in the existence of peace on this disturbed Earth, which will bring faith into a human's life. With his sword, Archangel Raphael will cut all stressful feelings from a human's thoughts, which will create a flow of positive thoughts and feelings. Raphael's presence reminds humans that everything that happens in life is meant to be, and that every experience occurs only to let a human hope and believe that there is always a tomorrow for him, and when tomorrow comes things will change for the best.

Archangel Raphael is the one that will help you and your soul mate to heal yourselves. The best way to do this is to meditate together with the help of Raphael; mentally and spiritually revisit your past in this lifetime so that you can clear your minds completely of any attachment to your past experiences. Let Archangel Raphael guide your healing meditation. He will help you revisit your childhood memories, and then to move forward to the present time. Go through it – see it as a movie. Stop, pause, and evaluate any thought that you feel should be evaluated. See the incident that you paused on and see the person or people that were involved in it. Talk to these people. Tell them how you felt about what happened. Tell them that at the time of the incident you kept all your feelings inside you, and that you hurt yourself by doing this. Tell these people what your feelings are now about that incident; tell them that you forgive yourself first for holding on to this memory for a long time; and tell them that you forgive them, if they did or did not know that they hurt you or how. It is very important for you to express yourself the way you think you should. You can cry, scream, yell, or do whatever you feel like doing. The important thing is that you talk to them. Tell them that you are now a different person and you understand that what happened was an experience for you and for them to learn from. Keep on going forward through this movie – to another and then another incident and thought that occurs to you – until you are cleared of every thought and fear that you had. By doing this, you will be clearing everything from the past that was still bothering you. You will appreciate for real all that happened, and you will not condemn the past anymore. With help from Archangel Raphael, you will clear and heal that part of your life and you will love all experiences that occurred, because you will see them as great lessons that will help you to appreciate life, and to finish it the way your soul planned.

If you prefer, your meditation could be accomplished in more than one session. Time is not an issue. Let it take however long it is meant to take for you to go through everything that ever happened in this life that is still bothering you. The important thing is that you both go through it together because you can help each other to understand and figure out how to get over all that has been stuck inside you for so long. This meditation will make you understand for real that however you reacted to your experiences – good or bad – was your own doing. No other human did anything to you that was not meant to be a tool for your learning; and you did nothing to any other human that was not meant to be experienced. You chose the experience, and you chose your reaction.

Never forget that in any experience, feeling bad will lead you to resist the understanding of its meaning; feeling good will lead you to accept the experience and the lesson learned by it. Either way, you cannot change the fact that it was an experience that was meant for you. I assure you that with this change of heart and mind, past incidents will not bother you anymore. You will feel like a big burden has been lifted from your shoulders and your heart. This awareness will help you heal yourself first, and also other people, through a wiser you. It will clear your Subconscious, allowing you to change the way you see and feel about incidents in your past, which is an understanding you must have if you are going to help other humans the way you are meant to.

I love you both and always remember that all the angels and the whole universe are already with you. You have to believe it and accept it, and then your life will go on to let you finish what your souls planned on for both of you.

Chapter 5

GOD

When I pray, who am I praying to? Who am I requesting help and wisdom from?

Every day I sit with you and we talk. We talk about everything that bothers you, and other things that do not bother you but you want answers for. Until now, you never asked me about who God is and who responds to your prayers when you pray. Let me tell you that when you pray, you are praying to the God that is in you. You pray to the Source that you came from and to the Power that keeps you going every day. The God that is in you always talked to you. He talked to you through images, dreams and voices that you heard. You might have thought that you were talking to yourself at that time, but it was not you talking. Other times you saw God's answer through books when you read something that made you think twice. You also heard God's answer through the TV or radio when you heard something that had an effect on you; and now you and I talk one–on–one through your heart. I assure you that since you were born, God has always talked to you... and He has never stopped.

God is the love that comes from your heart; that is why all the choices you have ever made that were based on love came from your heart. You can only choose from the love in your heart if you have heard God's words – even if you do not remember or are not aware of it. From now on, start practicing aware communication with God.

Take you and me as an example. The way you and I communicate makes our relationship stronger. You and I have a beautiful trust between us, and we share unconditional love for each other that lets you open up, so that you can see and understand the real God in you. Sometimes you still refuse to listen to the God in you, so you feel that you have to ask and pray, and you think there is no answer to your request. This is because you are not always paying attention to what is said to you. Here and there you ignore the words that are being communicated to you. You might hear but you shut down God's words, and pretend that you were not listening, just so that you can follow your desires. You then feel fear in your heart; you worry, and feel down and upset.

The times when you only hear your own voice answering you, you sometimes do not believe that this is God's voice; so you stop asking and praying, and you start to feel very lonely. But let me tell you, when you really listen to the voice that is talking to you, you will realize that it is the voice of God in you. When you for real understand that your voice *is* God's voice, then you will love yourself and every other human on Earth. When you listen to God's words all the time, you will stop feeling sorry for you, and you will stop thinking that the world is against you. You will not compare yourself to any other human, and you will not care what other humans think of you. With no fear or judgment, you will accept the life that you are leading, and you will live it the best way that you can, without feeling hurt or cheated. You will accept the real you.

Let me help you understand by comparing your past with your present life. Remember the kind of life you were leading before? Like every other human, you had all kinds of feelings and emotions. You faced many problems and felt sorrow; between now and then you also felt joy and happiness. These were all experiences that you have successfully finished, so you will no longer suffer this way because now is the beginning of the new you. All the rough times and struggles that you went through are now a part of your past. From now on, you will not think too much about what other people think of you; you will only care about what *you* think of you. You will not care if other people judge you because you will not judge yourself. You are now kinder and care way more about others than you used to because you love you more and more every day. You are discovering the new you and you are happy doing it. This happiness will lead you to love all other humans the same way you love yourself. Your thoughts and actions will now come from your heart.

Let me remind you that way before your book is out you will be in a stage where you will be in your higher self all the time. For now, you are still new to this and you are still teaching yourself the right way to be. You do realize that now there is a big change in you that is making you love the life that is coming toward you. Now you are believing more and more in the God that lives inside you, even though now and then you ignore God's words. Your belief and faith in the wise words that you are hearing on a daily basis is growing.

Remember what I told you before. When you are listening to God or to me, do not be moved by one word – do not worship the word. Worship the idea behind it. Adore the *purpose* of it, which is what is meant by the whole sentence that you hear. The most important thing now is to see how you could use all this information that you are receiving to keep healing yourself and to help heal others.

You now observe your daily progress, and you are allowing the experiences that your soul planned for you to be completed the right way. Make sure to never let the truth scare you or put fear in your heart. Always keep an open mind about everything that is happening to you. Having an open mind will lead you to a great understanding of how things really are. Always listen to your heart, and trust that the love you have for you, will lead you to finish this life in love and happiness.

This morning I am not feeling good about myself. I feel a big change in me. I look at life differently now. When am I going to get used to this new life and how can I tell that this new me is the real me?

Listen to every word I am going to say and, as I told you before, do not focus on the meaning of each word; understand the whole sentence. By doing this, you will see and know exactly who you are, where you were and what you are going to be.

Now let me answer your question. You are partners with a Source, Energy or Power. Let's call it God. You and God are very close to each other – or we can say that you and God are one. You promised God that you would come to Earth to play a certain role and have fun. You also discussed your plan with a lot of different parts of this same Source that you are from. You decided to come to an earthly existence to have many experiences using you and your Source–mates, with a lot of help from your Source. When you came to this Earth, you came as three beings combined into one: your soul, your mind and your body. Your soul is from your Source, Power, Energy or Superconscious. Your mind is your Subconscious, which is connected to your Conscious, and both are non–physical. Your body, which is your physical feature, is the tool that carries the mind and the soul. We will talk about this in more detail later on but for now just understand that you are these three parts. Put all three together and the whole is what created you. So, you are the God that created the *you* that exists as Sami for now.

Your physical body changes shape and form from lifetime to lifetime. Your soul will choose and create the appropriate physical figure for each lifetime it will have on Earth depending on what it wants to accomplish. Each physical body it creates will be different – appropriate for the satisfaction of the soul's desired experience. Your soul and your mind are the same and stay with you always, so you are the same *you* in every lifetime you experience.

In each of your lifetimes, you have countless experiences – some that you finish and others that you do not finish. Your soul and your mind store this data from all your lifetimes as collected information and experiences for future reference. This information will be used to help the soul create the appropriate conditions and physical body for the next earthly journey. Remember, each lifetime will start only when the *All You* chooses.

Sometimes you start an experience and you get stuck on it, not knowing what to do. As a human, you start to worry and let yourself get upset and mad. You become furious up to a point that the stress causes harm to your physical body. But let me tell you, all you have to do is pause for a minute and evaluate the way that you are approaching the experience. Look at the experience with different thinking. Focus on what the goal is, and then decide if you need to change your approach toward the experience or if you should stay on the same path. Either way, after you evaluate the experience, promise yourself that whatever the reason was that made you get stuck, you will never let it happen again. This approach will keep you happy and it will also allow the experience to flow and pass as it was planned.

Now that you know who the real you is, take this information and use it to run your life in happiness, as it is meant.

Chapter 6
THE DEVIL

One night during my meditation, I went through an experience that I have never had before in my life. It was one of the most beautiful experiences that a human could have. I saw my life in its different cycles. I saw how I used to be – then I looked into James' eyes and I saw the real me and what I have become. I saw the power that we earthly humans call "the devil." I felt who I am right now and I saw the devil and his demons fighting with my guardian angel for my soul.

The night was Thursday, December the eleventh of the year two thousand and eight. At eight in the evening, I was home watching movies with my daughter when suddenly I felt heavy energy and pressure over my shoulders. I stood up and went to my bedroom and with my hands I cut off all the dark energy that was attached to me. I closed my eyes, shielded myself and put mirror shields[3] around me. Then I went back and sat down with my

---

[3] A human can imagine outward reflecting mirrors all around him that he can use to shield himself against any dark energy that might affect him. When a human uses the mirror shield, the negative energy will be deflected back to the entity that is causing this dark energy.

daughter again to finish watching movies with her. Around ten o'clock, as we were watching a very funny movie, I felt the same weird feeling again. I felt strong energy and pressure all over my body, the strongest pressure being over my shoulders. I did not want my daughter to notice anything strange about me so I stayed with her for the rest of the movie.

Around eleven forty-five, I went to my bedroom again. I lay down on my bed and in my thoughts, I started evaluating the day. I started seeing and sensing all the actions and experiences that happened during the whole day, down to the last shielding that I had done a few hours ago. I was still feeling heavy energy and pressure over my body when I saw James sitting on my right, next to me on my bed. He stretched out his arms and held my hands. He said nothing. He was just sitting there holding my hands. I think he was giving me Reiki[4] because I felt the energy coming from his palms into me – and as he looked into my eyes I could see and feel strong, beautiful energy entering my body.

Suddenly, strange things started happening around me. I began to see things flying and floating in my bedroom, over my bed, and all over the room. I saw dark and light colors in all kinds of shapes, including human figures. The most interesting thing that I saw was a figure of a man with long, fine black hair covering his shoulders and a black trimmed beard on his face. He wore a black robe and was flying closely over my body. In an instant he landed on my bed and sat to my left. He stared at me with small, black, beady eyes. He was frowning and he had a very hard, mean-looking face.

A few minutes later the light colors in the room started to change to very dark green, very dark red, dark orange, dark blue and black. I did not see

---

4. *Reiki* is a relaxing, healing exchange of energy between a human and pure universal energy. Every human has energy surrounding him and sometimes this energy will be corrupted, according to the thoughts and feelings that a human is allowing himself to have; and *Reiki* is what will clear, purify and heal this energy.

any white or gold colors like I usually see. I saw only dark colors changing, sometimes slowly, sometimes very quickly, and sometimes mixing together. The mean dark figure was still sitting on my left. He looked at me and said things that I did not understand. Without warning, James hugged me and pulled me toward him, closer and closer. I felt the power that James was using to pull me toward him and tears dripped from my eyes. It was something I had never experienced before; not in this life, and not even in the nightmares that I used to have. James then started whispering in my ears to calm me down.

Everything is o.k. and it is fine for you to cry now. Let these tears wash out all the evil and dark energy that is in you. Do not stop until you clear your body from all this energy. Do not be scared. Take the fear out of your heart right now. I am here with you; I am holding you. I will protect you from any harm, physical or mental. Do not let any fear control your feelings. Feel my hug; you are safe between my arms. Nothing is going to harm you. You are receiving from me the beautiful unconditional love that you now carry for yourself. Cry as much as you want; this is good for you. Don't be scared. I am here to protect you, to love you, to provide you with all the comfort that I can give you. Just go with what is going on. Nothing is going to harm your physical body.

The other mean figure was still sitting on my left next to me, still saying things that I did not understand. His hands did not touch my body at all, but they were very close to my body. He was moving his hands in circles, and he was going up and down around my body. I felt a lot of heat and energy coming toward me from his palms, but I did not feel any physical touch as I feel from James when he touches me. The mean figure had a very angry look in his eyes and on his face; I could see the hatred coming out of his eyes. Suddenly, more and more ugly and disturbing figures wearing black robes started floating and flying around in my bedroom.

The energy colors were still changing from dark to darker, then a little bit lighter, and then dark again. The situation was very scary. It was way scarier than any nightmare I had ever had. I began to hear the sound of a blowing, howling wind; I heard the sound of an airplane taking off or landing; the noises were changing from high to low tones. My body felt very cold. I was shivering and my hands and legs felt ice cold. I also felt a very cold, freezing breeze in the room even though the windows were still locked and the heat was running in the house. Through all this, James was hugging me tighter and tighter as he continued to whisper in my ears.

Do not be scared; take the fear out of your heart this instant. No harm will come to you. Follow my lead; feel my arms around you. I will protect you. Put your trust in me. Close your eyes and keep them closed tight. Empty your mind. Clear your mind of all thoughts. Close your ears tight and only hear my voice singing in them. Feel the love that I am giving you and this will keep you warm and relaxed.

This lasted for about an hour when I stopped hearing the roaring, howling and the other weird noises. All I could now hear was the voice of James whispering in my ears as he spoke to me about my experience.

You were trembling; you felt terrifying fear in your heart and extreme cold in your body. You panicked and doubted me. You got very anxious and you did not know what to do, you wanted out of this experience. Then, when you started listening to the words I was whispering in your ears, you finally felt my soft, warm touch and embrace; you felt the clean, pure energy coming out of my palms. Then you looked into my eyes and felt trust for me again. You started to really believe that nothing was going to hurt you on the physical, and that was when you put yourself at ease. You started to relax and believe in me again, especially when I told you to take the fear out of your heart, to follow my lead; to keep your eyes closed, to empty your mind and only listen to my voice. I tell you, we did it the right way! We went through it the way it was supposed to go and I am glad that you saw all of it. I am happy that you felt it for real. Next time you fly,[5] you will see similar things, but they will not affect you anymore because now you know that it is an illusion that will pass.

I felt my body getting warm again, but I was very tired so I dosed off. When I fell into a deep sleep, I started seeing nightmares like I used to see up until a few months ago, where for hours all I would see were scary dreams. This nightmare was even worse — even worse than the experience I had just gone through with James. This time, I saw many experiences from my past and from the present; but the scariest thing was when I saw harm done to my daughter. I could take pain and misery in my life, but I cannot tolerate anything happening to my daughter. The threat on my daughter's well—being was way worse than seeing and feeling scary figures and dark energy flying around in my bedroom.

At ten minutes after four in the morning — which has been my wake—up time for a while — I opened my eyes, looked around and started remembering what had happened a few hours ago. Tears came down my face. None of the dark energy was with me in my room anymore; no lights, no energy, no demons, and nothing fearful. It was quiet and calm. All I felt were tears coming down my face. I was not sure if these tears were from panic and fear, or from relief. I looked at James, who was sitting next to me quietly, and I asked him what this was all about.

---

5. Through meditation, I am able to leave my physical body and see and experience all kinds of situations and energy. Leaving my body, which is the same as flying, provides me with more and more information and knowledge about what this power that is in me right now really is, and how I can use it without fear or doubt about who I am.

All the crying and the experience that you went through were very good for you. These tears purified all the bad memories you had and they cleaned your eyes to let you see clearer. All that happened was to bring forward the best part of you, so you can handle your life better and better. I gave you Reiki to relax you and I tried to have you say whatever was on your mind – but you said nothing. You did not ask me any questions and you also made no comments at all. You and I stared at each other for a while, and you still decided not to even whisper a word. You know that usually I will not bring anything up to you unless you mention it first.

Now let me tell you what happened and why. You see, there are angels all over the universe. Some of them are labeled good angels – these are the purified ones. Some of them are labeled bad angels – these are the evil ones. Keep in mind that all these angels were created from the same Source. The angels that are labeled bad or evil rebelled against their Source and tried to take over the universe. Another strong power – the good angels – fought this power, conquered it and scattered the bad angels all over the universe.

I want you to listen very carefully now to what I am going to tell you. When a part of Source decides to come to this Earth to become a human, this human will have his guardian angel, good angels and evil angels with him. The guardian angel is always with the human – stuck to him, attached to him – always trying to protect him in all his experiences, whether they are good or bad. If this human is not aware of the existence of his guardian angel, the help and protection will still come to him but it will be through a dream, a sign or by talking to the self or through a thought – but this human will not understand how this happened. Other times a human will understand and he will be able to connect to his higher self. When he can do this, he will see and hear directly from his guardian angel.

Many times, good angels come in a human physical form. These angels used to be humans before, who finished all the experiences that their souls needed to experience. They come to protect and give advice to and comfort humans, only because the souls of the humans they are helping have planned it this way. These angels will help no matter if the human experiences are good or bad. There is no need for them to be thanked because they have no ego that needs to show off. They will do what is needed and they will disappear as mysteriously as they showed up. The good angels' job is to encourage humans to love themselves with pure unconditional love, which they can then extend to include all of humanity. This kind of love will keep every human connected to his higher self all the time.

The evil angel is with every human, the same as the guardian angel. An evil angel is an angel that rebelled against Source. This angel loves himself, not the human that he is with. He always tries to win the human over, to make him his friend in duty. The job of these angels is to create new experiences that were not planned by the human's soul. Their aim is to make evil, which comes from the human's ego, conquer good, which usually comes from the heart. They will show a human how to love himself but this love will be based on selfishness, not on a beautiful unconditional love where there is no blame or judgment. They will convince the human that bad is better than good; that wrong is better than right. Basically, their main job is to teach a human how to judge himself, to make it very easy for that human to also judge others.

Evil angels are the enemy of the soul. Their most clever trick is to approach a human as a guardian angel. They will lead a human and they will protect him the same way a guardian angel will, but they will do it for a way different reason. This kind of angel will do his best to make a human love the power that they provide him with, so that he can be led their way. If a human chooses to follow evil angels, then when the human's soul goes back to Source, its mission will not have been accomplished as it was planned. That soul will then come back again and again in different physical bodies to finish all these experiences that were missed.

Now remember, every human has enough wisdom in him to have good win over evil. When you have good angels and evil angels, as they are labeled on Earth, there is always a big struggle between them. Each will do his best to attract you and keep your attention only so that you can follow either what your soul planned on, or what you desire, which will corrupt the plans of your soul. When these angels fight, they are fighting for you. Each one of them will try to win you over so that you will either be who your soul decided it wants to be, or a slave to the demon that will not let you finish what was planned.

One of the most famous purified angels is Archangel Michael. He is the most loving angel who is known as the fighter. He fights evil and demons – the devil himself, if you will. He is a great power in the universe, using his sharp sword to cut the evil angels' lousy energy, to protect whoever asks for his protection. You always asked for Archangel Michael's help indirectly without even knowing it, but since you discovered him and learned about him, you now ask for his help directly, but still not all the time.

I want you to remember something: you came to Earth to experience many different physical and emotional experiences through your free will. If I tell you what to do all the time, and if I push my power on you to lead you in a certain way, the experiences that your soul planned on will never occur. My job is to go along with whatever you choose. I will always protect you and do my best to show you the best way to finish what you planned. Sometimes you do not listen to me. You ignore what I am advising you and you follow the other angel. I know and you know that you are not doing this to hurt me or yourself. You are doing it only because you do not know better. But guess what? I will walk with you the path you choose. I will be with you all the way; I will never leave you alone, but I will always do my best to bring you back on the right path.

The truth is that angels are and always will be here to comfort humans in pain and in death. Sometimes humans will doubt the existence of angels, especially when a disaster happens. Humans will question and wonder where their angels are and why they are not being protected by them. When a disaster, catastrophe or big problem occurs, a human may not feel the angels beside him who are doing their best to comfort him. Keep in mind that angels cannot change whatever souls planned on doing on their trip to Earth. None of us can change the experience as it is meant to be and finished. We can only help a human go through the experience the way that was planned by the soul, regardless of how tough or easy, happy or ugly the experience is.

Everything you saw and felt last night was planned for you, so that you can understand that whenever you are in your higher self and you stay there – where there is no more judging or blaming, no more right or wrong, no more good or bad – nothing will affect you anymore. The angel in black that you saw sitting next to you staring at you, the demons flying all over the room and the dark shining light, all resembled what your life was about before. They were an expression you saw with your eyes, as a confirmation to make you understand that these things do exist and that you did follow them in the past. A lot of the experiences that you went through were planned by your soul; and I tell you that there were others that were added by the demons. All of this is history now.

Everything you saw, felt and experienced was revealed to you through your Conscious; and it has now moved to your Subconscious data bank, as you move to a different level of purity in your life. If you ever need to experience such things again, the information will be available to you through your Subconscious at the blink of an eye; so next time you will experience it without the same fear that you had last night.

Now let's talk about what you saw happening to your daughter. You saw what you thought was causing physical harm to your daughter and you felt fear of losing her. You have to understand and believe that your daughter has her life to go through on this Earth. It does not matter what you think is right or wrong for her because her experiences are different from yours. She is going to experience what her soul planned if you like it or not. So worrying about her is not helping her or hurting her, but it is hurting you. Stop that right now. Get over it and help her instead. She loves you to death so she will always pause and listen to your advice; but do not expect her to change the way she runs her life because of you.

Understand that the nightmares that followed your experience also came as a lesson for you to realize that nightmares are scary, but there are scarier things in this life than a nightmare. These nightmares were meant to make you understand the life you went through so far, and to help you recognize that you were strong enough to handle it. All the real things and experiences that happened so far in your life were way worse than any nightmare you saw in your dreams. What you see in a dream is like a movie of emotions, and reactions to these emotions that happened throughout your life. Most of the time, you are the main character where your Conscious and your Subconscious add more and more incidents and activities to your dream to make it a nightmare.[6]

---

6. When a human sleeps, the soul leaves the physical body, but the body remains attached to the soul by a silver cord. The mind, which takes information from the Conscious and the Subconscious, leaves the body with the soul. The Conscious brings the physical experience to the movie that a human sees and the Subconscious gives it meaning, making it either a pleasant dream or a nightmare.

The Conscious and Subconscious both provide the scenery, but only your Subconscious provides the emotional response – and you are the leader of your Subconscious!

When I settled down, I realized that for the first time since I started talking to James, my soul mate was not with me.[7] I did not see her as I usually do every night. Usually, we bring to us the souls of humans that my soul mate and I, as humans, care about, and we do Reiki on them. This morning, I did not have my soul mate's soul or any other soul with me. Only James and I were in my room. I came to the conclusion that it would be better for me to be alone this morning. The main reason for this decision was that I was scared of passing on to my soul mate and the others the heavy energy that I had experienced. I thought that I would be hurting them rather than giving them love. I also did not know if all my crying came from bad energy that would have caused harm to the souls of the humans that I would have given Reiki to. After I put myself in all this confusion, James started talking to me again.

You did not see your soul mate with you last night or this morning because you wanted to be her protector. You did not have her over so that she would not be affected by all the power and energy that you were experiencing. I tell you, it is fine that she was not with you. You chose this only to protect her; but remember, she does not need your protection. She can take care of herself. She would not have been physically hurt, but she might have felt a lot of the negative energy that you were experiencing. This would have caused her to feel disturbed

---

[7.] Since the time I started talking to James, my soul mate has been with me on a nightly basis, but I am not referring to a physical presence. Her soul is always with me in all sessions that James and I have. Every night, we bring to us different souls of humans that we are close to, only to give them love and to help these people relax so they can finish with ease any experience they are having.

the whole day without knowing what was going on unless you told her. The same is true with the souls of the humans that you usually give Reiki to every morning. You decided not to do Reiki on them this morning, and that is also fine. They might have also been affected by the heavy energy that you experienced, and they too would have felt different the whole day. Maybe they would have felt upset or angry without knowing why. All they would have known is that they were feeling somewhat different than their usual feeling every morning after you give them your love.

I want you to have no doubt that this experience was very beautiful for you to feel, live, see and hear. The wisdom that you have gained from it is that you now know that it was not a bad experience, as you always labeled the nightmares you had in the past. I wanted you to see and notice the old part of you that you are still somehow attached to. Seeing what you saw last night was to help you understand the real you. Knowing the real you will help you recognize that in this life, there is not only white and gold light that resembles purity and the God that is in you. There is still a lot of dark energy that represents bad energy and part of the past that you went through. Now it is time to clear, clean, and change the data that was causing you to run your life the way you did in the past. This change will allow you to follow the right lead to finish this life accordingly. It is a beautiful road that you are traveling and I assure you that it is going to be all good; full of pleasure and happiness and many new surprises. I promise you again and again that I will stay with you until the end.

Yesterday, I took my soul mate through a hypnotherapy session where she relived the part of her current life when she was about eight or nine years old. I saw and heard a lot of things about the abuse that she went through. I got very upset and I wanted to avenge her. Now I discovered that I can

use the power that I have within me in a different way. Please tell me what
this is all about and why I reacted the way I did.

What happened yesterday is a new and beautiful experience that
added to your discovery of the power that you have now. You discovered
that this power can also be used for revenge when you allow yourself to
be controlled by dark angels, which are also a part of earthly life. As a
human, you have free will, which provides you with the choice of how
to use this power – and now you choose to be a loving healer.

You figured out that while another person is hypnotized, you could
see what he is seeing – in his current life or in a past life. I want you
to know and understand that you are not a psychic or a fortune teller;
but when you go to your higher self, you are able to go places and
perform spiritual accomplishments in contentment, knowing that you
are learning and giving whatever you can. I tell you that for now if a
human is not physically sitting with you and if this human is not in a
state where he could be hypnotized, you will not be able to see his past
by yourself. You have to be connected to that human and that human
has to also be connected to you. You can figure things out better
than the human himself when you have this connection between you.
Things, for you, look clearer; and the images are brighter than they are
for that human. This is because the human will see something but he
might be scared to go through it, so he might reject it and refuse it.
He might also mix experiences from different lifetimes, jumping from
one to another; but you will be observing what he is seeing without any
effort on your part, and you will be able to figure out which lifetime
he is experiencing at that moment. Keep in mind that the skill of the
hypnotherapist plays a role in the way the human will experience a
hypnotherapy session. A good hypnotherapist knows how to lead his
client with the right questions and suggestions, to help the client accept

the process and be in control of his emotions as he sees his past. As a hypnotherapist, you already know that the only way you can help a human is through his own free will to allow you.

What you experienced with your soul mate yesterday is not something new for you. Your soul mate and you meditate and hypnotize each other very easily now. You both help each other get rid of any fear or past dilemma that you think you still have. Your soul mate did not need to go through hypnotherapy yesterday, but she did it for her and for you to experience, in a different way, the new stage that you both are in now. Your soul mate knew that if she went through hypnosis she would feel better, because she would be releasing some of her past anger; and she also did it for you to experience more through her. Remember something – your soul mate and you go from lifetime to lifetime helping each other, so your connection and the trust between you are very strong. This allowed you to see everything very clearly, and it was meant for you to see it all. It was a great benefit for both of you.

For you, the experience started when you saw what she was seeing and realized that she was mixing experiences from different lifetimes. This is when you got involved to help her focus on one past life at a time. As I said before, you were able to do that because you were the observer. Your soul mate's aim was to see the past of her current life and to get rid of the fear that she was still holding on to. Even though you had heard it all before you had not felt or seen it the way it really happened. If you remember, when you first heard about your soul mate's childhood experience, you got pissed but you did not make a big deal about it, only because you did not see it at that time. Yesterday, when you saw it, you felt it with her and you lived it, which made it a different experience for you. The old Sami, who was guarded and controlled by dark entities who were always protecting and leading the way he used to run his life, came back into you yesterday. You felt hurt, strong pressure and helpless.

You were seeing what was going on, but you could not do anything to protect her; and you felt bad that when these things occurred in her life you were not there to help her. Because you both are so close and emotionally tied, seeing and experiencing what she went through made you want to protect and avenge her. The truth is, whatever you went and did was to avenge both of you, which is *you*. Yes, you were trying to take care of your soul mate, but you were also trying to take care of your own emotions.

All this is good. Keep on practicing hypnotherapy on each other and on other humans. The more you do it the better you will understand the difference between past lifetimes and the past of a present lifetime in various humans. With practice, you will be able to hypnotize each other, and any other human that requests it, without involving your feelings and emotions in the session.

Now let us take a trip that will open your eyes even more to the power and methods of the dark angels. We will visit someone that you would never have thought is who he is by the way he looks and lives.

The three of us flew through the universe and we ended up in an old beautiful village with old, small houses next to each other. We entered one of these houses and found ourselves in a living room that was also a bedroom and a kitchen. We saw an old man with white hair and a white beard dressed in a black robe. He was sitting on a wooden chair behind a wood table, writing. The room looked beautiful. It had stone walls with a couple of pieces of furniture and a bed in the corner next to a table. It felt very pure and peaceful.

We approached the old man. He raised his head from his writing and welcomed us. He offered us a seat and we sat on his bed. He looked at us and said, "I am Jacob. I help people to stay in this life and get the most they can out of it. They stay because they love their earthly bound existence and they do not want to leave it. I cannot make anyone stay a second more than they want to, but I am good at convincing them to stay as long as their physical body will allow them." He paused, smiled, and said, "I know you both – and you both know me. We have seen and talked to each other in different lifetimes. Now I am happy to have the chance to talk to both of you again and to welcome you to my humble house." Then Jacob looked at me and said, "I am happy for you having discovered this beautiful power in you. You have it, but you do not know how to use it to benefit the most from it. For all of your present life on Earth, I have been offering you help. You were promised a great life, which you deserved. You always accepted our giving indirectly until recently, when you thought that you discovered yourself, and started rejecting the way you used to run your life. A few weeks ago, you went on a trip with your guardian angel where you met with me at the river. I looked different to your eyes, but it was me who offered you all the help you need, only so you can be with me. I promised you a beautiful, controlling, powerful life that you can finish on Earth and you refused it. I had offered you the same great power of the anger and revenge that you experienced yesterday. I hope you are listening very carefully to what I am telling you. Now you have discovered a different power and you used it in the first experience that hit you after your discovery. By using this kind of power, you showed me that you still miss the life that you led in the past, and that you want to experience more through me. Come back. I am extending you this offer. I promise you that if you agree and we join hands together, you will be the most powerful human and the most comfortable one on Earth. I will teach you exactly how to use this power that you have and how to take advantage of it to satisfy your earthly needs. This is your life for now, so why don't you get the best out of it? Why don't you come back and let me help you? We have been together before, from one life to the other. In some of them, you stuck to me and in others you rebelled against me. Hypnotize yourself. Go back to these lifetimes and see the beauty and the misery that you experienced. Maybe after you see you will decide which way you want to go."

*I looked at Jacob and said, "I hear you, and I can still feel the beginning of this life up until recently. I can see and feel how it passed and how everything in it went fine for me – but now I know Who I Am! I know What I Am, I know what I want to do and I believe in everything that I am going through and doing now. Yesterday, I did what I did and then realized that I allowed weakness to make me feel discomfort; then I blamed myself for trying to avenge my soul mate. Let me assure you, I am a different human being than I was in the past and I know that I am a different man. I understand that you might be meaning well by extending your help and your hand, but this offer is only to make **you** happy and to give **you** satisfaction in accomplishing what you want, not because you care for my happiness. If I agree, I might be satisfied in what you are offering me, but I will never be happy following you rather than following Who I Am. I know that in my past days in this life I used to be your puppet, but I want you to know that now I am free and I belong to nobody except me. Now I know that I have a purpose, which is to finish whatever my soul decided and planned on doing in this life." Jacob then put a smile on his face and said, "You will be back."*

James, my soul mate and I left that place. We came back and we sat down to discuss what had just happened and why.

The love that I have for you is similar to the love that you have for yourself when you are in the stage of unconditional love. Let me explain to you what happened on our trip today and then you figure out what kind of wisdom you both are going to gain from it.

This was a very valuable lesson for you to realize what kind of power a human can have. I said this before and I am going to keep on reminding you. The dark angels are always going to use your soul mate to make you feel weak. They are going to use her against you and you against her. I want you to understand that if what happened yesterday was with a different human, you would not have blinked an eye or given a thought to revenge; but you reacted the way you did because this was all about your soul mate.

You now know that you have the power of hurting…and loving… and it is always up to you to choose which way you want to go. You cannot have both because they contradict each other. They are like black and white so it has to be either/or. I want you to believe that I am with you in whatever you choose to do. I have always been with you and I always will be, until we finish this life together. It is up to you to decide which route to take and I will help you all the way to do what you decide; but I will tell you, the worst thing you can do to yourself after any experience that you go through is to feel sorry for yourself or to blame and judge yourself for the way you reacted through the experience. Feeling guilty is leading you nowhere except to confusion.

If you think back, you will agree that in this life you have lived the good, the bad, and the ugly. You laughed, you cried; you put your trust in a lot of people and felt betrayed; you were stabbed in the back and at the same time you stabbed others in the back. Rewind your thoughts and see your past. See how you judged yourself and blamed yourself for whatever you thought you did wrong. Now pause for a second and look at where you are now. All these experiences were training for you to make you understand that life has its ups and downs and it has its beauty and ugliness; and to show you that it is up to you to choose which route you want to follow. You have always had the wisdom to choose; only now you are wiser than you have ever been. The wisdom that you now have is your source for understanding that whatever experience you choose to go through – good or bad – you will do it with happiness and satisfaction and according to what your heart tells you.

See this power that you are in now? Every human has it. You are not special, but now you choose to recognize that this power exists within you. You talked to the devil. He offered you his hand. He offered to take care of your earthly existence as long as you are on this Earth. You refused. *You* chose the refusal. No one pressured you or forced you to refuse. You did this because in this stage of your life you feel deep inside that you are a healer. You believe that you can give, and you know that what you are giving goes way, way beyond the physical experience. You felt great refusing Jacob and I felt great with you. This refusal came from your heart and from your belief that you now really know Who You Are.

Chapter 7

ENERGY

I want to know more about how energy works. How could it be used to heal for real? What kind of good or bad effects come from energy?

Energy is a power that fills, and links to, a very important Force; it expands through the whole universe and every human is a part of this indivisible Force. Energy exists everywhere, on every level of human understanding and beyond. Humanity cannot exist without Energy and it is also the human tool for decreasing anxiety and stress, and for providing a healthy living. It does this by letting the human connect to a higher energy – Universal Energy – that is always available. This higher Energy creates energy fields within a human that help balance the unstable energy that occurs when a human gets sick, stressed or distressed. Understand that human energy is always connected to Universal Energy; it is a human's awareness that will let him accept, and apply to himself, what the universe is providing for him. This is why a human can help in the healing of his own physical and mental/emotional condition, and that of other humans; which is the power of healing that you know as Reiki. Universal Energy or Reiki, will balance all the chakras[8] in a human body, which will make a human feel peaceful and relaxed; and it will provide the best conditions for the greatest possible healing.

Do understand that when a human places his palms above his own or another human's body, even though he is not touching the physical body, he will in fact be moving energy that will release the stifled or congested chakras that are found in that human's physical body. This healing can happen only if the human giving energy and the human receiving it have faith in its power. Without faith, energy healing cannot occur. Energy, with all its power, is still engaged only through the unconditional love and faith that is in a human's heart when he is in his higher self – a state of being where only pure love is flowing from him. This is why the transfer of this pure energy can never hurt any human.

Energy is very flexible and has no limits. It could be used in person or it could very easily be sent and transferred between humans over a distance using the connection of Universal Energy. I tell you, giving or sending pure energy to another human is a beautiful gift with great power. Its power can heal a human even without a physical touch – only by a motion of the hand or by a look of the eye that is full of love. It could heal a human with or without the help of medicine, or it could help medicine work with fewer side effects.

Energy has been used for ages and ages to heal many of the human body's problems, but the way the power of energy works has never been completely understood by humans. Many studies have been attempted by humans, since their first days on this Earth, to try to understand the mystery of this power; but so far nothing definite has been determined

---

8. Chakra is a Sanskrit word meaning "spinning wheel." The chakras are energy centers on the human body that are constantly spinning, the major ones located along the spine.

about how it heals. I say, it all comes down to faith. Not one master who walked this Earth has ever claimed that the power he has in the palms of his hands has healed another human. These masters always told humans that it was their own faith that healed them. I tell you again, energy will only heal humans through faith if the giver and the receiver believe that it can. This is why you might hear of energy healing that has occurred without the use of medical intervention being labeled a miracle. The word "miracle" is mostly used to describe something that cannot be explained by humanity. On Earth, labels provide a way for humans to somehow make sense of what they are experiencing; so labeling something as a miracle will let a human believe and have faith in its existence.

At the beginning of time, humans used to believe in and use the power of energy in all their healing. They used it to heal themselves and others. These days, humans are slowly going back to the old beliefs, and they are beginning to use the power of energy to heal themselves. Humanity is beginning to recognize that every human can heal himself through the power of energy if he knows how to use it, and if he has faith that it will heal him. Some humans that do not yet have faith in their own power search to find the right healer to help them. This is happening more and more on Earth.

I want you to know that there are humans who will twist the real purpose of energy healing to get rich, completely missing the faith component. Some humans allow their needs and wants to control them to the point where they will do the impossible for the dollar. When the dollar becomes the human's god, there is no more faith in healing through this power tool that is called energy. In this case, the energy giver is a phony; he is not even a business person who really believes in what he does. A human's goal to get rich by tricking others is based on selfishness and need; and this is definitely not Reiki. If the receiver also does not have faith in energy healing, it is like a double-edged sword that cuts both ways. This non–existence of faith will prevent real healing from taking place. The giver's only intention of greed will prevent pure energy from flowing through him; the receiver's lack of faith will stop him from creating his own miracle. A giver's lack of faith and belief in the fact that the power within him can heal, will also prevent him from healing himself.

Now, remember, life is very valuable for humans on this Earth, only because they fear what they do not know; so they will do everything possible, and also aim for the impossible, to keep their life going. When a scared human reaches a point where he has only two choices, to die or to live, he might see energy healing as the only tool to keep him going. That is when he will convince himself to believe that this tool will heal him. This is where a real miracle, by earthly definition, happens. In this case, the receiver's faith will be so strong that even if the giver's intention is to give energy healing only for the money, the receiver will still be healed. The miracle will happen, but it is basically manifesting because of the receiver's faith in the power of healing energy. I hope you really understand that I am talking about the power of faith and free will that manifests through a human's Subconscious.

But let's say the receiver did not heal because he went through the energy healing session out of obligation and fear, not out of faith that he is going to be healed. If you think about it, he lost nothing because this type of healing experience is not harmful in any way, but he also did not help himself to gain any benefit. In this case, the sick human wants to be healed regardless of the medicine, even though he understands nothing about energy and is full of doubt. For sure the giver also wants the sick human to be healed so that he can become famous, gain a good reputation and attract more clients. There is a total absence of faith. I tell you, the best healing will be when the giver and the receiver have faith, and when both believe in the power of Life. That is when miracles will happen that humans will talk about and trust in.

Now let's talk a little bit about the energy field that is within and around a human. The aura is an energy field that floods the body and is absolutely essential to human life. This energy field makes it possible for the human body to be alive and to function as it does – physically, emotionally and mentally. The aura consists of a colored glow that sometimes is a single, steady color and other times a combination of different colors, which surround and take the shape of the body. It is a reflection of a supernatural energy field that fills everything and anything on Earth. A human can see auras coming out of the chakras, or energy centers, of the body only after he connects to his higher self. It takes a lot of practice for a human to reach that point; not all humans will be able to achieve it.

Let me explain to you in detail what a chakra is and what it does for the human body. *Chakra* is a Sanskrit word meaning spinning wheel. Chakras of the human body are spinning wheels of energy that exist everywhere on the body and each one has its own necessary job to do for a human to exist and function on Earth. The seven major ones are located on the spine, from the top of the head to the root of the spine.

The Crown chakra is located at the top of the human head. When this chakra is pure, the energy around it is seen as a violet color. The crown chakra is the chakra of Consciousness and it is the point of connection to the higher self.

The Third–eye chakra is located on the center of the forehead between the two eyes. In its purity, its energy is seen as an indigo color. This is the connection chakra between your Divine Self and your human self. This is the chakra of light, time and awareness; awareness of your Divine Self, transcendence of time, and of your connection to your higher self.

The Throat chakra is where the human throat is. Its pure energy is seen as a blue color, and it is the center of communication and feelings.

The Heart chakra is located where the human heart is. In its purity it is seen as a green color. This is the center of giving and receiving love.

The Solar Plexus chakra is between the heart and the navel. It is gold or yellow in color when it is pure. It is the storage center of emotions – although emotions are not created through this chakra.

The Navel chakra is on the navel and its pure energy is seen as orange in color. It is the center of the human body's sexuality, creativity and emotions.

The Root chakra is at the bottom end of the spine, and its pure energy is seen as a red color. This is the only chakra that does not grow with the growth of a human's physical body because it is fully developed at birth. It stays the same in size and energy flow from the time a human is born and as long as the human is still on Earth. The Root chakra is related to the survival and security of a human.

The balance of the chakras is always important for energy to flow through the whole body; to heal the body and to help keep a human in his higher self. I want you to always remember that a human cannot be in his higher self if he is not balanced, and he cannot be balanced if he is not in his higher self. This is the only way that healing can take place. If a human is angry or unhappy, in a lousy relationship or always worried, confused or in emotional distress, these emotions will be stored in the chakras of the body and, over time, they will create an imbalance in the body's energy system. This results in slow-spinning chakras, and it leads the human to exist in his lower emotions like fear, doubt and anger, preventing the human from reaching the love, happiness, health and success that he is aiming for. As a rule, the older and wiser a human gets, the better he will handle his life and himself, which means that his energy will be more balanced and aligned with his soul…if he chooses it to be.

Love is the most important part in creating balance. Love increases the count of active chakras in the body and enlarges them. You see, love is pure energy. When the pure energy of love interacts with the body, the number of chakras that are energized increases and each existing chakra expands and spins faster and faster in order to purify the body. The more the body becomes aligned and balanced, the more it will be connected with the human's personal power, which will keep the human in his higher self all the time.

Energy healing engages and affects delicate energies as they relate to the experience of healing, consciousness, and the human's potential; which means that energy healing allows each human who believes in it to achieve the highest possible healing in accordance with his soul's plan. When you are doing Reiki on yourself or on another human, you are placing your hands on an area that needs to be balanced, so that universal energy can flow freely to heal that area. It means that you are sparking the chakra wheels to spin the way they are supposed to for the body to function to the best of its ability.

A woman in her nineties came to our wellness center to receive Reiki and muscle release treatment. She was surrounded by dark entities and black energy. My soul mate and I did our best to clear most of the energy that was around her. What was this dark energy? Did we do the right thing by clearing these energies from this woman?

This is the *new you*. You concentrate for a few seconds and then you can see angels, energy, and any entity that is surrounding other humans. What you saw on the older woman is what the new you is showing you. Let me just tell you that every human on this Earth wishes for what you can do. Every human will have an urge to see what you can see. I am telling you this not for you to feel that you are better than anyone else. I just want you to always remember that whatever is happening to you is coming from the love that is in you. Any human that reaches the stage of love that you are in, will be capable of doing the same as you are doing, if not better.

So now open your eyes and ears, look at me, and hear me as I explain what the situation is with this elderly lady. This ninety-two year old woman has been living her years allowing dark entities to run her life. She did not do it on purpose all these years, and she is still not aware that she is allowing it. The dark and black entities that you saw surrounding her and going in and out of her root chakra are her protectors. They will never leave her alone, and especially not with someone like you who can understand and figure out, by taking one look, how to clear another human from their power and control. What you saw on this woman were the same figures that you saw in your room the other night. Remember what we talked about? When a human comes to this life, good and bad energies, or good and bad angels, come with him and stay with him all his life. Each one of these angels works in a different way to attract the human to his side. As a human grows older and older, he has a longer period of earthly time to gain the wisdom to choose a way to live and finish his life; which will allow his soul to finish its experiences as they were planned. Understand that if the soul decides to leave early, it does not mean that the human did not gain the wisdom that the soul had decided for that human to gain during this lifetime. It only means that the soul had planned to leave early.

Now let's go back to talking about the elderly. Sometimes, if demons are controlling the human's life, they will prevent this human from leaving this life. They will do this by showing the human a lot of goodies so that he will be attached more and more to the beauty of earthly needs. This will make this human get stuck in an experience and put himself in a loop. His soul will survive through this experience of being in a loop, but it will not have a chance to finish what it planned on doing in this lifetime through this human. At this time, the soul is still gaining wisdom and the human is still healthy and able to function for that soul's experiences, even though they are different experiences than the ones the soul had originally planned on. The soul will keep on going with it until it reaches a point that the body, or shell, of this human cannot function anymore. This is when the soul decides to drop that body and go back to its Source without finishing what the real plan was. It will then come back in a different body to finish what was initially planned.

In the case of the elderly woman that came to your center, she is a healthy old human that somehow has discovered and believes in the existence of universal energy. When she met you and learned what you do at your center, she did not stop telling you story after story about energy and meditation, and how she was able to heal herself most of her life without using too much medication. She has been doing this her entire life; but all this was done with the indirect help of her demons. These demons gave her way more help than her guardian angels could provide her with, only because she chose to listen to them. They were showing her the beauty of surviving by giving her advice on how to stay healthy and do the impossible. They did all this so that they can prevent her from leaving this earthly life – so she can remain their servant as long as possible. Even though the demons played this role in her life, in the end, she is going to leave. When she does, she will come back, and they will be waiting for her with open arms so she can be their puppet again in different lifetimes to come.

Meeting this woman did not happen by mistake. It was meant to happen. Let me explain why. She had a therapist that she always went to who she felt very comfortable with, and they always talked about energy and about a human's life and lifetimes. Her therapist was connected and she loved learning from him; at the same time, he was learning from her. When this therapist got sick and could not help her anymore, she missed the comfort she always felt with him. It happened that one day you and your soul mate were at the senior apartment complex where she lives, providing free information about yourselves and how you help people. Even though you were sitting in the far corner of the hall, her demons showed her the way to come talk to you. Finding you was to satisfy her hunger for the same wisdom she used to share with her therapist, so that she can keep going. Your soul mate and you chatted with her for a while, even after the event was over, and she saw the real love that you both carry. That was why she started coming to your center to satisfy her need. You worked on her muscles a few times and released a lot of the pain that she was feeling. She felt great about herself and she felt at ease with her body, but she still needed a person to talk to about what she used to discuss with her therapist.

On the woman's last visit to your center, you saw a lot more dark entities than what you had seen before. This time you saw the dark energy going in and out of her root and surrounding her, with her demons holding down her shoulders, arms and hips. These demons were attached to her to prevent her from feeling better as she had felt after her previous sessions. The demons wanted her muscles to feel well, but not her emotions and needs. You were now a danger to them.

You decided to stop working on her muscles so that you can work on relieving her of this dark energy. The more the dark energy was broken, the better she felt, as if a load was off her back. She put a big smile on her face and started to relax. You started to see the color of the energy surrounding her change from dark to bright, and you saw the dark entities that had been attached to her begin to disappear. The team effort that you and your soul mate gave was the most beautiful thing that humans can do for another human, especially because this woman thought that she knew all about energy – even though she really knew nothing about it. She had never felt the peace of this beautiful energy.

I'm telling you, you are now upsetting the black angels. Her reactions made the black angels angry only because they felt they were losing her. They are very smart and they do not accept losing very easily; especially when they feel they are losing a human they have been working on for a long time, through whom they were able to fulfill and accomplish their needs. They are going to use their power to convince the old lady not to come and see you anymore. She is a strong human that will not give up easily, especially since now she feels great about herself. A war is going to start between her and her black angels and her and her white angels. You and her white angels are a team against the black angels because of what you are providing for her. The demons want her back. Be ready. They will be with her next time she comes to visit you. They will be attached to her the same way you saw them last time, only this time they will be more prepared and more powerful. They are not going to let go that easily. You two, with the white angels' support, are also ready to get her to your side. Be aware now that the more she starts coming toward your side, the weaker she will start feeling. She is still feeling good, but now she is going to question this beautiful new feeling. That is when a lot of doubt will arise in her, causing confusion and disturbance within her. She does not know what is going on and I tell you she should not hear it from you either. Keep on doing what you are doing for her. Keep offering her rides to come and see you. Keep on giving her all the love that you can give. Whatever the end result is, it will be her own choice and decision and no one can change it for her, except her.

Yesterday my soul mate and you talked through me about the symbols that she saw the day before. Would you explain this to me a little more? Also, I want to know what that dark energy was that I saw around my soul mate's neck. Then could you also explain to me the feeling that I had after I cleared dark energy off students at the center without their knowledge?

Your soul mate and I talked a little bit yesterday during the day, but it looks like she was not ready for me because she was in a hurry to do something else. I also think that she did not understand what I told her about the symbols that she was seeing the day before. Let me explain it to you and you can tell her later. It will help her in understanding what she asked for.

When a human meditates and goes very deep into his meditation, it will be like he is hypnotizing himself. For this, it is very helpful if a human can meditate in an almost dark or completely dark place. When a human goes into a deep meditation, he will start seeing characters or signs that resemble a mark or a symbol. Every time the human sees that symbol when he's in deep meditation, it will be a reminder that will help take him deeper and deeper into his meditation, starting from where he left off the last time he saw that symbol. Every incident that the person is meditating on will have its own symbol.

Meditation in the sun will be different because the sun has very strong energy. This energy is powerful to a point where the human eyes will start seeing a bright yellow or bright red color and the shadows of symbols. Even though the eyelids are shut, the character or the sign that the sun draws will look like electric shocks or lightning. Every time a human thinks of and sees that sign again, it will be a reminder of the incident, or the thought, that the human was experiencing when that sign was created. The symbol itself has no meaning or power. The symbol is created by the human's Subconscious, using the energy of the sun, to make it meaningful and unique for that human. Basically, it is a personal creation and interpretation.

Tell your soul mate that she is doing better and better every day in concentrating and clearing her mind. Tell her not to stop talking to you and asking you about what she is seeing. The important thing for her now is not to put much effort or thought on her own into what is taking place in her life right now. The more she asks me to explain things to her, the more she will be satisfied in handling all the new things she is discovering. This will lead her to love herself. By loving herself, every incident in her life will be very easy to handle. She should know that she is going to be way more successful than she is now. I am going to repeat myself. She loves to help. She loves to help others heal. She wants to do it and she believes that she can. Every day, she wakes up looking forward to doing more and more. The more she practices, the more she will be able to do. All she has to do is be herself and not try too hard. The more she relaxes, the clearer she will see to heal.

Now let's talk about the dark energy you saw around your soul mate's neck. This dark energy was a reaction to things that she was trying to do. She started to see energy behind you on the wall and she asked you if it was real. You also told her that there is a lot more in the room to see. That was when she started putting more effort into seeing the other energy. All her effort made her judge herself, which was an invitation for dark energy to approach her.

I want you to know that dark energy works in a mysterious way. It crawls into a human body very easily. It will start to control the chakras of the body that are affected in the experience that is occurring. Remember, the throat chakra is for creation, and what your soul mate was doing was creating a scene of what she has been aiming to do for a while. As soon as she saw some energy, she tried too hard to see the rest of the energy that was floating in the room. The more effort she applied, the greater the attraction for dark energy to seep in.

Since she started seeing this new energy a couple of weeks ago she is inviting dark energy because she keeps trying harder and harder to see. You had not yet seen dark energy so strong on her, but I tell you, this time you had help. Your soul mate had on a crystal necklace this time, and crystal is a power and energy revealer to a person who can see energy. When she tried the same thing two weeks ago, she was not wearing her crystal necklace. Yesterday, she had it on, which allowed you to see the energy around her neck clearer and stronger than at any other time. When you cleared the dark energy off her, she felt great. Then after a while she was seeing energy again. Again, she started putting effort into seeing more and more, so dark energy started to crawl back into her. You saw it again, and you cleared it again. Then it happened for a third time. When you told her about it she decided to clear herself. She wanted to clear herself so she can feel more confident in herself, but she was not ready and could not do a good job. You did not say much about that. All you told her is to take off the crystal necklace because you thought that her necklace was attracting all the energy you saw around her neck. After she took it off, you did not see any lousy energy on her anymore, but it was not because she took the crystal off. It was because she stopped trying so hard to see more energy after the crystal came off, so no dark energy approached her all night long. You were happy to see her cleared, but always keep in mind that dark energy does not like what you are doing, because now you can see it and clear it very easily. You should still keep looking and seeing. Don't be scared. Keep telling your soul mate what you are seeing and offer her help to clear dark energy off her. If she accepts your help then do it, and if she rejects your help, let her handle it herself. Do not take anything personally because she has to experience what she chooses to experience. Keep offering your help; and it should not make a difference to you if your offer is accepted or rejected.

Now that you will be seeing a lot of energy on people you care about and love, it is important for you to understand how your emotions are affected by what you see. Go back with your memory and think of the time when you saw in the classroom the small plant fairies or entities that you labeled "plantakies,"[9] crawling toward your soul mate. At that time, you did not say anything to her only because you did not see any harm being done to her by these small entities. But I tell you, it is always better to tell her what you are seeing so she can learn, but let *her* decide how to handle it; either by allowing you to help her or by doing it herself without your help.

Now to answer your last question, let's talk about the energy clearing that you did for the students in the center's classroom. This was a very beautiful and wonderful experience that you wanted to have. You enjoyed helping to clear the lousy, dark energy off all these humans that were in that room. The idea came to you and you asked Archangel Michael to help you in clearing all these humans and the center itself. You were thinking of how you can do this without having anybody notice what you were intending to do. Out of nowhere you heard my voice telling you to stand up and leave the room, and to take your soul mate with you and tell her what your intention was. You went to another room at the center and told your soul mate to go back to the classroom. You relaxed your body on the sofa and then you left your body while Archangel Michael and I stood beside you in case you needed our help. You left your body and flew all over the center. You started by clearing the classroom first. You started with your soul mate; then you went through all the humans that were in that room, one by one. While you

---

9. Everything in this world has energy around it, whether it is a solid object or something that has life. Plants, trees, shrubs, etc. all have life and they have small energy entities around them. The first time I saw them, my soul mate and I jokingly labeled them "plantakies." Every time I see them now I call them plantakies.

were going through them, you got confused for a few seconds because the seat that you were sitting in before you left the room was now occupied by another human. For a split second, you thought that you were clearing your own body, but right away you realized that another human was sitting in your spot. You finished clearing the place, then with the help of Archangel Michael you bundled all this energy and took it out into the universe. When you came back to your body, your soul mate was coming back to the room to check on you. She talked to you for a couple of minutes and made sure that on the physical you were o.k. After relaxing for a few more minutes on the sofa you followed your soul mate to the classroom. Anytime you do something like this, you do not have to talk about it, or tell anyone else about it. The more you say, the more questions you are inviting from people that do not yet understand what you are doing. This will cause them confusion and doubt about you, and they will question what they are doing being around you.

On Earth, there are all kinds of rules and regulations. One of them involves invading another human's privacy. But let me ask you: what is privacy? "Privacy" is a word used on this Earth that has a value based on rules and regulations that humans created. If you want my advice, I will say, for now you shouldn't even think about telling others what you are doing. The minute you start questioning yourself about what you are doing, the less confidence you are going to have in what you are doing, and the less healing you are going to accomplish. I assure you that what you did was wonderful and it was meant for those humans to be cleared by you. Do not worry about what others think. If you do not tell them, they will not know. Keep on doing what you are doing – keep accomplishing – and soon you will never doubt your purpose for being here.

My soul mate and I went to New York City for the day. I saw and experienced all kinds of energy. Can you help me understand what I saw?

The trip happened out of nowhere, but you went there for a great reason, which is for both of you to see and learn a lot of new things that are happening now in your lives. Your soul mate came up with the idea. You hesitated but went with it, and you both loved every second of it. You saw the good, the bad, and the ugly. New York City is a very busy place that is crowded with humans and energy of all kinds. The city is a great place to experience so that you gain more information and wisdom.

As you left New Jersey and reached the tunnel going to NYC, you noticed all kinds of energy that is keeping the tunnel from collapsing. You saw darker energy more than lighter energy floating inside the tunnel. You saw ghosts, figures and spirits that are still nesting in there refusing to leave. They decided to stay there because of their love for that place, where they spent their last moments as humans on this Earth. Some of them died building that tunnel, others died in car accidents there; some of them are there trying to finish an experience that they still need to finish; and some are still hanging around to learn how to finish an experience that was not completed.

When you reached the city, the first place you went to was the underground main bus terminal. You wanted to see the energy, you wanted to see entities – so you did. All over, energy was floating in different colors and shapes. The humans that were there each had a story and a thought on his mind, which created the energy around them. Some of them were worried and frustrated that they had a long wait for their bus; some could not take being underground in a closed, crowded place and some were there for the experience of seeing the city. You wanted to see more so you and your soul mate decided to walk around the city to see what kinds of energy and entities there were in a place like this.

The sun was up but it was a cold day. You walked for a while and then decided to go into a pizza place to have lunch. As you were eating, you noticed one of the people behind the counter preparing some food. You saw dark energy on him and you saw the same energy crawling into the food. That energy was still active all over the food and all over the people behind the counter. I tell you, if any of the customers or workers ate this food it would not have had any more effect on them than being in contact with the human himself. This is because energy is like a cloud, and it could very easily go in and out of a human without putting any kind of pressure on a particular part of the body. This means that even though energy enters a human body through the mouth with food, it does not mean that it will affect the intestines. Energy is always in and around the body, so the energy that you saw around the guy, even though it was going into the food that humans were going to eat, would not affect a human any differently because it went through the mouth instead of through the hand by a handshake.

You left the pizza place to walk on the street. You saw energy floating in the air everywhere. The area was crowded with people even though it was a cold and windy fall day. You saw people surrounded by their angels and energy of all different colors. You saw black, white, green, and blue energy – any color a human can imagine. Seeing crowded energy and colors mixing this way was a new experience for you. You were like a kid, seeing so many entities and different energy combinations.

As you were walking, two people walked toward you, hugging and kissing each other. That is when you saw, for the first time, white sparks of energy all over humans. When a human is sexually excited, the energy around him will look like sparks. The color of the sparks depends on the situation. If there is a mutual excitement between humans, then usually the sparks will start off white and then turn to gold. There are occasions when the energy sparks start off blue, turn to green, and sometimes they even end in black, depending on the situation.

You were very excited telling your soul mate all that you were seeing. You told her about the sparks, you told her about the different colors of energy mixing together and about the fairies and figures that were surrounding the kids who came out of a theater. What you enjoyed seeing the most was the pregnant woman who had just passed you on the street, where you saw the woman's energy and also the baby's energy on her tummy.

The most exciting event of the day for you was when you saw your soul mate's face in the sun, shining gold with beautiful energy. You had never before seen this brilliant shine around her. The reason for this was because she was connected to her higher self at that moment, not having a worry in the world. You should know that any time a human is in that stage he will look more purified and more innocent than usual. Your soul mate then started seeing the symbols that she has been seeing lately, and she told you about it. You explained to her that anytime she sees any of these symbols again or anytime she meditates and they pop into her eyes, they will be a reference to this trip that you both took together and the experience that you both gained from it. You both had a lot of fun experiencing together even though she did not see a fraction of what you saw. I assure you she had a lot of fun, the same as you but in her own way.

You were acting like a small kid who was seeing and discovering new things in his life. I know you want to go back to visit this place again, and I say you should. Just know, when you decide to go on an experience like this again, do not go by yourself. I say this because the second time it will be a lot easier for you to see and absorb, and you will learn a lot more than what you learned the first time. You want and need a companion that you trust to talk to about what you are seeing. Have faith that all these new experiences you will be having from now on are for you to gain more wisdom and knowledge. They will make you the human that your soul decided for you to be.

Lately, I see a lot of figures, ghosts, entities and angels. I see them in my car, in my house and everywhere else, whether I am alone or with company. Tell me about the old man figure that I saw yesterday and spent some time speaking with. What is the reason for this experience?

You reached a point in your life that even though you are still learning and gaining more wisdom, there are a lot of entities, figures, and humans that will seek to learn from the wisdom that you have already gained in your life. There are a lot of lost souls who ended the human life of the human they were occupying, but are still in the transition stage. These souls are still around to learn how to handle most of the experiences they had desired to accomplish but did not finish. They are preparing themselves for when they come back in different bodies to finish these uncompleted experiences.

Now let me tell you about the figure you talked to yesterday. Seeing and being with this elderly figure, who is really a replica of a human – not a physical human – rarely happens to ordinary humans. Because you have reached a high stage of awareness, you are ready to show other souls how to handle experiences they missed or did not finish, so they can be completed as they were planned when these souls come back.

You are never alone now. Souls are always with you and around you. Wherever you are – in your car, at work, in your house, or anywhere else – you are surrounded by figures, ghosts, and angels. They are around you because if you pay attention to them and talk to them, you will be helping them by giving them the wisdom from a human perspective on the experiences they have not completed; and also for you to gain more experience, to know exactly how to help heal real humans when they seek your help.

Now let me tell you in detail why you saw the old man; and let's see what kind of wisdom you gained from this experience. You were all alone but you had a lot of entities hanging around you. Your eye saw an older figure sitting by himself, looking at you. That same night when you were home earlier meditating, you had seen the same old figure. He looked very old to you; older than any figure that you have seen since you became aware of figures around you. You asked him why he was with you and what he wanted from you. He said that when he was alive, he reached the age of 102. He told you that he was a shepherd in the mountains somewhere in the Middle East, and he had a small herd of sheep that he took care of since he was a little boy. Every day he took his sheep out early in the morning. Sometimes he went back to his farm, and a lot of times he slept with the herd wherever his heart decided to stay for the night. He slept surrounded by his sheep all night long. His food and drink were whatever was available that night. He smoked whenever he found tobacco and paper to roll his cigarettes. He was a lonely human – always alone, never had a friend. This old man had a handmade flute that he made out of bamboo which he loved to play. For most of his days, he sat under the shade of a tree playing his flute while his sheep grazed or stood around him. As far back as he could remember, since he was a kid, he always saw figures and entities that he sometimes feared; other times they were his companions. He always knew that these figures were not real humans. These entities preached to him and taught him different ways to keep his life going and to be happy and satisfied in what he was doing. He knew, somehow, that he was talking to angels, but he never realized that there are different kinds of angels.

One day, as he was alone with his flock, sitting under the shade of a tree playing his flute, he felt sadness. He felt tears coming down his eyes but he did not know why. Suddenly, a few feet away from him he saw a beautiful, gorgeous, glowing lady. He was shocked because all that he had seen before were figures of men and ordinary women, but none had ever had the shine that he saw on this beautiful lady. He paused and wondered to himself, what is such a beautiful figure doing in the middle of nowhere? She was so close to him that he could smell a beautiful aroma coming from her. She looked at him and said, "Hello," and called him by his name. He answered her and, in a blink of an eye, he saw her sitting next to him without even walking toward him. She put her hand on his hand. He felt fear in his heart. She told him not to be scared of her because she was the Angel of Love and she was there with him to teach him how to take care of and love himself. She told him that she felt his sadness and that she would take care of him for the rest of his life. She would always be with him to protect him, keep him happy and relaxed. All he had to do was follow her lead, her instructions and her teachings. The old man could not say no or reject what she was asking of him. He was taken by her beauty, and the smell of her strong perfume was making him feel more and more attached to her. She told him to trust her and let her control his life. She would make sure that he would stay on this Earth for a long, long time. The old man became more scared and his fear controlled his emotions. He did not know or understand what was going on. He wanted to refuse her offer – deep inside his heart he was refusing it – but his mouth was accepting everything she was asking him to do.

Life went on and it was all happiness and contentment for this old man. Every now and then the same pretty figure came to visit him. She spent hours and sometimes days with him, talking to him and showing him that life on Earth is very beautiful. She told him that he would live forever only if he followed her teachings and if he always stayed focused on her.

On the last day of his life, he was over one hundred years old. He was a very, very old man. On this day, he was walking slowly with his herd on a path that he always took on his way back to his farm. This path was next to a deep valley. The old man was trying to climb down a huge rock that was in his way when his foot slipped and he fell way down, deep into the valley. He felt terrible pain and was hurt very badly. Some of his bones were broken and he was bleeding from every part of his body. Exactly at the last second before he died, he smelled the familiar beautiful aroma coming closer to him. He opened his eyes and saw that gorgeous, glowing woman for the last time. He asked her, "I thought that you were here to always protect me. What happened? Where were you when I needed your help the most?" She told him that she was next to him when he slipped and fell, and that she tried very hard to hold on to him to stop him from sliding all the way down to the valley. She told him that she did her best to protect him but a different power fought her for him. This time, the other power won and was able to stop her from finishing her job. She failed to protect him and could not provide him real protection anymore because of the power that was weakening her. She told the old man that now he could go in peace and she will be waiting for him when he comes back so together, they could again finish another journey.

After this old man died, his soul got stuck in its earthly thoughts, feelings and emotions. It felt sorry for all the time that the human wasted while it was occupying his body. This old man's figure discovered that the glowing woman was a dark entity angel that kept him alive throughout his life, showing him how to be a good–for–nothing bum. She kept him happy and healthy only to make him miss all the experiences that his soul was supposed to finish in this lifetime. As a human, he did not know better. He loved every moment of the life he lived. It was a very easy life, away from problems and sadness – unlike other humans' lives. But what he really missed on his journey was the *real* feeling of happiness. He did not know anything better than his limited experience. He did not know that for a human to be happy he has to get sad, or else the human cannot know what happiness really is.

The old man's life ended when he fell down, and all that he had been promised by that beautiful woman just evaporated in the blink of an eye. She gave up on him at the last second when he needed her for real, so his physical body died. Now he has to go through a new lifetime to experience a lot of what his soul missed in that lifetime.

The reason this old man is with you now is to learn from you how to know the difference between white and black angels. He is around you because he realized that you can talk to white angels any time you want. Even though black angels whisper in your ears, you refuse to keep them around you, and you can get rid of them very quickly. He also knows that you are at war with these dark entities. They will win a battle between now and then, but they can never win the war. This old man wants to learn how to tell the difference between black and white entities so that when he comes back to another earthly life, he will be able to finish the experiences that his soul planned on. By his intention, he will be following the white angels' path all the way in his next lifetime.

Last night James came to me early, a few hours earlier than the usual time we meet in the morning. He told me and my soul mate that we are going on a new trip, and we will see and experience many new things. I told him that I did not want to go, that I had enough experiencing for now. My soul mate opened her big mouth once again (always a joke between us) and insisted that we go with James.

So, there we were, floating and experiencing the beauty of the universe. A few minutes later, we reached a very beautiful, shining, white and gold energy cloud. We went through that energy cloud and in it we saw bright white golden angels that looked merry and happy. In the middle of this crowd of angels we saw a floating golden chalice with beautiful stones and jewels on it. My soul mate grabbed the chalice and the look on her face suddenly changed. She looked purified. Happiness was all over her face, and she told me to go over and hold the chalice. I put both my hands on it and I felt beautiful energy like I have never felt before. I hugged the chalice and did not want to let go. No words could describe the feeling I was experiencing. The feeling was similar to what being in heaven or paradise might feel like. It felt like this was the right place for me to stay. I felt attachment – I did not want to leave – but James said it was time to go. There were still more places to go to and we would not have time to finish if we didn't leave at that moment. When we left the chalice, a lot of angels left with us. They accompanied us during the whole trip from this point on.

As we left the chalice, from a distance we saw another white cloud. The closer we got the more we saw clearer white energy surrounding the cloud and mingling within it. As we approached even closer, we saw a beautiful crystal castle. We felt purity and humbleness through these clouds, so we kept going until we reached the castle. Inside the castle we saw gorgeous, pure, fine crystals and many gold and white angels that were filling the whole place. My soul mate, James and I – with all the angels that had come with us from the start, and with the new angels that came with us from the castle – were enjoying the scenery and the sound of golden harps and flutes that were being played by some of the angels. All we heard was beautiful, fine, relaxing music. We felt this beautiful energy and, again, we did not want to leave. But once more, James insisted that we move on. The beautiful, relaxing, angelic music was still with us.

We started heading toward a light blue cloud. The deeper we went into this blue cloud, its color became purer and purer. Behind the cloud we reached a green prairie where the sun was shining with its golden rays. The edges of the prairie were full of old, huge trees whose branches created shadows. It was the most beautiful scene that the eyes could see, but it could never be described by a human. My soul mate and I spent some time enjoying the beauty of this prairie. We also felt that this was a place where we wanted to stay and never leave. But once again, James told us that it was time to leave this paradise and move on to another place.

We reached a dark red cloud and even more angels joined our group. The deeper we went into the cloud, the more rejection we felt. A lot of pressure started to control us. We wished that we had never come here and we wished never to return. At the end of this dark red cloud, we hit land that was rough; and the environment was dull and depressing, like a gloomy day that leaves a human feeling stressed. We walked a little bit and reached a deep cliff. Deep underneath the cliff there was running water. We jumped into the water and went with the flow. All kinds of rocks and blockages were in the water, getting in the way of our course. All the white angels, dark angels, guardian angels, and the three of us, were going with the flow of the water.

The water then began to flow faster and faster. The energy started changing from dark red to dark green and to a very dark gray that looked almost black. That's when James told my soul mate to stay back on one of the rocks that was in our way. He told her that many angels would stay with her to keep her company. I looked at James, and I told him that if she stayed, I would stay, and if she went, I would go — we were going to stay together. James insisted that the experience that I was going to face was only for me and that she was not ready to face it yet. James assured me that with the help of the angels that were going to stay with her, she would be more than fine and she would be waiting for our return. I agreed to go, so we kept floating in the fast current of the water, stuck in very dark gray energy. That was when Archangels Michael and Rafael joined us.

Without any warning, the water stood still. No more movement. A dark, huge, black figure appeared in the middle of the river. He had shining red eyes with smoke, and sometimes fire, coming out of his nose and mouth. He raised his arms up over his shoulders, and all we saw were different colors of energy coming out of his palms. He looked at me and said, "I like you. I like where you have reached now in your life, but I do not like the way you stick your nose where it does not belong." He lowered his arms and started pulling me toward him by putting his hands over my shoulders. As he was trying to pull me closer to him, he told me again, "I want you to be with me. I want you to always stay with me. I can provide you with help that no one can provide to you as a human. I will always keep you safe and protect you from any harm." I felt fear in my heart and became very scared as I strongly refused everything he offered me.

He ignored what I was saying and kept insisting that he could help me, and we could both be of great help to each other. Then, by and by, his hands very slowly loosened their grip on my shoulders. He was still insisting that I was a very good candidate to join him in doing miracles in this life. All I did was continue to refuse all his offers. I was telling him that my place was not with him, and that my heart was telling me that my place is somewhere else, where I can help humans to understand what this life is all about. A few minutes later, he gave up on me and his hands let go of my shoulders. That's when the water in the river started moving again. But this time the river flowed in the opposite direction. We started heading back to where my soul mate was waiting for us. The energy was brightening up a little bit even though it remained dark for a while. When we reached the rock where my soul mate was waiting, she asked me if I was all right and she also had many questions about what I saw.

We floated together again, and we reached the cliff and the cloud we were on when we began this journey. From there we came back to the blue cloud and to the prairie behind it. We stayed at the prairie for a while, enjoying the scenery and the gorgeous rays of energy from the sun. James had only a few words for us.

This trip was one of the best that you both have taken because you experienced seeing and feeling all kinds of energy, from the lightest to the darkest. All human beings' lives run on, and depend on, the energy that you saw. Without this energy there is no life on this Earth or in the universe. No matter how rough, tough, or beautiful the energy is… it is needed in human life so humans can experience new things on a daily basis. The soul itself is energy. Angels are energy. Even guardian angels are energy. I tell you, the human physical body cannot exist for one second without this energy.

Chapter 8

GHOSTS

I am seeing different figures from the souls that hang around me all the time. Are these ghosts that I am seeing now?

On Earth, it is said that seeing is believing. You have been seeing, hearing and feeling me for a while. You see angels and dead people's souls around you all the time, and you just started to experience something different from what you already know. You are right – you are seeing ghosts. A ghost is a replica of the physical body in every feature, even with the style of clothing that the human had on before he died. Usually, these ghosts will stay around the area where the human body died. What you are seeing lately is real, and you will see more and more of them. Pretty soon, you will be able to very easily distinguish between a soul and a ghost–soul.

Now remember what we talked about. For a human to exist on this Earth, he has to have a soul that resides in him. When a human goes into deep sleep, the soul will leave the body but it will stay attached with the silver cord. This is considered a temporary death because the soul has not left the body for good. Final death is when the soul drops the body for good, where the silver cord fades and the soul never comes back to that same body. Some souls of dead people will stay very much attached to their earthly existence. Even with the help of their guardian angels, and other angels who are around them to help them, they still cannot be convinced to leave the earthly realm and go back to their Source.

A lot of humans have seen figures that could be lost souls or ghosts, and they may have heard voices coming from them. The way a ghost is seen and heard by a human depends on the eyes and ears of that human. Seeing or hearing a ghost puts fear in the heart of humans because there is no logical explanation to satisfy them. They might call these figures ghosts, lost souls or demons. Most often, even though the human knows that what he saw and heard was real, he will deny that he saw a figure only because he will be scared that other humans will judge him and consider him insane, according to what is considered insane in the society the human lives in.

What is a lost soul? What is a ghost? A lot of legends created by humans tell stories about ghosts and lost souls. Even holy books talk about ghosts – from the Torah to the Holy Bible to the Koran. These stories speak of how the prophet or the master of a holy book took care of the lost souls and got rid of ghosts. Some human–created legends say that ghosts are the souls of humans that died and are still around to get revenge on whoever killed them. Another story is that the person himself, when he lived as a human, was a very bad human and as punishment his soul is still left on Earth, not knowing how to go back to its Source. All who hear about or read these stories will let fear into their hearts, and they will create stories to feed their fear.

On occasion a human will be sitting alone and he will see a strange light passing through the room; or he might notice movement from the corner of his eye; or he might hear a sound that is an abnormal noise for his ears. Deep inside this human will fear that there is a ghost next to him or around him. His fear will prevent him from considering that there might be a logical explanation for this light or sound. I tell you that this is true most of the time; but sometimes these incidents might occur because there really is a ghost staying around where a human died, and it is refusing to leave. For a human who never questions what he has been told, this kind of experience will terrify him because through movies and horror books, humans are taught that ghosts are very dangerous and that they could harm a human very easily. But remember, this theory is only a human creation and it has nothing to do with the truth.

The fact is, to get rid of his fear a human has to understand and believe that there is more than a graveyard waiting for him when he dies – there is an afterlife. Ghosts and souls are proof of this. When a human understands what the purpose of his existence on Earth is, then he will understand that life exists after the graveyard and that death occurs only for the body and not for the soul. Knowing this will let the human understand that a ghost is a soul without a body and that it should not be feared. He has to know that there is no entity or energy that can cause physical harm to any human on this Earth. This kind of understanding will open a human's eyes to believe that angels also exist, but he will question what the difference is between the two.

Usually, angels are protectors that are always attached to the human from the second the human sees light on this Earth. A ghost is a soul that had come here and occupied a human on Earth. After the human died and the soul left the body, that soul decided to stay here, refusing to listen to its guardian angel and all the angels that tried to help it go back to its Source. Ghosts refuse to leave because they are very attached to their earthly experience. They are always looking for a physical body to live in, but they cannot find one because every physical body that is alive is already occupied by another soul. A human will find relief from his fear when he understands that the difference between a ghost and an angel is that a ghost is on Earth refusing to let go of the earthly bound experience and go back to his Source; and an angel is here providing this ghost with wisdom to lead it back to its Source.

What you saw in the city and what you have been seeing for the last few days is real. You are not daydreaming or hallucinating. Remember what I told you days before. Now you see, hear, and feel a lot of things because you reached a very high stage of awareness and love. These experiences might scare you, but they will scare you in a different way than what scary movies and horror books describe. I promise you that you will get over this fear and you will learn a lot from these experiences. While you still have a little bit of fear left in you, you might still wonder if you ever asked for all this in your life. Let me tell you now as I did before – all that is happening to you is occurring only because you asked for it.

A few days ago, you helped heal a girl that came to you seeking help. She walked in like a zombie and left feeling like a beautiful smiling angel. When you first saw her, you noticed dark entities and dark energy attached to her. When she left, most of this dark energy was not with her anymore. This experience helped you accept that entities, ghosts, souls, dark energy – and energy you have yet to see – do exist. This kind of experience will become very normal for you.

Now let's talk about what you saw a few mornings ago when you were at a business meeting. You sat next to a human being and you and the man were chatting about nothing important so you were relaxed. You have the habit of touching people's hands when you talk to them, only this time when you did that, your hand went through his hand and you realized that you were not talking to a real human. That pissed you off and scared you because you thought that now you would not be able to tell the difference between an entity and a human. Your fear was in fact good because it was useful in confirming the experience for you. Pretty soon, you will find your ability to see these entities a soothing relief for all kinds of panic and stress in your life. Let me assure you that very soon you will start to distinguish the difference.

For now, do not allow your ego to make you judge yourself or blame yourself for whatever is happening in your life. Many of these experiences will happen to you on a daily basis – so get used to it. I assure you again that soon you will drop the fear from your heart just as you have already done with me. When you first heard and saw me you were scared and confused but now, we are together all the time and you talk to me all day and all night long.

Whatever you see is going to look as real as me, and soon you will recognize that what you are seeing is help that you have asked for; to help you heal yourself and others. You are a human that believes by seeing and hearing. If you do not see and hear, you do not believe. This is the main reason why all this is happening to you in this way. My advice is to always remember that even though this is a new experience, nothing is going to hurt you on the physical unless you choose to hurt yourself through fear. For now, sometimes you will experience first and then you will start seeing and believing. Other times, you will see and believe and then the experience will begin. It does not matter which one happens first. Both will give you needed knowledge and teach you how to provide help for yourself and others to heal.

Always remember that these experiences are very important for the reason of your being. They represent the whole of what you are. It means that your physical, your Subconscious, your Conscious, and your Superconscious, all work hand–in–hand to show you what Life is all about. This will be normal for you now that you are in connection with all kinds of energy and power from the external world. You are not connecting to your mind alone. You are able to combine your energy with the energy of the universe, which makes you a human that could talk to and discover through external reality. So, fear and weakness should be expected from you sometimes for the time being, until you get over these feelings and emotions and get used to what you are. New experiences will happen and new discoveries will always be recognized until the end of this journey.

I want you to understand that this is not a competition with yourself. It is an experience where you are not only representing the human that you are anymore. You are representing the whole you, who is seen as the image that is the physical you, as represented by sense data. You are a human who is able to access and understand the whole you, not only what your physical sees, hears and feels. You are always in touch with your angels and the archangels, and they are great sources of information for you; which leads you to experience beyond the capacity of the physical; you now consciously exist and experience in the awareness of the whole you. I assure you that you do not have this gift to give you something to show off. This is happening for real because your soul had planned to be the great healer that you are – for yourself and for the humans that will accept your help.

I need to understand more about what I'm seeing and the difference between all these entities.

O.k. I will try to make it easier for you this time. There are many different types of entities and angels that you see. Most of what you see are guardian angels, ghosts, lost souls and dark energy entities. They come in different shapes, sizes, and colors. They are male and female, young and old, big and small, black and white or floating energy of all colors. These entities are spiritual beings without bodies of flesh and bones, though they apparently have the ability to appear in human form.

Guardian angels are assigned to each human when the human is born to a new life on Earth. These angels are stuck to a human like his shadow. They never, ever leave the human alone. They are with the human they are assigned to from the time the human occupies a womb until the soul goes back to its Source. Their job is to lead the human, to protect him, and to execute his soul's plan as much as they can. But always remember that a human has free will so he can always corrupt the soul's plan. If the human chooses not to follow his soul's plan, the guardian angel will still remain with that human, to help him go through his life as smoothly as possible. The advice and wisdom that a guardian angel provides the human with is given without any judgment or expectation.

The ghost is a soul without a body. A ghost is a replica of the human that died, whose soul decided to stay on Earth for a while because of its love for earthbound experiences. A ghost is always looking to reside inside a physical body, but it cannot do that because living human bodies are already occupied. Ghosts are not dangerous and should not be feared.

A lost soul is a soul that decides to stay earthbound for a while after the human dies, but for a different reason. A lost soul will stay around because it knows that some of the experiences that it planned on going through were not done before it dropped its physical body; so it stays to gain knowledge on how to best finish its unfinished experiences. It will look for humans that have discovered their higher self, and it will stick to them, trying to absorb everything it can before it goes back to its Source. Then it will decide to come back in a different human to finish the experiences that were missed in the previous lifetime.

The dark energy entities, which are known as dark angels or demons, also come with every human when he or she is born. Their job is to corrupt what the human's soul planned on before it came to Earth. They never give up – not even at the last minute of a human's life. The dark energy angels do this only to make it very hard on humans to leave Earth. For some humans, the older they get, the stronger these angels will be attached to them, affecting their emotions to fear death. Their main job is to influence the human to believe that physical life can be forever and that being earthbound is the best experience that he could ever have. They will put fear and worry in a human's heart, which will keep a human deeply attached to Earth. Fear causes worry, and worry keeps a human confused. They will try to keep a human stuck in a loop so he can never experience what his soul had planned on. When the human's soul comes back, it will come back to complete its unfinished experiences and to also have new experiences.

Now that you have a better idea about what you are seeing, it will be easier for you to distinguish between all the figures. Do not be scared of anything, and always remember that none of these entities can physically harm you. They will try to put fear and confusion in your heart, but now you are in a stage where you will not allow it. And if you do, you will not allow it to last long enough to get yourself stuck. I want you to always know that I am your guardian angel, and I am here to protect you as much as I can and as much as you will allow. You are doing great, kid.

How can I control the way I see so that I can turn it on or off anytime I want?

Why do you want to turn off what you are seeing? Give me one reason why you would want to turn it off, and I will teach you how to do it. There is no good reason for you to turn anything off. You should hold on to what you can do and keep it going. Now you understand what you are seeing and why, so you should be happy that you have eyes that work with your heart to let you see. You know how to tell the difference between all figures and entities that you are seeing. You know what is what and who is who. Isn't it beautiful to be able to see all this? Do you know how many humans would love to do only a part of what you are doing? And you want to turn it off? Stop all this nonsense. Keep talking to yourself and keep convincing yourself that you want to live with the new gift that you have – do not be scared. Deep inside, you love who you are and what you can do. You love every second of it. All you have to do is to follow your heart; that is where you will discover that you do not want to turn this off at all. Now stop being annoyed and stop being scared every time you are introduced to something new. Go back with your memory a little bit and ask yourself these questions: Have you ever been hurt physically or emotionally since you started to discover who you are? Has any harm come to you?

Let me tell you, if you allow fear to make you judge yourself, you will only lead yourself to negative thoughts; and this will put more fear in your heart. But if you follow your heart, you will never hurt yourself with worries, blame or judgment; and everything that you intend to go through will be positive. Stop this fear in your heart, and stop it now. Start following your heart every minute. When you cry now, just believe that these are tears of joy and not tears of sadness and fear. Your heart is used to all this by now so there should be no fear anymore. You are going to see and do a lot of new things – a lot more has been planned for you. I know that you can handle it and I believe that you will. Believe me when I tell you that you are going to do and be what your soul planned on doing and being.

Chapter 9
THE TRIPLE CONSCIOUS

What is the difference between the Subconscious, the Conscious and the Superconscious? Please make it easy to understand.

This is a great question. It is going to take some time to explain so stay focused – I know you will get it. You can write while we are talking, and I will pause for you to finish writing. After we are done, you can read it again and again until you understand it for real. Then if there are more questions, you know where to find me. I love you, so settle down and listen to me.

The Subconscious, Conscious and Superconscious complete each other. The Subconscious is required by the soul to fulfill its human earthly lifetime. Basically, it is the data bank for the knowledge gained from its present human lifetime. The Conscious is the information and knowledge data bank for the present lifetime and past lifetimes of the same soul. The Superconscious is the data bank of pure and clean information that is stored from all souls from their experiences of all lifetimes lived on Earth.

A human's Subconscious leads his daily action. It decides how the life of this human should run. It creates the love, want and need for earthly materials and it teaches the human how to judge. The Subconscious is an opinion of a relationship to a situation and between humans. In other words, the Subconscious (with the help of the Conscious) provides the human with the choices of who to interact with, and how to deal with other humans and all incidents. It engages passion, opinions, feelings, visions, temper, self–awareness and sensations. It represents being alert to follow what drives you instead of being unaware – so the Subconscious is useful in providing facts toward a human's accomplishment – which means it provides a human with the truth that he believes in.

The Conscious itself provides an experience that moves every feeling in a human. Actually, in fact, feelings themselves do not have a direct effect on human behavior. A human will be affected by emotions, ego and the programs that he has within him; the effect will then create a feeling.

The Subconscious and the Conscious always work together to let a human bring to mind an incident or activity that occurred in this lifetime, or a past lifetime, so that the human can use this information as a reference. The mind's job is to check what knowledge and wisdom the human gained from this experience or from one similar to it. So, the Subconscious, the Conscious and the mind work together to feed the human all he needs to help him choose how to act or react. On Earth, this is labeled common sense.

The mind is the tool that connects your Subconscious to your brain. The brain is the shell that contains the electrical activity of our existence, as guided by the mind, from second to second of our being. All information that is received by the brain is not somehow stored outside the brain in special veins or arteries; nor is it stored inside the brain in a vessel or other physical information storage place. It is stored in a non–physical storage place where it stays until the physical body is dropped. After physical death, this information will be transferred from the Subconscious to the Conscious then to the Superconscious.

A human's Subconscious does not go to sleep when a human sleeps at night. When a human dreams, his Subconscious will show him a movie of things related to incidents from his present life, in which he is the main actor. In his dream he will see himself and other humans, which will make him believe that he is living it for real. The brain, with the help of the Subconscious, creates these scenes and they are seen by a non–bodily space.

When a human is dreaming, he will go to places and put himself in situations that he would not do on the physical in real time; so he is seeing and experiencing in a non–physical state, if you will. This does not mean that the experience is not real. In fact, it *is* real without exaggeration. These dream experiences are acknowledged by the soul, which will let the human have a full understanding of his free will, which is the engine that drives the dream experience. Free will means that the human is free to create scenes and experiences without obligation, fear, blame, or any earthly wants and needs – and it could be done very easily – even in his sleep. When a human understands his ability to create with his free will, he will freely and consciously partner his Subconscious with his Conscious, which will lead him to a very high stage of self–awareness.

Self–awareness itself permits an anxiety in every human for continued existence, and this increases his will to stay alive. Staying alive is, in fact, the main purpose and aim in a human's life. Being in a high stage of self–awareness will confirm to a human that his control of his life is beyond any other determination; and if he claims this control, he will not be scared of what his life will be. By conclusion, any human that goes to his higher self all the time is mostly using his Conscious, while retaining his necessary connection to his Subconscious, only because he is deeply aware of his free will at every moment. This equals great awareness and great creative power.

Remember that the human's Subconscious, with the help of the Conscious, creates an experience that moves the human's feelings. The human will then evaluate this creation and decide, using his free will, if he is going to follow it or not. If he sees value in following this experience, then he will start acting it out in the exact path that the experience requires. If a human does not evaluate and just acts on the thought, which means that he does not know what he is looking for in the experience, he will start the experience but he will get lost and turn back. For example, if I am sitting in the car with a goal of going to New York, I will start driving to get there. But, if I am sitting in the car and I do not know where I want to go, I will just drive around and get anywhere. Remember again, either way there is no good or bad, or any judgment to any experience or choice. Whatever the human decides is being done exactly the way it was planned, and it will be added to the Conscious, through the Subconscious, as a completed experience. Basically, in life there is no useless or wrong choice or experience.

Humans usually say that their conscience talks to them using words, but let's take an infant as an example. An infant does not know how to understand or speak with earthly words, yet this infant still has feelings through which he expresses himself; and these feelings are created by his Subconscious. So we can say that the Subconscious is the tool that lets a human think; and it will communicate with the human in the way the human understands, if it is in baby talk, adult talk, sign language or any other way that will be understood. The process is the same but no two humans think the same way. Every human has different thoughts, following his own Subconscious. Sometimes the thoughts of two humans can be very similar, but they will never be the same. Even if two humans have the same physical experience, each of them will gain different knowledge and wisdom.

A human's thinking is a busy procedure which involves the Subconscious and the Conscious, but the human usually is not aware of the procedure. All he recognizes is the thought itself. Most humans do not know that all thoughts they had, have, and will have in this lifetime – from hate, dislike and revenge to happiness, love, etc. – are attracted to the mind by the Subconscious. All these thoughts are stored in the Subconscious; and all thoughts from past lifetimes are stored in the Conscious. When a human starts a new experience in his life, a quick reaction from the Subconscious will be to check with the Conscious data bank. It will look for incidents and experiences that are very close to what is needed—good or bad, it does not matter, as long as the soul went through it before and gained the knowledge that it needed from it. Now let me ask you, do you think this means that no new ideas are allowed to develop, or that a human does not know how to act toward a new experience? Do you think this means that a human is stuck in the past, from this life or the previous lifetimes, and that references from his past will be the only solution to finish a new experience? The answer is a big NO! No human is ever trapped in any past ideas or experiences because he has the power of his free will to create new ideas and thoughts, which will lead to new experiences. For example, a human might decide to totally change the way he is running his life – from positive to negative or from negative to positive. Whatever the choice, he is deciding through his free will. All these experiences turn into knowledge and wisdom, according to the way each human reacts toward his experience.

Let me say that a human's mind is always uptight, jumping from a thought or idea to the next. A lot of feelings and thoughts pack the mind; even unwanted thoughts reside there. As I said before, these thoughts are Subconscious and Conscious references from the past. The trick for a human to produce new thoughts rather than using the stored ones does not require using a special tool or technique. There are no rules. Because you are a human with free will, whatever seed you plant will be the seed that creates your experience. So, to find new ideas to reprogram your thoughts and to change your goal, you have to create and follow an understandable objective, which will be the seed you plant. Most important is to have the desire to complete this new objective. A lot of humans know what their goal is, but they fall short of giving directions for what they want to their Subconscious.

To get what you are aiming for and to complete your goal, ask yourself how you could do it. I tell you, when you know your goal, you are halfway there. To establish the other half, all you have to do is to shut down all your thoughts and meditate by yourself. While you are in meditation, see the objective that you are aiming for. Feel good about yourself. Love *All You* with unconditional love. Clear your thoughts from selfishness and see the God that is within you. Follow your heart... then all kinds of new ideas will start popping up in front of your eyes. During this change of character, you might feel miserable because you are following something new of your own making, not the same routine that you are used to. So when you reach that point, always meditate and see with your heart, not with your eyes – until you get yourself used to the new ideas. Start filling your Subconscious with new ideas, and you should especially fill it with gracious considerations of yourself. That is when you will become a different human who will still be running the same experiences that your soul planned on, but with a different approach that will make you enjoy finishing them.

Creating new ideas from your feelings and not from old experiences is not an easy task; but I tell you, it could be done very easily if you want to do it. The more you see it, the more you will convince yourself to follow it. Start by writing it over and over again; keep thinking about it every second of the day, no matter what happens to distract you. The more you practice this, the more you will be training your Subconscious to accept the goal as a permanent idea. This goal will then be one of the routines in your Subconscious, and it will be accomplished very easily. Make sure you understand what I said: for a human to change himself he has to make the changes in his Subconscious, not his Conscious. When he can do this, he will have mastered himself.

The Superconscious could be defined as a vibrating energy that serves as the primary house post for every possible outcome into time without ending. The capacity that a human has to define himself to him, as well as his free will to choose what he wishes for his thoughts, all reside in his Superconscious. The Superconscious is the intelligence, cleverness and shrewdness that reside within every human. It is what makes the human what he is. It contains pure knowledge, and it is what makes you represent yourself following your heart.

The past, present and all possibilities of the future reside in the Superconscious. It has no limits or margins, from the smallest to the largest thoughts. It is the beginning and the end, which creates the I AM. It includes all things from the known to the unknown. The Superconscious could visualize, understand and hold a thought regardless of what it might be. Whatever thought comes to the mind from the physical, or from any other place that a thought comes from, it exists in the Superconscious. The truth is, the Superconscious feeds the Conscious, and from the Conscious it feeds the Subconscious, leading the human's mind to follow the right path to accomplishment according to his soul's plan; and for this to be done in the best way possible. Keep in mind that a human himself, and all the other humans that are close to him, including his family and friends are all a part of his Superconscious. In other words, the human's Subconscious exists as part of his Conscious and his Conscious is introduced with an important part of his Superconscious.

Through the Superconscious, goals are reached. All that it requires is for a human to concentrate on the thought to make it a reality. The way a human chooses the experience, regardless of the choice, happens as a result of a feeling or a plan or a consideration. If this experience does not occur to the Subconscious, then the experience will never exist on the physical. But since the Superconscious carries all the known and the unknown, the experience will be there waiting to be picked up and to be experienced. This could happen in a current lifetime or in future lives to come.

When a thought occurs, it then becomes an opportunity. With the needed support that is full of the right passions and realizations, this opportunity will be allowed to become visible, and to become a fact that will lead it to be an experience. This means that for a thought to become an actual experience, the Subconscious and the Conscious will be engaged. When a thought becomes an accepted experience, then the creation of the experience will begin. It does not matter if the experience is good or bad. Any event or creation that occurs is in response to what the human is looking for.

Look at you. Since you came to existence, your Superconscious has also existed. So far, you have already discovered three lifetimes that you have experienced on Earth. But I tell you, you have existed for billions of years as energy floating in the universe, and not only as a human physical entity. You came from Source, and your Conscious and Subconscious came from the same Source. It means that everything in this existence is energy, and you have been given the gift to express this energy; and to form your beliefs based on the type of consciousness that your soul decided on, giving you the choice to run this life through your feelings and dreams.

Life is where it is now for you because of the creative beauty, love and ideas that are created by the Superconscious. You are in a stage where you consciously access and operate from your Superconscious almost all the time. As you have discovered, the Superconscious is the final data bank for all information. Any answer that is needed for any idea or thought is there. The Superconscious is always ready, and it will accept any new ideas or proposals that a human comes up with. You are one of those humans that uses his direct line to his Superconscious, where you discover answers to everything that you are meant to know, in the way you are meant to know it.

By accepting and loving your new understanding of life, you have made yourself a free man. You know that there is no use or reason for judgment, blame, or weakness in any choice that a human makes. By accepting new ideas, thoughts, experiences, etc., a human can create new progress in his life using a new approach and new feelings. He will then become a custodian of his life that will express a change to help create a new him. He will become a lover of himself and his own best friend, where he will trust himself in everything that happens in his life. Through this, he will start to develop a feeling that will make him aware of the values that he wants to finish this life with; and he will be giving hints to his Subconscious to support his new thinking.

The Subconscious guides brain power in the direction that the soul decided on. It elevates self–feeling from lifetime to lifetime up to its final goal of unlimited freedom. Every human, with his enormous power, is able to raise his Subconscious mind. The easiest way is to focus on what he wants from his life and not on what he does not want. He should concentrate on what his goal is, not on how he is going to fix what has been broken. If the human always looks at what he wishes for, if he knows exactly what his goal is and believes in it, he can be sure that he is getting his power from his Superconscious – even though it may be indirectly, through the filter of his Subconscious. The result will always be success in establishing his wish.

I have told you a few times that what your eyes show you is different from what your heart shows you. This means that you exist as a human with the capacity to choose to see with your eyes or with your heart, and this will determine your reach. You, as a human, exist in relationship to the endlessness of the universe. Being a part of the same Source, you and your Superconscious are very important parts of this endless universe. From the minute the idea of you is considered, the Superconscious is constantly providing you with any experience that you wish to grab from it. From its field of endless possibilities, anything that is not here on the physical yet, will stay stored in your Superconscious, available for you to choose it. All you have to do is to come up with an idea, believe in it as if it does exist, and it will be very easily sent to you. Being free and having unconditional love for you – which means seeing with your heart – will really let you create whatever you desire. There will be no limit to what you can do and the only one who can stop you is you. Always know that for every choice, action, thought, or experience, there is a result...and the quality of this result is also only determined by you.

I hope I made it simple enough for you to understand. Actually, I am sure you understood. Whenever we talk, it's better not to focus on any single word of what I say; always try to understand the whole sentence I speak to you. If something is not very clear, talk it over with your soul mate then you can always ask me to discuss it further. I love you and I am here for you always, to help you finish this journey with peace and happiness.

Chapter 10

THE SIXTH SENSE

Talk to me about the sixth sense. What is it, and how does it help humans?

This a very beautiful question that I was waiting for you to ask. Understanding the sixth sense can do miracles in a human's life. Listen to me carefully, write every word I say and I will do my best to answer in a way that will be easily understood by any human who reads this book.

Life on this Earth is not a life without the senses. For all humans, it is known that there are five senses, and some even know about a sixth sense. Now, the first question that should be asked is: how would humans know about their sixth sense? It is actually very simple. Think back to your past and also think of the present. Have you ever had a correct guess or an accurate sense or suspicion? If you have, then you have used your sixth sense indirectly, without knowing it. Think about it this way. Most of the time, your thoughts, answers and understanding – from good to bad – for all your past and current experiences in this lifetime, are a result of incidents that occurred and how you related to those incidents. Some of your answers were in line with your beliefs and understanding of life – let's call it a reference based on your past – and some were not. So let me ask you, where do you think these other answers came from? I tell you, if you did not have a sixth sense, these answers would not have been given to you directly or indirectly. Listen carefully to what I said. I said that some of the answers you got were in agreement with your beliefs and understanding...and some were not. If you have a doubt about the existence of a sixth sense, ask yourself why would you sometimes come up with a conclusion that goes against your beliefs and understanding, or that you have no point of reference for? It is easy to accept an answer if it agrees with the way you see and experience life, but it is something to really think about if you come up with a different or new conclusion. This should make you pause and think of why and how you came up with this conclusion. This is an easy way to prove to yourself that you have a sixth sense that offers you solutions and wisdom to help you go through this life.

The six senses are tools for the human survivor. They provide the greatest help to a human to help him know himself. If a human knows how to control his senses, then he will gain real peace of mind. On a Subconscious level, a human has thoughts or ideas, and he comes up with answers and conclusions for these ideas or thoughts. Some of these answers may be based on experiences that the Subconscious recorded as the human went through experiences in life. Other answers will come when the Subconscious uses the help of the Conscious to reference a similar experience from a past life, to provide the human with the answer. These answers will help the human to adjust the way he is relating to what he is going through, according to what is convenient for him or what his goal is at that moment.

There are a lot of humans that will respond unconsciously to an event; sometimes, they will even know this event is about to happen even before it happens. How can a human do this? It is because, as I told you before, the mind knows ten seconds before an experience happens that the experience will occur! The responses for these experiences are always a result of the information that comes from the six senses.

Now let's talk about the senses in detail. Eyes are for seeing; ears for hearing; tongue for tasting; body for touching; nose for smelling; and mind for consciousness. Most humans believe in and understand the five physical senses but the mind is rarely considered. Most humans never think about the way they use their mind, and they do not consider it a sense tool because it cannot be seen or touched, and also because it is not understood. But let me assure you, if you take care of and follow all six of your senses, they will take good care of you by doing their best to serve you, as they were meant to.

You can "come to your senses" by paying attention to all six of your senses. All of your senses are always working together for you, to make an experience of every minute. If you think deeply about the way your senses work, you will know and understand that the way they work for you is a real miracle. For example, how does your nose tell the difference between one smell and another? How do your ears hear and know the difference between one sound and another? How does your tongue let you taste the difference between one food and another? How does your body tell the difference between rough and soft, cold and hot? How about the human eyes? Light comes directly into the retina of the eye, which causes a reaction by certain cells, which sends a message to the brain to let you see color. Not even the newest technology, with all the research behind it, can tell you how a light wave of certain energy comes to the retina to make it see color. Last but not least, how does the brain take commands from other organs or parts of the body and act accordingly? Aren't all these labeled miracles here on Earth? I tell you, do not be surprised at the way you were created, including the miracle of your senses.

Paying attention to your senses will bring you to the center of attention, so that you can train yourself to notice and understand what there is to be noticed, instead of only what you want to notice. This pleasure comes from bringing your mind to the moment, which will give you a chance to be free of stress and full of happiness.

Understand that the senses cannot cause a problem for a human as long as it is understood that whatever the experience is, even if it causes temporary suffering, it is for the human to learn and gain wisdom through it. If a human understands this and has no attachment to an expectation from an experience, then the senses will for sure be a fact of happiness for this human. Keep in mind that expectation is way different than having a goal.

All humans are happy using their senses when they feel that the experience is going the way they believe it should go, regardless of how beautiful or ugly the experience is. For example, let's say that you have been living like a slave all your life and suddenly you realize that there is something called freedom. You try to gain your freedom, but you allow your emotions to make you feel miserable about all the years that you have been living as a slave – even though you are finding the hope of freedom. When you see and realize that your experience living as a slave has made you miserable, you will attach to the hope of being free. So now you will love what your senses are showing you, even though this has caused you temporary suffering. In the same situation, sometimes a human will reject the idea of freedom because this means that he will be facing the unknown. This human would prefer to stay in darkness rather than accept the unknown result of freedom; so he will hold on to the shelter of slavery. Either way, the senses were engaged by the human's free will.

The most important thing about using the five senses is that together they provide knowledge to the sixth sense, even though each experience is led by the sense that is most dominant in that experience. The dominant sense, with the help of the other four physical senses, collects data and knowledge that is gained from the experience and this information is sent to the sixth sense. The sixth sense collects its data from the experience itself and from the Subconscious and Conscious. When all this information is collected, it means that the experience is over. Now the human will face similar future experiences with no fear, because he has gained the knowledge needed to help him go through the new ones easily. Understand that without these six senses, a human cannot function and cannot exist.

The only way a human can gain the benefit of keeping himself happy and content in his life is by consciously having his six senses work together all the time. The best training for teaching your senses to act together is accomplished through a special meditation. The best time to practice this balancing meditation is early in the morning. While still resting in bed, let yourself relax. First, shut your ears down. Do not allow yourself to hear anything for a minute; then listen to every sound or noise your ears can catch. Next, open your eyes and visually focus on only one thing. See nothing except that object that you are focusing on; then let your eyes look all over the room and see everything around you. Next, be still in your bed without moving a muscle for a minute; then stretch your arms and legs in different directions; release and relax. Inhale slowly for eight seconds…hold your breath for 4 seconds… exhale to the count of ten. This exercise is for the nose and the throat. The last exercise is for your mind. Empty it of all thoughts for a minute. Allow your mind to be an empty vessel in your head; then fill your mind with thoughts of all the activities or experiences that you had the day before. Mentally visit these experiences with no judgment. This will help you to get rid of negative thoughts that were stressing you. Then slowly empty your mind again and let your body relax completely, as you focus on your breath for a few minutes.

Do not be concerned if you do not meditate on all your senses, because meditating on *any* of your senses will help to balance the ones you did not meditate on. The more you train yourself, whether you meditate on one sense or all of them, the more you will be purifying the whole you. When you can create balance between all your senses to help them work together, you will be able to accomplish things that you never thought possible. You will also become a human who appreciates creation and all that he is. When a human stops taking everything for granted he will be wiser, happier and aware.

Think about this for a minute – have you ever thanked your eyes for seeing or your ears for hearing? Have you ever, in your whole life, thanked any of your six senses for doing their job? Most humans have not; but I tell you that you can choose to do it starting this minute. Through your free will, you have the choice to experience life through awareness of the senses, which will make you very powerful in creating whatever you want through every experience you go through. You can be the happiest human on Earth if you understand what your six senses do and by being wise enough to know that your senses will always help you to create what you wish for. This will allow you to enjoy every moment and to live that moment to the utmost, understanding for real who you are as a human.

Chapter 11

PSYCHICS

I talk to you. I ask you questions about myself and other people and I hear your answers. Society labels a person like me crazy. Am I going insane or am I a psychic?

Let me assure you that if you are for real going insane, then you would not have the sense to ask this question. A lot of people that you know, and others that you do not know, will think that you are insane when they read your book, especially when they discover what you can do now. For them, whoever speaks to himself or to angels is insane. But it does not matter what others label you. You are discovering the *real you*. This will let you do miracles and heal others with the touch of your palm or sometimes with the tip of your finger.

As you now know, every human has a guardian angel. The way you and I communicate with each other is through transmitted message. In fact, an angel cannot make an impression upon a human unless the human believes that there is such a thing as angels. As I have told you before, guardian angels do not interfere in a human's daily life, but they will drop messages or signs to keep a human from getting himself into deeper confusion. So if a human believes that angels exist and he can clear his mind, he will be able to hear his guardian angel talking to him. Understand that an angel comes down to the level of a human so that he could be understood. These angels always have answers for questions that are asked, according to what will protect and keep the human as safe as possible. As you know from your own experience, we also have a sense of humor. Asking funny questions will give the human silly answers.

Infants and children do not doubt so up to a certain age angels communicate with them using words and signals that these children understand. As they get a little bit older, society corrupts these little humans' knowledge and wisdom. Their wisdom will change over time, according to new, different data that is provided to their Subconscious by their society's rules and standards. This new training will cause children to lose their connection to their angels.

It is not uncommon for humans to hear about the existence of angels and some even say they believe in them, but the same humans will also somehow doubt their existence. Since angels are not physical creatures for human eyes to see, it is easy for humans to have doubt. That is why every guardian angel expects that his human will ask for proof that he really exists in that human's life. You already asked and you got your answers. You received a lot of messages from me and I received a lot of messages from you, in an indirect way. Then you asked me how you can see me, and what the best way to communicate with each other is. I told you to be open to receiving everything from me without any expectations. I told you to teach yourself to get used to me, as I also will teach myself to get used to the new you. I asked you to trust me as I trust you. But the way you are – a tough macho man – made it very hard for us to communicate. So I learned your words and adopted the way you speak. Then I took the shape of a human figure that is familiar to you, only to let you see and hear me in a way that you understand; this allowed us to communicate with each other very easily. Now you know that I exist, and you are comfortable communicating with me. So, now I know and you know that nothing should make you worry anymore. Remember to just go with the flow, and know that what is meant to be…will always happen. So for now, I assure you that you are not going insane; you are only getting wiser and wiser every day.

The other question you asked is if you are a psychic. Let me explain to you what a psychic is and what a psychic does, and then you can tell me if you are a psychic or not. Psychic readings supposedly are spiritual methods used by humans to obtain information about themselves and others. Psychics use a selection of specialized teachings that may involve an outside factor such as a crystal ball, tarot cards or informants that give information about the subject to the psychic. But these outside factors or tools are not essential to achieving a reading. People who declare themselves psychics are basically people who know how to go to their higher self and be there most of the time. On Earth, they are labeled advanced spiritual people. I tell you, they are regular humans without any extra powers over others; they only pay more attention to things that normal people overlook. The power they claim they have is a talent and cleverness, and the more they practice and experience it, the more talented they become.

Being "a psychic" is a profession. To be one you have to have the ability to control the self by clearing the mind. The psychic must believe that he sees and feels energy and angels. By having this belief, the psychic is able to connect to his higher self any time he chooses to. The higher self is the stage of unconditional love where a human can best clear his mind. A psychic will then go deeper and find his angels, and he will get used to communicating with them. On Earth, when a human has this ability to connect and communicate with angels, he is considered special – someone who has limitless powers of the spiritual realm. But these limitless powers do not translate well into the material world; so psychics must be able to see the object of the reading in relation to earthly physical reality. Some psychics also use empathy, which is their ability to identify with the human's emotions. Using both, the mind and the heart, will lead a psychic to a better understanding of the high self, which will then lead to a balanced heart/mind relationship within him. This balance will allow the psychic to give a reading that makes more sense, relative to human reality, than if he was only using the heart or the mind alone.

You should also know that the truth is not relative to time. The truth deals with now. The truth does not deal with space – it deals with here. Here and now is one joined idea that the psychic lives in at the moment of a reading. He reaches out and sees whatever he can, and he tells about it the way he understands it. Now listen carefully. When a psychic gives a reading, he will feel and see and connect with angels, and whatever he understands of that connection, will be his reading. That will be the truth that he understands about what he is seeing. Keep in mind, and never forget, that whatever is true for one human might not be true for another. A psychic is human also, so his reading will be delivered according to his beliefs. A different psychic might give a different reading to the same human because what is right for one psychic might be the opposite for another.

I tell you again – whatever a psychic says is valid only for that exact moment of the reading within those exact circumstances. The second the subject of the reading moves a limb or gets up from his chair, the circumstances have changed. Basically, because the psychic deals with the here and now, whatever he says will be what he is seeing or feeling at that exact moment. A psychic will ask his client a lot of questions and he will go with the flow depending on the answers. Through a lot of practice and experience, he will have a nice relationship with reality. This means that a psychic will know how to present the information in a way for the human to get his satisfaction out of the reading. Many humans will listen to what the psychic says, and if they believe in what is said, they will depend on the psychic's words rather than looking for their own solutions.

So, the question now is: are the talent and abilities of a psychic real? And I tell you that on this Earth, every human has the ability to be a psychic, but not every human chooses to be one. The souls of these humans that choose to be psychics had already planned to occupy the shells that would play the role of the psychic experience.

Other humans notice and pay more attention to people that appear to have more physical or spiritual power; and they label these people super talented, supernatural, or super spiritual humans. Many humans will question why this power is available to these super humans and, not having a real answer, they will make up stories. They might guess that these people were lucky enough to be born to a rich family where they were provided with extra affection and love, which created this talent that is their power; or the desperate condition of poverty led a human to an awakening. . . and so on. The truth is these psychics are really very normal people. They are not supernatural and they come from all kinds of different backgrounds.

As I already told you, all humans are born with psychic power, but most of them lose it as they grow up because of the way they are affected by the community around them. Most of this rejection will come from the idea that it is insane for a human to speak to angels or to speak to the self. When kids start telling others what they are seeing, they are judged and made fun of. The majority of these kids will not dare to talk about it. As time goes by, they will forget about what they can see and hear. Very few of these children are strong enough to stay unaffected by this judgment and to grow up still believing that they can see and connect. These few are the ones that will have the ability to become psychics. But keep in mind, some societies reject psychics and they will not accept them to be part of the community as normal humans. But let me assure you again that every human is psychic and every human can use this ability if he chooses.

The energy of this universe works in a mysterious way where it could provide things that are not accepted as normal in most humans' beliefs and traditions. These out–of–the–ordinary happenings are often called miracles. Energy will let a human generate his own miracle, which is a fact he believes he could create. This kind of human will be different from other humans on Earth only because he believes in this power. You are one of these humans who now believes in himself, and you are ready to follow your heart and to help others through this gift that you have discovered within you. But…there is a big difference between being psychic and being "a psychic".

Let me remind you what I said before. When a human is born, his skills and abilities are born with him because they were planned by his soul. It is the human's choice and, in his power, to use these skills and abilities. Every human can choose to be in his higher self, which will lead him to communicate with angels. This communication will give him the ability to know about another human's past and what that human's soul planned for its earthly journey – but nobody can predict the future for real. The future can only be told as it was planned by the soul, not as a certainty of what will occur. Did you hear what I just said? Humans have free will to recreate a different future from what the soul has planned! A psychic can never tell how a human will use his free will and what he will create in his future. For this reason, I say it is not wise for a human to run his life according to a psychic reading.

Every human has the power to see the *now* and the *here*, which is the moment that he is in. Seeing and living the *now* will create the future, so the future depends on the *now*…and every second is a human's now.

Some humans choose to make a profession out of psychic readings. They do this only to make money. By doing this, they are losing the truth of what this power is all about. Understand what I am telling you. This kind of professional psychic is not real. He will use all kinds of methods to pretend that he is seeing the past and predicting the future. This professional psychic will manipulate other humans into unknowingly giving him hints about their past in their current life. He will use this information to make the other humans believe in him, which will build trust between the psychic and the human he is doing the reading for. When this trust is in place, then it is easy for the psychic to say all kinds of things about the other human's future, which in fact will only be lies and guesses. This human will believe the psychic and accept what the psychic tells him as a fact, so he will expect it to happen in his future. When things do not turn out in the human's life as the psychic predicted, it will cause him pain and confusion. Instead of questioning the psychic's predictions he will instead blame himself for the predictions not coming true. A human should always use his free will to choose a trustworthy psychic that he can trust so he can save himself from this confusion.

Now that you know a little bit more about what a psychic is and what he does, and now that I gave you more information about our connection, do you consider yourself a psychic? Do you think that you would do this as a profession to make money? I do not think you are this kind of human. But you could do a lot of what a pretend psychic can do and better. So, if you choose to do it, go get a crystal ball and I will lead you.

I tell you, never forget that you are a healer that is going to do miracles for the rest of the days that are left for you on this earthly journey, and you will not need a crystal ball.

Chapter 12

EGO

———————————————⊙

Talk to me about the ego. How does it start? How does it work? How can a human have control over his ego? Please tell me everything I should know about my good friend "ego."

A human's ego begins at conception. As the fetus grows in the womb, so will his ego. The second a human comes out of the womb he will begin gaining wisdom and feeding his ego through his experiences. This information will keep him growing and experiencing until his soul decides to end the human's life. It means that the second a human is born he begins to define his reality and runs his life accordingly.

Let me go back a little bit. I will repeat myself, but be patient. It is important that you really understand. A human's ego, with connection to the human's Conscious, brings forward events that occurred in the human's lifetimes. The Subconscious will get all the recollections and feelings from the Conscious which holds every experience from past lives, besides his current life. When an experience occurs, the Subconscious initially will not accept any feelings or scenarios from

135

past lives; but gradually, the Subconscious will accept the data from the Conscious, and it will react to an experience using this data.

The main questions and experiences that a human faces in his current life come up when the Subconscious brings from the Conscious, to this lifetime, the experiences that the soul did not finish in past lives in different physical bodies. These experiences were unfinished because the human did not clearly follow the soul's plan, or because the human's choices changed the path of life in a way that prevented the soul from doing what it had planned to do. All these experiences that came from different lifetimes will finish only if a human clears the path by reaching the higher stage of consciousness – which is full of unconditional love – so that he can deal with himself and other humans without any need, judgment, or blame.

Every human has the capacity and the ability to create, and he has the knowledge of how to react toward his creation. I tell you, a lot of events, experiences, and issues are going to face every human in his life. When they are understood, the human will free himself of all confusion that might keep him from finishing and accomplishing what is meant for him. But, many humans cannot keep up with all the creations and experiences that they face on a daily basis, so they feel stuck and the time they spend on this Earth is not enough to help them finish all these creations. Sometimes it does not matter how much a human tries to finish an experience. When he gets stuck, he will not recognize his own creation. Instead, he will start looking for different outlines that are very close to his creation to help him finish it. Sometimes it will take the human a lifetime to do this, and sometimes it will not be accomplished in a lifetime. The only thing that can prevent this confusion is unconditional self–love through the higher self.

Understand that the Conscious and the Subconscious use most of a human's energy to let him create and experience. Being in his higher self will allow the human to recognize the easiest way possible to help an experience satisfy the soul, by recognizing and referencing data from experiences of past lifetimes. This will allow the human to use less energy this time, because he will not have to create the experience from scratch. It has already been done, it has been recognized and the data accessed, so the human just has to run through it.

Anytime a human uses his Subconscious and his Conscious to re-create himself, he will be free to create and to go through all kinds of experiences without distress. No matter what the experience is, if it is happy or sad, good or bad, it will not make a difference. The human will be able to control his emotions and his ego by understanding his general benefit from the outcome. When a human is in the higher stage, no matter what the result ends up being, it will be a learning process for the human to gain more knowledge and wisdom; and for the Subconscious to gain more data from this experience. This human will always have confidence in himself, and he will never feel like a casualty. He will allow himself to see what a beautiful creator he is. When a human realizes who he is and what he is doing here on Earth, he will always be stable and in control of his ego.

The truth is, most of the time, the older a human gets the more his ego will prevent him from bonding with his pure thoughts. His ego will make him deaf to the voices of his angels that have been leading him since the first second of his life, so he will become more confused in understanding the truth. He will accept what his ego is telling him as a fact, only because it is the only truth that is known to him. This truth – his truth – is a result of all the data that was poured into him since the day he was born.

Now, when a human is confused, he attracts all kinds of stress energy that will create within him a volcano of built–up energy, which has no exit except through that human's emotions. This human will then be fuming, sad and mad, and he will feel like exploding. He will either erupt within himself causing his body disruption and disease, or he will anchor externally, unleashing his energy on another human or object. This does not mean that there is no hope for change in that human's life. He can always create miracles through his free will, which is the same way he created chaos!

Now let's talk about your ego. The stage that you have now reached in your life lets you look back and evaluate where you were in the past and where you are today for the sake of wisdom. You are in your higher self most of the time, but here and there you still have some doubt and fear coming from your ego. This is normal because you are still human, but you know in your heart that you can heal others if they accept your help. In your life you always loved to help others, but now you want to do more – you want to help heal others. All your feelings about healing others are not by accident; it is a part of your soul's experience. From now on be sure that every time you meet another human and talk to him, it is not by mistake. It is something that was meant for both of you. You will notice that when you offer a human your help directly without him understanding who you are, this human might feel scared; but don't let this stop you. Anytime you see or feel energy or entities on others, I want you to understand that it was meant for you to see or feel so that you can help these humans. You have the special job of being a tool of souls, to help humans reach where they are supposed to reach.

Your ego will play a role in this experience because it will create emotions of doubt in you. Some humans will accept your help but others might reject it. Do not allow your ego to control your feelings! I know, and you know, that you want to help and that you are meant to help. Even if your help is refused, do not feel bad or disturbed and never give up. Keep trying. The human might eventually accept your help, or he might reject it completely and be out of your life. This will be fine for him because it means that his experience was meant to continue somewhere else, not with you anymore; and it will still be an accomplished experience for you, because your benefit does not depend on the other human's choice to accept or reject you.

When other humans reject your help, it is because the dark entities surrounding them want them to be confused. Dark entities will stop these humans from accepting that you are in their life at the right moment, to provide them with the help they need to heal themselves. These entities will convince their humans that whatever you are doing is wrong and that it might hurt them. They will try to make them believe that what you are doing is invading their privacy, to create rejection that will prevent them from finishing an experience the right way. Let me tell you again, if it was meant for you and another human to be at the same place at any time, and you have the feeling for helping him heal, it was meant for you and him to be together at that moment. When you feel an urge to heal others, it means it was meant for you to give and for the other to receive, for you to find each other so you can help the other human to move through an experience very quickly without struggling to finish. If a human refuses your help, it will only be his ego and his dark entities that are playing a role in leading this human to stay confused and stuck.

I want you to know that, now, a lot of your dark angels do not like you. They do not like the stage that you have reached. They do not like that you are trying to help other humans. These dark angels are going to use their power against you through the humans that are very close to you. These humans know you and understand you like no one else can, so they are perfect tools for dark entities to take advantage of. These entities are going to try to convince these humans to reject your help, even more than the humans that are not close to you. The dark angels are going to pressure these humans' egos to demonize the power that is within you, only to make your ego react in a way to lead you back to them, or to stop yourself from helping other humans. They will do their best to affect your ego in a way to convince you that what you are feeling and accomplishing is only a dream – that it cannot be real. If the dark angels succeed in doing this, they will win. So, remember, mastering your ego and healing yourself is part of the experience of helping other humans. If you do not succeed, then when this life ends your soul will come back again to try to reach the end result for the purpose of its being on Earth.

I want you to listen to me very carefully and understand what I'm telling you. Whatever you are doing in offering help to others, keep on doing it. Do not allow any rejection, whatever it may be, to stop you. You are helping people heal themselves. If they do not want it today, they might accept it tomorrow, and if they do not, then it was not meant for this to be part of their experience. Always know that you are not alone on this mission. All the archangels are with you to help and support you; I am also with you, helping you and leading you. Do not lose faith in who you are now. Do not give up on anything that you have already achieved. Do not allow any reason to stop you from accomplishing what you are aiming for – helping and healing others. Do not even think of stopping what you can do, even if others refuse and reject what you can provide. Believe me when I tell you that all this is an experience that your soul planned on and you are doing great.

Tell me about jealousy. What is it? What effect does it have on human beings?

On this Earth, you see humans whose ego makes them believe that they have the power of owning something – if it is material or another human. This is where jealousy comes from. Jealousy is the result of a human's uncontrolled ego, which produces fear and worry, and negative thoughts and feelings. The human will believe his Subconscious creation of these thoughts and feelings, not realizing that they are his own creation. This belief will affect the human's emotions up to a point where the human will be in fury, misery and hatred only because he is afraid of losing what he believes he owns.

When a human is born and opens his eyes to the world around him, he will begin to understand just a hair of what life is all about, and he will start recognizing what the word "own" means. This little human will hate to lose any possessions or his feeling of comfort, if it is material or love. This is when jealousy will start to build within him. This jealousy will give a human the power of feeling safe because it makes him believe that he is protecting his needs. Jealousy will always affect a human's reaction to what he believes is hurting him.

Keep in mind that when a human is born into this life, love and jealousy are born with him. Jealousy always starts with love, if it is love for another human or love for material. Love can stay throughout the human's life; or it could vanish in a split second. The minute a human confuses love with lust, real love vanishes very easily. But jealousy will not vanish when love does. It stays way longer, and it will cause anger and stress to a level where a human will not understand why he is feeling miserable or what to do about it. When a human feels that he is losing a human or something else that he believes he owns, this threat will put a lot of pressure on his ego.

Now follow me closely. A human's ego, with the help of his Subconscious, will always provide the human with whatever he expects from an experience, according to the data it holds. The job of the ego and the Subconscious is to protect the human from harm, as defined by the human himself. This means that if a human has trained his ego and his Subconscious to react in a jealous way, they will always provide him with his satisfaction. Keep in mind that preventing jealousy or getting rid of it is very easy to do. Every human always has the free will to choose to provide new data to his Subconscious, so it could provide him with different solutions and reactions. All the human has to know, understand and believe is that nothing on this Earth will go with him when he dies. If a human believes that anything that is on Earth is for the earth, he will allow his life to run the way that it was planned by his soul, without giving himself the burden of jealousy.

In humanity, jealousy arises when love starts to fade between two humans, where a human will feel that he is losing a partner to a competitor. Another common situation where jealousy occurs is when a human feels a threat to a material possession. Jealousy will kick in slowly, and it will begin to create an enemy out of the other human who used to be seen as a lover, or of the human who is a threat to the material possession. Panic will control the human's emotions when he feels this threat. Since jealousy explodes through emotions, the jealous person will anchor this energy within himself – where he will cause damage internally – or externally, on a solid object or by lashing out on another human.

The best way for a human to handle his jealousy in a positive way is to recognize that it will create fear, worry, rage and sadness for him. With this awareness, he can then decide which of these four elements is the biggest problem, and then he can ask himself this question: am I hurting myself by acting like this? This question has either a positive or a negative answer. A positive answer might be that rage helps him release his emotions, which allows him to cool down. A negative answer might be that his self–judgment and the residue of his reaction create a feeling of guilt and shame. It is up to the human to choose which answer he would like to follow, and then he should address his partner accordingly without any blame, judgment or finger–pointing. There is no right or wrong answer. The human himself will choose the answer, and this will be the right answer for him. If he feels that the answer he came up with makes him feel miserable and angry, he can easily change it to a different one. This will help him reach a stage that is beyond his ego which is the higher self.

It is very important for you and your readers to understand that all souls come from the same Source, and they all occupy humans so they can experience together on Earth. When there is jealousy between humans, it is like a physical body having a hand and a leg that are jealous of each other. It is like the leg being jealous of the hand because it can only walk and not grab. When a human is jealous, he is seeing the situation as if his body parts are pieces separated from each other rather than being bonded as one body. When he comes to the wisdom that his body parts actually work together as one piece, he will be relieved to see that there is no place for jealousy in this life. He will then understand that human beings need each other to live and experience together on Earth. Having this understanding will prevent a human from feeling hurt if he does not have what others have, or if he does not experience a certain kind of love as others might. Let me assure you that jealousy is the worst disease a human can bring on himself. Believe me when I say that a human can only bring this sickness unto himself, and only he can bring the cure.

Remember, jealousy is another experience that is meant for humans to have on Earth, and it could be a lesson for similar experiences that might happen later in life. When a human understands this, then he will always have a positive answer for himself, without blaming or judging himself. He will be able to let go of old beliefs and traditions and be open–minded to new data. There will be no room for a negative answer; he will be able to see a happy solution and grab it, without anger or sadness. Love will take over and happiness will reside within this human, who will drop all jealousy from his mind.

If a human reaches a point where he feels he is stuck in his beliefs and his thinking and he cannot find an answer by himself, he could always ask someone else for advice. But always remember, all humans are different in their thinking, so a human should not blindly do what others tell him to do; he should listen to others, evaluate what he hears, and then decide which way is best for him. The right choice will be whatever he chooses by following his heart.

Humans always have the resources they need to find solutions for making themselves happy. Since the Subconscious controls the human's feelings and emotions, it is always there to protect the human by helping him to find a solution for his problem. If the Subconscious does not have a solution that is acceptable by this human, it will go to the Conscious and the two will work together to come up with an answer. All humans, through their Subconscious, share the gift of the knowledge and wisdom that the Conscious carries; accessible through the human's free will.

As humans, we are taught that life is supposed to be filled with self-sacrifice to help others, and that helping others should be the measure of our happiness. Since a human is born, all the data received by his Subconscious from his human guardians – whoever they are – is about helping others in order to succeed and be happy in life. But I tell you, if you do not help *you* first, you cannot help anybody. Since the Subconscious controls the human's feelings and emotions, I say a human should first fill his Subconscious with positive thoughts and feelings about who he is and what he has. Then he can be happy for the success and happiness of others, and he can also help others, allowing his heart to always guide his emotions. This will lead to a happier life, full of joy in accepting whatever Life provides him with. For this human, every moment will be beautiful.

If a human can train himself to believe that he is the God that he is, he will entrust himself in the knowledge that he can create miracles in his life. If he deeply understands that this life in the body he resides in on Earth is limited and will come to an end, he will not attach himself to what he owns – material or other. He will then be the happiest, wisest human, living his life knowing that his job on Earth is to experience; and when the experiences that were required of his shell are finished, he will understand the true significance of the experience itself. So, a human should trust himself to have fun in whatever he does or faces in his life. He should always be himself and look at the good in everything that he experiences because every experience a human goes through will, without a doubt, improve all future experiences for this human. Believing in this action will make a human content with himself and happy for the success of other humans.

When a human has the power of believing in himself, his words will be spoken without any effort or contemplation about what he should say or do. Remember these words when you are faced with an experience involving a jealous human and you will be all right. I love you and I love every moment of the beauty that you have brought yourself to. Trust me when I say that this is the beginning of a beautiful change in your life, and a lot more of this happiness is yet to come.

Last night I lost my temper. I had not done this in a long time. My buttons were pushed and I lost it. It did not take me long to snap out of it, but I hate what I did. Can you tell me why this happened? How can I control myself not to do this again?

Let me first say that what happened last night is good because you learned something very useful. The important thing for you to understand is that feeling bad, hating what you did and judging yourself is taking you nowhere. Blaming yourself will hurt you a lot – so stop it. So you got mad; you yelled and screamed. You realized what happened very quickly and you stopped yourself from reacting more. Then you dropped your pissed–off mood very quickly. This shows you what a great change has occurred in you, and it will only get better in the days to come.

Now let's talk about the ego in detail. What you experienced last night is the I AM within you. This I AM controls your emotions, your mind and your body; and your ego is a big part of this I AM. Last night your ego controlled your I AM. Take a minute to think back to what you already went through in your life. In the past, your ego was always your best friend. Your beauty and peace of mind had been conquered by an ugly stain that controlled your consciousness. It controlled your hate and your love, your dreams and your hopes, and everything that you did; and all this created your personality.

Ego exists to help a human deal with the challenge of fulfilling the needs of his earthly existence. Without exception, every human's ego controls his consciousness, because it filters every feeling that a human experiences. Every incident that occurs has a big effect on building a human's personality, which is a big part of the ego in that human. Because the ego is created by all the experiences that a human goes through in his life, it is different in every human. A simple way to think about it is that a human's ego is the result of how he defines good or bad. Some humans see the good as bad and others see the bad as good; and it all goes back to the way the ego was created in each human. For example, if a human chooses to help another human and he does it because he wants to, without any expectation, he will think that it is something great that he has accomplished. His pleasure will come from the action itself, not from the result. If a human does the same thing only to be recognized, then his action will be the reaction of his ego; and if his expectation does not occur, he will be very disappointed.

A human always has the choice to allow his ego to run his experience or to follow his heart; but most humans are missing the awareness of having this choice. Very few humans stop to consider the whole of who they are. Think about this for a minute. If I ask you or any other human, who are you? You will answer me with your name, your age, where you live, your sex, what you like and dislike and so on. All this is not *who you are*. You are describing to me parts of your personality and your answers only tell me *about* you and not *who* you really are. You are describing yourself in relation to external factors instead of answering my question. If any human can figure out that there is way more to him than physical descriptions, he will have found the key for all that he is looking for in this life – the key to happiness and peace.

I tell you, the ego controls every human's feelings and actions from the minute he is born. When a human is a child, the ego starts forming through the reactions that a child has in relation to his experiences. For example, if you give something to a child and then you try to take it away, the stored data of the child's ego will make him huff and puff and reject having that object taken away from him. But, if you leave that object with him and after a few days you give him another object, the child will not care for the first object at that time. The child's reaction will be one hundred percent different than if you just took the same object away from him. The same thing is true for mature humans. If you lose anything that you believe was taken from you, your ego will make you fight to get it back. But if you keep it and a new thing comes in its place, you will be o.k.

It is not only the material that makes a human's ego react. It is every experience that he faces – from falling in love, to friendship and so on. Now remember what I said before. If a human's wants and needs come without any conditions in all situations, then that human will feel good in every situation; but when they come with any kind of condition, the ego will be controlling his emotions so he will not feel good at all.

Actually, the human will feel miserable, and he will keep suffering until he understands what he did to himself.

In fact, when the ego gives a human what he wants, it will be very hard for the human to give it back. Some humans commit suicide because they were trying to give back what they had and they could not do it. They feel miserable up to a point that it will make them end their life just to get rid of the pressure that their ego built up inside them. The worst part about this is that the more a human has, the more he wants. As long as he is controlled by his ego, a human will never be content; because his ego wants him to want more and more. This causes a human to live in misery without ever finding satisfaction and happiness.

You should also be aware that your ego does not stop at making you miserable by pushing you to judge only yourself. Your ego will use your own emotions and data to also pressure you to focus on and criticize others' needs and problems. It will make you feel that you are smart enough to give other humans advice on how to run their life. If the others do not take your advice, you will believe that they are wrong, only because your ego will tell you that your way is the right way, and every other way is wrong.

Ego will also convince an unaware human that other humans are a threat to him. It will show him how to cause pain to others for revenge, making him believe that taking revenge will make him feel better. It is a tough lesson for a human to learn that revenge might make him feel better for a short time but it will not relieve his confusion or anger. If you are honest with yourself, you will agree that, as a basic rule, no human can ever hurt you mentally or emotionally unless you allow it. You and only you can hurt you, with the help of the feelings and thoughts that your ego provides you with, which are always created by your own free will; basically, by the way you manage your ego!

The minute a human becomes aware of what he is about to do before he acts, he could control his ego and direct it the way he wants to, not the way he feels he has to. He will know how to control his ego emotions that are always trying to conquer him; which means he will know how to stop his ego from dictating to him what to do and how to do it. When a human can train himself to control his ego in this way, he will raise his consciousness to its highest level – the level of freedom – where he will know that he has choices in whatever he does, rather than following what he has been told; and he will have great power in creating his own happiness.

But, thinking about controlling your ego does not mean that it is done! Knowing and doing are two different things. You will agree that everything begins with an idea, and then your ego tells you how that idea should be carried out. By intentionally thinking of different choices, a range of different options will start flooding in, from good ones to strange ones. Some of your thoughts will put you at ease and other thoughts will stress you. It does not matter what the thought is – as long as you recognize and know how to overcome the thought that is coming from your ego. It is the way you *deal* with a thought that makes it a miserable one or happy one; and it is also what will determine your action.

Whatever a human's thought is – it controls his feelings without the human realizing it is happening. He will live in his thought, unknowingly accepting that this is the best he could do. Most of the time this leads to sadness and unhappiness; which ends up in stress and the need to release the increasing pressure that he created for himself. Releasing this energy internally will cause him physical problems; releasing it externally will cause him physical or mental problems; both will cause him misery. But, even when a human is depressed and miserable, he will still do the best he can to protect his thought, only so he can feel that he is in control. This is his ego protecting his pride from being hurt. If a human becomes aware that his ego is causing this chaos, he can work on changing his thought by letting it pass, and then elevate his faith and belief in his power to change his thought, so he could be at peace.

It is true that humans' thoughts cause them to worry mostly about what is going to happen tomorrow or the next day. Every human can change his worry to joy by making a strong effort to think pleasant thoughts, by believing the certain truth that whatever is going to happen will happen, if he worries or not; worry will not change the fact of an experience that is waiting for him. I say, take care of today and let tomorrow take care of itself, if tomorrow comes. If a human can convince and train himself to adopt this routine, then very slowly he will be able to change his thoughts so he can finish the rest of this life without too much stress. Realizing and believing that it was his thought that caused his reaction, will create confidence in the human which will lead him to a beautiful self–control. He can then live in happiness, always coming from the heart. With this new wisdom he will know better how to finish this life the way his soul planned.

Understand that your ego is not always wrong. It is the way you use it that will create a wrong reaction, which will make you miserable. The worst thing a human can do is fight his ego, instead of controlling it through his free will. If a human yells, screams and fights or if he speaks and acts wisely and calmly, the fact of an occurrence will remain the same. It is up to the human to decide which reaction will make him happy. I tell you to always remember that there is no right or wrong – but there is a difference between happy and sad. When you are happy, you will be in your higher self where there is no judgment and no difference between good and bad, because your interest will be focused on the knowledge and wisdom the experience is giving you. Your higher self never asks anything of you; but it will lead you to unconditional love, which will allow you to gain the world, if you can stay in this state. In the higher self stage, the ego just knows that it is, so it does not create problems for you. When you are not in your higher self, your ego asks for a lot from you.

The ego's role is to keep a human attached to his physical existence and to make sure to keep his anxiety for life ongoing. For a human, there is always a big difference between life and death, success and failure, good and bad. These differences create a problem for the human who tries to accept one and refuse the other. The truth is that none of these can work without its opposite. These opposites complete each other. But when the human ego kicks in, it shows the human that success is better than failure – this is where the fear of failure begins. The ego will show the human that good is better than bad – this is where the fear of being bad starts.

The worst thing is when the ego shows the human that life is better than death. Worries like this are created when a human does not understand and does not know where he came from, who he is, and where he is going after he dies. Because a human does not know what death will bring to him, he fears death for as long as he is alive. For a human, death is not part of his sense of logic. Death is a problem to be faced by him, and it is very hard for a human to accept that it will come. The denial of death is how the ego assures itself that the human is still alive and it is also why, on a daily basis, a human does all he can to survive and stay alive. The death scare created by the ego terrifies the human internally and results in certain behaviors externally. This will lead a human to feel that he must always provide himself with self–protection so that death will never come to him. This is how a human comforts himself and controls his fear of death; but when a human has a fragile personality, no amount of self–protection will help him control his fear of death. But think of it this way: if there is no life, then there is no death. So a human should not have a problem with death alone; his problem should be with life and death combined together.

Understand that in a human, the ego itself could die without the physical body coming to an end. This occurs all the time when people seem to be unconscious and near death. We will discuss this some more when we talk about death in detail.

Things are going great in my life. I understand who I am and what my mission is, but every now and then I allow fear to control me. How can I get rid of this fear once and for all?

When a human is born, fear is born with him. Think of an infant. If anyone yells, screams or makes any loud noise next to him, he feels troubled and cries. Once an infant takes his first steps and falls down, he will cry even though he is not hurt. Fear starts unconsciously and it comes from an emotion that is built inside the Subconscious and the ego, to help protect the human on his earthly journey. Fear is actually very useful only if it is controlled the right way by the human. If fear is not controlled it will lead to anger, nervousness, horror and depression.

Fear can weaken a human being to a point where guilt, blame and judgment of others will take over all his thoughts and actions. When a human judges and blames other humans, then he is definitely judging himself; and he is also feeling powerless. Judging others is a way for this human to fool himself into believing that he has power over others. In fact, he will never judge others if he really believes that he, himself, is powerful. But I tell you, it is a human's ego – a tool of the Subconscious – that steers the judging and blaming. Unless the ego is controlled, a human will never find a solution to get rid of his fear. On the contrary, his fear will grow stronger and the human will get weaker and weaker.

Think for a minute what fear is all about. It is based on thoughts and ideas that the human ego creates for him. The more he thinks these negative thoughts, the more he will believe in them. Soon after, he will start running his life according to what his new negative belief is. These negative thoughts will create weakness, where he will have less confidence in what is ahead for him.

The beautiful part is that a human always has the choice of staying in his fear or letting it go. For you and for every human, the easiest way to balance the ego and get rid of fear is to think positive, happy thoughts all the time. For example, you can think of happy experiences that you went through, or you can think of a place that you have been to that made you feel like you were on top of the world. When a human does this, his positive thoughts will conquer the fear that most of the time creates negative thoughts. Making a habit of this method will help a human trust himself and his belief in internal spirituality. Then, nothing will scare him.

Controlling fear is an easy task for you now because you are in a very powerful stage of your life – so control it, do not fear it. I will tell you that fear can be a very valuable tool in a human's life if it is controlled and directed in the right way. Fear could create emotions in a human to trigger this human to act in a way that changes his life for the better. If you think about it, fear of misery is what pushed you to be the angel of love that you are today. Fear helped you discover a great power that is in you, which is the unconditional love that you carry in your heart. I promise you this is just the beginning. Go with it and finish it to the end. Do not get stuck by fearing fear.

Chapter 13

FREEDOM

I am tired of depending on others and I am tired of others depending on me. How can I depend only on myself? What can I do to be free? Talk to me about freedom.

A human can be in a lot of confusion when this question comes up. Believe me when I say, when you are in your higher self the answer will come very easily. When you are in a stage where you do not judge or blame yourself or others, your higher self will give you all the answers that you are looking for. But let's talk about it.

The first step a human should take to feel free is to become independent. To be independent, your emotions and feelings have to come from your heart and not your ego. Let me explain. Every human feels and knows that his family and his close friends provide a very important support system for him. To free himself and to be able to follow his heart, he has to first provide himself this support, without depending on any other human. This means that he has to love himself to a point where he will not need confirmation from others to feel good about who he is.

Another part of being independent is for this human to find something that he loves to do and keep himself busy. He can start by finding an occupation he enjoys so he can support himself. Even if he does not make too much money, it is a great start that will help him feel great about accomplishing on his own. The minute he believes in what he is doing, money will start coming in with no problem. As long as he understands that money is not the only thing that made him earn his freedom, he will be satisfied in believing that getting rich is not the only tool for happiness.

The second step to reaching freedom is for a human to make the best of the situation that he is in. Making the best of a situation is not the same as settling with dissatisfaction out of obligation to please others. Let me repeat myself. To move in the right direction, a human should always act using his heart and not emotions or feelings that come from his ego. This means that the human will not be scared to be fair to himself; and creating this balance has to start at home. If a human lives alone without a partner or family, it will be a little bit easier to start a routine of freedom. If he lives with a partner or family, he can still do it, but he will have to include the family members. A very important rule to follow is to discuss everything with his partner to make sure they are in agreement with everything they are planning to do together – good or bad – as long as it is coming from the heart.

The first understanding should be that each partner is free first, and no human should tell another how to run his life. Then these two humans can help each other do what they need to do together. They should support each other and both of them should have financial freedom. I say both because it is important for them to understand and believe that neither of them is better than or unequal to the other.

When this agreement is accomplished, they will see how their lives will improve and be full of happiness.

I tell you, even though a human has a partner, it does not mean that he should shut himself off from other humans. He should always look for new friends so that he can gain wisdom from his new relationships. This does not mean that he should forget or ignore his old friends. All he has to do is to pay a little more attention to the new people in his life, which will help him evaluate and figure out who his real friends are. He will know which humans will provide him with relaxation of the mind, and who will be there for him when he needs a shoulder to cry on, without wanting or needing anything from him.

Even though a human may use the support of his family and friends while he is working toward being independent, it is important for the human to start figuring out how to help himself. He should know and believe that the road to freedom starts with setting a goal. He should always keep in mind that he is the only person who can stop him from accomplishing and finishing what his heart is looking for him to accomplish. The only way he will fail is if he starts to doubt that he can do it. The most important thing is to never give up. He should see the goal that he planned on and follow it. It does not matter if others see it as good or bad. If he follows his heart, he will reach and achieve his goal the way that his soul planned on more quickly. Believe me, if he can do this, a human will prevent any stress that he might have created for himself otherwise. He will then be free for real.

I want you to always remember that the more a human follows his heart to make his experience look better to him, the better it will end according to the way the soul planned. A human should always enjoy what he is doing and he should do it in happiness with the humans that are included in the experience, no matter what their roles will be for its completion. When this is done with contentment and without blaming or judging, it will create happiness. This happiness will be the best medicine for stress, doubt or fear that he might try to cause to himself in his new way of life.

If a human lives with and shares his life with family, he should delete any data that he was taught as a kid about the way a family has to run. He should sit with his housemates and set up new rules; but do not call them rules. Call it a new routine for the family to follow. Responsibilities that will make the family live happily should be divided and shared equally. No one should have a bigger load than the others and no one should be the master and all the others his slaves. Equality does not mean that one person's needs and wants are to be taken care of and the others' needs and wants should be ignored. Because life teaches humans to be selfish, this might be a challenge to be faced while trying to create a new routine.

A family requires many chores to be shared to keep it running in a healthy way. If there is a routine that is considered very important for one and not for the others, it should be broken and changed. Where is the harm in breaking a routine and replacing it with another one that is good for the whole family? This is a must and it should be done so the family could live happily. If one of them cannot change a routine and help himself live with a new routine that the family decided on, he will feel miserable and stressed. If, instead, this human creates happiness and love for the self, he can accept the fact that he is not the only human in this family that should be happy. He could change his routine with happiness and contentment, knowing that this is the best way for this family to live together. If the change in routine is a must, and it happens that a family member cannot make the change by himself, then the other family members could help him do it or, the change should be made anyway and the stubborn family member will remain miserable about it. On the other side of this, if one of the family members feels very strongly about something, what is wrong with that human doing it himself? If he cannot do it himself, then there are always options to get help from outside the family.

Keep in mind that the family member who tries to suggest a change in the family routine will face resistance and rejection at first. If it is refused by the family members, it does not mean that he has to take on all the responsibilities by himself again. Saying the word "no" to a lot of the things that the other members are expecting from him will help him rid himself of the slavery and misery that he wants to stop. Sooner or later, the other family members will begin to understand that this human has chosen to live free, and he will no longer be that old rag they used to wipe their feet on. This rag has now changed to a beautiful wall carpet, which they can cherish and enjoy having, without stepping on it or dirtying it anymore. By doing this, the human will find the happiness that he is aiming for. He should rejoice in his achievement and not feel stressed or miserable if he fails to accomplish it – trying is also an achievement. As I have told you before, there is nothing called failure in life. The human should just see it as an experience that passed, which he should learn from so he can be more successful in similar experiences later in life.

If a human believes in himself and loves himself, he will believe deep inside that his life on Earth has a purpose besides being a slave to others. He will then be free, and he will be the happiest person on Earth. He will know that he is full of powerful love that he can pleasantly give to others, only because he *wants to* give and not because others expect it. Let me assure you that freedom starts at home. If a human cannot accomplish this freedom where he lives with the humans he lives with, then he cannot accomplish freedom in anything he does in this life.

It is very beautiful to be free, but does this freedom interfere with the soul's plan?

I have to tell you, this question is full of judgment and obligation.

Now listen to me carefully. When you come here, you are not here to discover anything. You are here to create the life that your soul planned on having before coming to Earth. When this life that you are living was planned, it was created with pure love because your soul does not know good or bad, wrong or right; so you can never "interfere" with what your soul wants. A human's free will can take the human off the route, but the soul will only accept experiences it can learn and gain wisdom from. Freedom and no freedom are both experiences.

Your soul and all other souls are a part of Spirit or Source. Anytime a soul starts planning on a new life to experience through a human on this Earth, another part of the same Source will be planning with it. So, every soul that comes from the same Source will have its plan to help itself be affected by the experience, and to help the other souls to be affected by the same experience. This planning is all done in a way that is full of pure love that does not judge any experience.

I want you to remember that when the soul plans, there is no time or date consideration. Everything for a soul is like a split second in earthly time, even though the earthly realm depends on time. For example, when two souls meet each other after a long period of time on Earth, the time it took for these two souls to meet as humans was not planned by their souls. When the two humans meet, it is because the two souls were to meet again in a new lifetime, at a certain point of progression, to play the roles they chose. For the souls, the planning of a lifetime was planned to take place in an instant and then be done. These souls also plan on leaving Earth together, but time is not a factor that is considered. Departure all depends on when each soul is finished with its plan and no longer needs the shell it occupies.

As I told you before, every human comes to Earth with three separate bodies – the soul, the mind and the body. These three parts work together as one. They cannot be separated, and neither one of them will function alone by itself. When the plan is created, it will consist of the plan for the roles that these three parts will play. It will be planned for the three parts to act together as one. In fact, the part of creation itself will also be planned, and every one of these three bodies has a role to play in it. The soul is the main planner who plans on the experiences that it wants to have. The mind comes up with the thought of how to create the experience that the soul planned, and the body creates the physical and mental experience that the other two bodies worked on. Now, if the mind has a thought and the body does not help create it, then it will be a stored thought that the human might come back to later; and it will become a hope. If the mind comes up with the thought and the body agrees to go with it and starts creating it, it means that the three bodies believe that it could be accomplished very easily and they have great faith that it will be.

Every master who came to this Earth was very sure that every thought that is created from pure faith will definitely be completed as it was planned. All that is required from you is to be thankful, grateful, and deep inside from the heart, believe that it will be done. Never condemn or judge any part of the thought. If you are condemning or judging what was planned before you came to this Earth, it means you are judging yourself. That is the worst thing a human can do to himself. The important thing is for you to always finish the creation or the experience with happiness and love; and when you do this, you can do miracles. You can walk on water if you want to. Every human follows this procedure directly or indirectly. This is the basic rule of life.

Some humans are aware of what they are doing and know exactly what they are following. Others will do it, but they do not know why. For the humans who understand what they are doing, all they have to do when a thought comes to mind, is to recognize it and see what accessories it needs. When the idea is complete, the creation and/or the experience will be completed as it was planned. Without hesitation, the human should always keep the idea in his mind, having a strong belief in his abilities to create it. This will make the human believe and trust that his thought is right for him and it is what should be done, without any doubt.

It is very important for a human not to let his fear control his thoughts and feelings. He should not be afraid of anything in life, and he should know that not everything his ears hear is right. He should listen, but only follow his heart. He should also immediately change any negative thought that comes to his mind. He should just wipe it out and change it to a positive one. I know that it sounds very difficult to do, but it is a lot easier than it sounds.

So, to answer your question, a human should let his mind think about what he wants to do and let the body help create what is planned, without judgment or guilt. Now you know the secret to freedom!

One of my clients asked me about his kids. When they were very young, he took care of them without question. Now that his kids are older, he wants them to take care of themselves, but they still live with him and depend on him for everything. He feels there is something wrong with his kids but he cannot figure out what it is. Educate me more so I can be even wiser.

Why does your client think that there is something wrong with his kids? Your client has to understand that in this life there is no right or wrong; no good or bad. If your client, or any human, understands what this life is all about, he will think differently about this situation because he will be aware of his own purpose.

Before a human comes to Earth, his soul already chose the way it will live life in the human it occupies. This soul has a lot of experiences to finish from past lives, and new ones to start and finish in this current life. Whatever your client and these kids are going through is a part of the experiences that their souls chose for them. So when your client worries about his kids and gets upset over them, do you think he is helping them? Or is he only hurting himself?

I want you to always remember that worries are a human's own creation. Worrying only makes a human feel lost; and it prevents him from seeing things clearly. Instead of worrying, there is a way for your client to help his kids if he wants to. He should think back to when his kids were younger and notice the personality of each one. Then take a balanced look at them now as young adults. According to his evaluation, he can give each of them the best advice he knows, and then let them be. They will listen to him and appreciate every word he says, but he should not expect that they will change the way they are running their lives. Each one of your client's kids has his or her own strong personality and they see life in their own way. Take, for example, the oldest one. This kid, especially, is not shy of speaking in public and he has no fear of expressing himself and convincing others of his opinions. He does not know how to express himself in a politically correct manner; he says it the way he sees it. He does not go by earthly rules that say he should respect elders or people in authority, or whatever, any more than any other human. So what is wrong with that?

Be aware that all kids are beautiful souls that decided to come to families of their choice, to go through a lot of different experiences. Your client's kids' souls came to Earth to be with a family that will help them do this. At the same time, these kids will help the other family members to also finish what they are here for. If a human tries to make another human change the experience that was planned, he will fail. Your client should understand that no human can decide for another human if an experience will end with happiness or misery. I am telling you that everything that happens on this Earth, in this life, has a reason for happening; and after the reason, there is the result. So, these souls will help each other finish their experiences either with love, happiness, and joy; or with sadness, agony, misery, and pain – whatever is planned. To the soul, it does not matter if the result is good or bad. What matters is the experience itself. All your client should do is to give his love and knowledge to his kids, which will satisfy all their souls' purpose. Period.

Now, if a kid's role is to play the dependent person role like another one of your client's kids, the parents' role will be to give this kid whatever they can to provide his comfort. So indirectly, these parents will make this kid dependent and he will rely on them for everything. The kid will reach a point thinking that whatever he says goes, and usually this is where the human ego kicks in and controls the mind. The more the family gives this kid, the more this kid will take and want. When the kid reaches adulthood, the parents might start trying to convince the kid that he is an adult now and that it is time for him to take responsibility for himself. The parents will tell him that now he should depend on himself, and whatever distress he is going through is of his own making. This kid will not be able to accept and believe that this is happening to him. He will start blaming all his misery on his parents for not giving him all the attention that he was used to. He will not understand that the people who took care of him all his life are now changing the routine. This does not mean that the kid is a no–good human. He just does not know better.

This kid stressed himself a lot when he was no longer getting what he was used to, which affected the health of his physical body. Now he is scared of what is happening to him physically and his fear is controlling his feelings and emotions, making him halt the experience that was planned by his soul, only because he is not using his heart to see. He is allowing his fear to create scary images of his future, without thinking for a minute that things could actually get better. This is making him weaker and weaker every day. I assure you that he has his own experiences to go through; and one of them that his soul planned on was the role that he is playing now. But this kid is not here alone. His soul also decided to come with other parts of the same Source to help him finish the experience. This is where the parents' role comes in. These souls decided to come together at a certain point to help each other.

Whatever fear and worries these parents are going through now about their kid's health and future is all from their own making. They need a good kick to snap out what they are doing, and balance themselves accordingly. The important thing that they should know is that when this kid came to this life through them, it was not a mistake or by chance for any of them. When these parents came to you, it was also not by mistake or by chance. The parents were meant to meet you, and they are learning a lot from you. You are teaching them self–control and how to behave differently in relation to their experience. They are helping their kid all they can, and it is being done intentionally – but they are missing balance. With your help, they are beginning to notice their emotions and reactions and how they are affecting the situation. You are helping them see that the most important way to help their kid is to show him how to see with his heart.

Because humans cannot exist without emotions and feelings, these parents and their kid are still going to worry, feel bad, and cry together as they go through this situation. You are in their life to guide them and provide them with wisdom and knowledge to help them get through it. If they listen to you and keep the channel of communication open between them, and speak from their heart without any blame or judgment, then the experience will be much smoother for all of them. The parents have to understand that their kid is going through an experience and they cannot change the fact. Whatever the kid's soul decided to happen, will happen.

Now for the kid – the way you can help these kinds of kids is mentally and not physically. Do not get directly involved with these kids unless they ask you to. If you are not asked, you can always send them love from a distance without any expectation. If you happen to talk to them, give them fatherly advice; tell them what you think and then let them handle their situation. If they listen, they might benefit a lot from what they hear. You can always talk to them, lead them, and show them how you see life. Give them advice and then let them do it their way.

I know and you know that you have been helping others since you opened your eyes to this life. Some of them you chose to help and you did a great job. Some of them you felt that you had to help, which means you did it out of obligation; but you still did it with love and without hesitation. With others, you did not know why you were helping them, and sometimes it did not even occur to you that you were helping – but you did it, giving all you could. Now that you know you can help, give, and heal, it is beautiful that you want to help even without letting the other person know that you are helping. This is where giving and healing will work the best. I promise you something: this is the start of a long healing journey for you, and I am convinced that you love it. As I told you many times before, you are a great healer. You will reach a point in this life where you can heal a human using your fingertip.

My client told me that his current job is providing income that allows him to take care of his mature kids' wants and needs, but he does not like his job. He asked me to help him figure out how he could start taking care of himself.

When your client says "their needs," ask him who assigned him a job of "need provider"? Who said that all his life he has to take care of other people's needs? His kids are grown–ups now and they do not need anything from him. He is the one that is spoiling them and allowing them to depend on him for everything.

His job provides security for him and the somewhat life of luxury he is living. It is also providing his family with their wants and needs. His biggest challenge is that he is having a hard time letting go of the idea that he is responsible for providing his kids' wants and needs – only because they expect it from him. He is putting himself in a loop where he feels guilty if he does not provide them with what they want. In fact, all he is really doing is preventing them from going on their own and putting into action the things he taught them. He already raised them, trained them, taught them and showed them how they can provide themselves with their needs and wants. They are mature and smart. He can always be there if there is an extreme need, but it is time for your client to free himself. He should understand that there is no reason for him to judge or blame himself for wanting to do what makes him happy. He already knows what he wants to do for himself. He wants to finish his dream, and he should do it. Your client should not allow anything to block his way or stop him. He should always follow his heart and make himself the number one person he loves. By loving him, he can provide his family with the love they expect, in a way that will also make him happy.

I want you to always remember that mastering yourself has put you in the position to help others do the same. Give others the knowledge they need to master themselves and let them fly. So now I will tell you to tell your client not to assign himself the job of taking care of the needs of others, but to assign himself the job of taking care of his dream. Hopefully, he will understand your message.

One of my male clients told me that his wife has a best friend who is male. He thinks his wife is cheating on him but he does not have proof. He is very jealous and lost and does not know how he should handle the situation. Tell me, who is he to try to limit his wife's freedom because his jealousy is controlling him?

Humans have to know and understand that no two people will come into each other's life unless it was planned. If the wife is cheating on him, it was meant to be for their souls to experience this situation.

All humans are free; no one needs to put rules on any other human being. If the feeling of a need is created, it will be of the human's own doing. If the need ends with hurt, this hurt is created by the human himself and no one else. Now, your client's wife and the male friend are very close friends; they enjoy talking to each other and helping each other go through life. Let me assure you, if the husband stops being jealous and thinks about the situation without hate in his heart, he will find the answers to the questions that his jealousy is bringing up, which are hurting his ego and his pride.

This husband is a man that wants more than he can give. He does not put any conditions or rules on his own wants, but his giving always depends on conditions and rules that *he* decides on. If his wife does what he wants and provides his needs, if she does not hurt his ego, and if she is that human he can order around to do whatever he says, then he will love her according to the way he is receiving. In this case, he sees no problem in giving what he decides to give – not what she wants from him. However, if all his needs are not fulfilled, his giving is shaky. Let me tell you, if he thinks hard and goes deeper into his thoughts, he can ask himself this question: what more do I want from my wife? I assure you that his answer will be that he did not want a wife who would express her feelings as she should, because his ego and pride cannot handle it. His joy and happiness is to go to his house and see his wife waiting for him with open arms, hugging him, kissing him and comforting him. So basically, it is always about him and his needs. If he goes home and does not get this reaction from his wife, then God help his family. He will allow himself to feel hurt and sad and he will become furious. Again, if he pauses and asks himself what he really thinks of his wife, he will see that all he wants is a robot, a machine – someone without feelings and emotions. He only wants a slave to say, "Yes, Master". If she does, then everything is great for him. If the wife does not obey him, he starts thinking and structuring a story in his imagination. Then he starts building his life, his thoughts, and his pride according to the way his ego is leading him. This human would be a different human if he paused and looked within himself, and allowed himself to discover the beauty that is him.

Let me repeat, all humans have free will and free choice in this life, so no human should be a slave to the pleasures of another human. The husband's jealousy is blinding his eyes from observing a real friendship between two humans, and learning from it. He has to understand that his wife and her male friend have a beautiful friendship between them that is not based on lust – they care for each other without any conditions. They need nothing from each other. Society condemns this kind of friendship because it is not understood. This kind of friendship can only happen when both humans care about each other without any wants and needs. Your client can learn a lot by observing.

Let me assure you that the wife is still in love with her husband, but he has to understand that there are different kinds of love: one is based on need mixed with lust – like the wife has for the husband; and a pure love that does not know lust and need, which is between the wife and the friend. He can be jealous all he wants but he will never have the fulfillment of such a friendship with any other human until he really knows who he is. If the husband discovers who he is, then he will understand that his wife is also human and that she has feelings, emotions and needs, like he does. For now, it looks like this human is not ready to do this. Instead, he would rather stick with his jealousy and the conclusions, which are his own creations based on his own selfishness. The wife is not hurting him at all; his ego is hurting him.

I was in a park relaxing when I saw a white dove circling above me. What was this dove's message to me supposed to mean?

The dove that you saw yesterday was a real one. It was not a daydream and I assure you it was not in your imagination; it was for real flying above your head. It was meant for you at that moment to see and feel that dove. She came to give you a very important message about freedom, which you are seeking all the time.

You asked her what she was doing circling above you. The dove answered that she was there to show you that she is free. She told you that she can do whatever she chooses to do at any time without causing pain to others. You told her that you are also free – she answered that you are not. She told you that you still act out of obligation, and you cannot do anything you choose to do anytime you want. She told you that there are many restrictions in the way you act and react, so your freedom is limited; but she can eat, drink, and fly anywhere she wants, anytime she chooses, without feeling a need from any other entity; you do not have this freedom.

This was a beautiful message for you to think about. You still, from time to time, have doubt and fear about what you are doing. Between now and then, you think about not offending others when you say, ask, or do something. You still feel that you are obligated to go with the flow even when you do not feel like doing it.

I want you to understand that freedom on Earth means that no other human can stop you from doing something good for others, even if the others are not asking for it or expecting it. You will face a lot of rejection from humans who do not understand you, and if you do not get rid of your feeling of obligation, you will not be able to finish what your soul planned for you. It is very important for you to always remember that no human can stop you from sharing your wisdom and helping others any time you choose. Do not allow yourself to believe that a human's freedom should stop when he feels that he has caused harm to others who do not like what he is saying or doing. Always know and believe that no human brings harm or fear to another; a human can only disturb himself, through his ego.

The dove is a symbol of love and peace. She came to you yesterday to give you this beautiful message that will help you do what you are here to do, with love and peace. She was preparing you for dealing with the many kinds of people that will find you, and also with the humans that will reject you. She was showing you how to deal with humans of different races, religions and traditions equally, and how not to judge any experiences that will happen in your life anymore. The most important message was to stop judging and blaming yourself; worship and love yourself instead. So, the bird's message for you yesterday was to take good care of you first so that you can take care of all humans with the same love that you have for you.

Chapter 14

LIVING LIFE IN HAPPINESS

How can I live and finish my life in happiness?

A human's life is like a stream, where water keeps flowing all the time. Depending on the weather, sometimes the water will flow rapidly and other times it will flow little by little; sometimes the stream will run very smoothly, and other times it will be corrupted when it hits rocks and blockages. So when a human thinks that his life is running harmlessly and smoothly, something out of nowhere will interfere, and it will change the way that his life is running. This will cause what was planned by the human's soul, to be experienced in this lifetime, to also change.

I tell you, issues turn into energy, and energy itself turns into issues. I will explain in an easier way for your readers to understand. Always in this life, a human's thoughts and acts will decide the life that he is going to have, and a human's perception of everything that happens to him will determine the outcome of his experiences. The outcome will be what he thinks it is. If a human being acts in what he believes is a good way, then he will expect a good ending for his life. If he acts in what he considers to be a bad way, then he will expect a bad ending for his life. I say, a human chooses and defines what will interfere with the smooth flow in the stream of his own life. If a human knows this, then there should be no confusion about what his fate will bring him. He will understand his life and what he could expect in his future.

It is a fact that life on Earth is based on contrasting experiences. Not all experiences will be good and not all experiences will be bad. When something goes wrong in humans' lives, they always face the truth the way that they were taught since they were born. When they think that something has gone wrong, they will label it a problem. The truth is, problems only come from a human's Subconscious; if he reacts toward what he calls a "problem" in a negative way then it will be a problem that will make him suffer. If he reacts toward the experience in a positive way, then it will not be a problem for him; it will be an experience that will feed his knowledge, and he will face it in a pleasant way. So the best way for a human to be problem free is to control his Subconscious.

For a human to control his Subconscious he needs to be wise enough to understand that nothing on Earth exists by itself. All of life is here to go through an Earth journey together; each life form helps the others to exist, even if it is not a recognized fact. At the end of life on Earth, a human's body turns into ashes that mix with the soil; leaves of trees turn into soil; a small seed in the soil becomes a plant; so seeds, leaves, humans, and everything that grows and dies on this Earth is from the same Source. If a human does something to destroy any of them, then a human is destroying himself. This means that everything that is an experience for you is not an experience *only* for you. If you can understand this for real, then you will be a humble and grateful human being for the rest of your life.

The main job of humans is to seek happiness and to stay away, as much as they can, from suffering. But suffering is part of humanity and it starts the minute a human is born. Think about it. The second a human sees the light when he comes out of the womb he starts crying; when he feels tired and physically unwell, he feels depressed; when he is with company out of obligation, he feels miserable even though he tries to make himself happy. When humans are in love and problems start between the lovers, they feel depressed and distressed; sometimes this might even lead them to end their lives. Then, as humans get older more aches, pains, and diseases hit their body. These humans remember their younger, healthier days and feel depressed that the end of their life is near. Even with all these experiences in a human's life, the wish for happiness always stays with him. Everything he does in his life is to try to accomplish this wish.

Many humans believe that if they improve material and physical conditions in their lives, their suffering will be less. But I tell you that improving the material and improving the physical will not get rid of their fear of sickness, aging and death. It will not make a human happy. Actually, the opposite will happen. Every improvement done for the material will have its own problems to be faced; and this will increase the suffering and problems the human will face. Even though he will try to be happy because of what he has accomplished, trying to accumulate more and more material, out of obligation or from his own want, will only make him reach a point of depression that will void happiness out of his life. All he will be doing is making himself a slave to the material itself, rather than trying to make himself happy for real.

The only solution for a human to gain happiness is to find the pure happiness that comes from pure inner growth of peace and love. If a human begins by looking for inner peace in a spiritual way, then outer peace will come automatically without having to look for it. This means finding peace inside you by understanding what your beliefs are and following them. It does not make a difference what the beliefs are, as long as you are content and you are following what your heart is telling you. This will lead a human to truly master himself, and find freedom from suffering. But, if a human does not look to find inner peace, and only looks for outer peace, there is no chance for him to know real happiness.

Finding inner peace starts when a human can teach his Subconscious not to depend on external conditions. A human does not need to wait for a better situation in order to be happy. Whatever the situation is, if it is negative or positive, good or bad – he can have inner peace. This will depend on how he looks at the experience. If the human practices seeing the bright side, if you will, then he will know that he is gaining knowledge and wisdom from all experiences, and he will be at peace. This can happen only if he practices living his life without having needs or expectations in any situation he faces.

If a human's need keeps him waiting for the perfect situation to occur for his satisfaction, then he will never consider changing anything in his current situation, thinking that his expectation is perfect. Let me give you an example. If a human wants to own the best house in the world, and all he does is look forward to his rich uncle dying so he can inherit his uncle's money to buy this dream house with, then he will not look to using different tools – in the present – to get what he wants. Rather than understanding that actively aiming toward his goal is an important experience for him, and that every experience helps a human master his life, he will instead be expecting a future situation to come up to fulfill his need and expectation. This human will spend a lot of time being stuck and lost – sometimes even a lifetime.

I want to remind you that life on Earth is limited. No one knows how long it will last, so by going through each situation in a meaningful way, a human will be able to finish a lot of what was planned for him, without too many problems or too much suffering. This does not mean that this human will never face challenges that will affect his emotions to make him suffer. Happiness, in fact, does not last forever because humanity is built on the basic rule of contrasting experiences. Ultimately in this life, every human is going to meet with a kind of suffering; and each human will decide how to face his suffering and what to make of it. Some humans will suffer a lot; wiser ones will suffer less. But remember, suffering comes from self–indulgence in wants and desires for pleasure, and from unawareness of the soul's plan. Indirectly, every human acts in ways to corrupt the peace of his conscience, which creates his dissatisfaction. This is part of life.

I tell you, happiness is not an easy place to reach, but when a human decides to put all his energy into following his heart, this will put him in a stage where he can master himself, to live in peace and happiness most of the time, regardless of the situation he is faced with. It is important for you to always work on how to live your own life in happiness; and when you do, you will be ready to know how to deal with all other humans without judging any human or anything you hear from them.

Chapter 15

LOVE

━━━━━━━━━━━━━━━◦━━━━━━━◦━━━━━━━━━━━━━━━

Talk to me about love. What is it all about? How does it start and where does it end?

Love is one of the most beautiful subjects that we can talk about. Love is accepting. Love is appreciating. Love is to want another to feel good. Love is tolerant. Love is having respect that does not come from obligation but from the pure feeling of fullness and contentment of the heart. Love is joy, and suffering. Love is freedom, and slavery. Love is to want the best for yourself and other people. Love is not possessing, but energizing. Love is like setting companionship on fire. Love is like a vision making warmth come true. Whatever description you have for love, it is all true. Love bonds two or more people together by improving the connection between them. When this connection becomes very close, it will soothe their souls.

There are two kinds of love: unconditional love and love. We will discuss unconditional love in detail some other time, but now let's talk about love in general. I tell you, it is very easy to create love. Basically, love is built on the desire to fulfill its own need. It depends entirely on the first glance and impression of the figure that a human's eyes see – what the eyes see sparks lust. The only thing this love needs is a mutual concentration on the spark between these humans. When this happens, love will be easily created. With this love, there may or may not be mutual respect for each other; there are terms and conditions, and if one of them is broken then this love will no longer exist.

The meaning of love changes with each relationship. It depends on how deep and how complicated that love is. The best love is when you treat other humans the way they want to be treated, and not the way that you want to treat them. To love another human is to wish for him the best that he can have and be, and to be totally honest about your feelings by sharing yourself emotionally, morally, physically and spiritually. This kind of love exists between family members, friends, lovers and so on, but it usually depends on conditions; even though these same relationships can also have no conditions, which is unconditional love.

I will tell you that love and unconditional love are divided by a very thin line and can be confused very easily. Basically, when a human has positive love feelings for another human without any needs, wants or judgment attached to this feeling, then it is unconditional love. This means that you can love another human unconditionally without the condition of expecting that human to love you the same way. An example of this is a situation where a mother and father love their kids unconditionally, but these kids grow up to reject their parents because they did not inherit their money. It is very important for a human to tell the difference, or else he will be living in a loop, finding no end to his confusion.

The way a human feels when he loves someone depends on his own wants and needs. As long as his wants and needs are provided for and satisfied, it will not matter who the other human is. Let me also tell you that a human's ego plays a big role in a love relationship. When the ego is satisfied, it will convince the human that whatever he sees and hears from the other human is beautiful, and it will be accepted with love.

It is normal for humans to try to find ways to show their love and acceptance to each other – I also have a few suggestions. I say, the best way is to see the beauty in one another; to hear sweet words, to speak the most beautiful words that the heart can express; to smell the best aroma that the heart can offer; to give a hug, where touching and holding expresses real love in the greatest way it could ever be expressed. For this love to continue, it is important for these humans to appreciate their connection, where they are always on each other's minds and in their thoughts.

Some love relationships are what humans call romantic. Romantic love is shared with a very close sexual connection. A lot of people think that sex is love but they are often disappointed and confused by their understanding. Women, more than men, usually look more for security and love in their sexual relationships. They can tell the difference between love and sex better than men can. Most of the time, women seek love but they could be satisfied with sex. Sharing sexual pleasure with another human is what gives a human the strongest push toward romantic love.

In a romantic love situation, a human will express love that comes from the heart and he will be generous with whom he loves, even though he will still have expectations from this love. He will give all his time and affection focusing on the other, and that is when he will start seeing the difference between feelings and appearances. This will let him confess what is on his mind without the fear of rejection. When both humans follow their heart without any fear, this feeling will make them behave with added power and energy when they are around each other. They will feel self-assured and they will act powerlessly silly. Now, if romance was a pure creation, without wants or needs attached to it, and if it was supported by reasonable proof, then surely most humans would want to have it and hold onto it. But humans are not taught about love in a way to help them create this pure romance.

It is also true that love could be very stressful when it comes only from one side because love is not only a feeling, it is also an action. There are always some logical reasons that will prevent a human from expressing that feeling – usually from fear of refusal – which makes a human's ego hurt his pride. Being scared to express love to another human will prevent a human from going through a very valuable, planned experience. Believe me when I tell you, life on Earth is limited by time, and the more a human wastes time in not accomplishing what he is meant to do by allowing his ego to control him, the more time he is losing in finishing what was planned.

One of my clients told me that she does not have sex anymore – she now only makes love. Could you explain to me what the difference is between having sex and making love?

Having sex is to pleasure the physical. A human's body has a need and it also has the need to express that need, so humans have sex for physical pleasure. Having sex will give a human relief, pleasure and satisfaction for a short time after the fact, which will have a positive effect on the human's emotions. Having sex and making love are almost the same in relieving energy, but there is a big difference between the two in other ways.

Making love comes from the heart, and only the heart – without any needs or obligations – and it is the most sacred experience a human can have. When humans make love, there is no fear or guilt, and no earthly emotions coming from expectation. Making love can only occur when a human feels that he loves himself and his partner as one, and when the feelings that these humans have for each other are very pure. Making love is very sacred, and it may or may not happen in a lifetime. It all depends on the feelings that come from both partners, supported by unconditional love and purity of the heart. It is a very unusual experience that occurs only when both humans are ready for it.

Now let's talk about your client who told you that she now makes love instead of having sex. I want you to understand that after she spent some time with you – talking and expressing her feelings – she now believes in herself, and she wanted you to know that she has reached a stage that allows her to understand and live in her higher self. She felt the urge to share with you, without any fear or regrets in her heart, that she loves herself and her partner as one. She told you that she sees the same love in her partner's eyes, and this makes her feel that they are both one now. She believes that she understands that making love is not the same as having sex.

Get used to this because from now on you are going to counsel and teach people how to live the rest of their lives in peace. You are going to hear, see and feel all kinds of gestures and stories from people. This is beautiful so there is no need to be scared – do not fight it or think too much; and always remember, whatever is meant to be...will be.

You explained to me the difference between making love and having sex. With all the social rules and traditions that are followed on Earth, is it o.k. for a human to just have sex?

When your soul decided to come to this Earth, before it decided which physical body it wants to reside and create in, it was in its highest feeling. It decided to come to Earth to go through new experiences using pure love as much as it can – without any judgment. The soul does not know good or bad; the physical is the part that experiences good and bad, according to the traditions and beliefs that are dictated by the society it lives in during its earthly existence. What is good in one society might be bad in another; and what is bad in one society might be good in another. Good and bad could very easily change places, where the good becomes bad and the bad becomes good. This depends on what the majority of humans in a society decide to change.

Most of your life so far, you had been judging yourself about everything that you did. Since your first day on Earth, you were taught to always judge yourself and others. One of the rules you were taught was that having sex, if you are not married, is bad and sinful. The best one was when you were told that you were born through sin. To purify that sin, you were told that a priest has to clear your physical body and your soul by praying from a holy book. The honest truth is a priest may or may not understand what he is saying; it is usually a routine repetition for him. He has already said the same words hundreds of times and he most likely cannot even hear himself praying anymore. Again, this priest believes that he is purifying your soul and getting rid of the devil that came with you when you were born. If you think about all this for a minute, the contradiction will be very obvious. How can humanity exist without the act of sex? Don't you think this should be the first consideration?

All earthly rules were made by humans for humans. Most of these rules were born out of different experiences that had occurred to humans, and their reactions to them. But the rules of a society were not made by ordinary humans. They were created by humans who had power over others and this is the way it still is. These powerful humans change old rules and make new ones according to their mood, their benefit and their ego. Their position gives them the power to convince the humans they lead that following their rules is the right thing to do. If a rule no longer pleases them, they will change it or make up another one. One of the rules created by these leaders with authority says that if a holy man does not unite a man and a woman by reading some words from a holy book, they cannot have sex; and if they do, it is a sin, sometimes punishable by death. In other societies, sex is openly practiced on alters. So, who is right and who is wrong?

You are asking me if it is o.k. to have sex, but I want to ask you, is it o.k. to whom? To the old you that used to judge and be judged all the time, or to the new you that is doing a great job being in his highest self? If I am answering the old you, then I would say that sex is bad because you used to believe what you were taught – that having sex is a sin unless you are married according to your community's rules. But for the new you, I want *you* to answer the same question without using any ego or judgment. *You* tell me. Is having sex good or bad, or a sin? By now, you should understand that what a human does is only for his earthly existence. All these rules are staying here. When the end of a human's journey comes and he leaves this Earth, all earthly rules will be left behind.

What is the easiest way for two married people to live together all their life, even though sometimes it is out of obligation? How can these people live together without guilt if cheating is involved?

The best way for two humans that are in love to deal with each other is to be in their higher self and understand what life is all about. When a human reaches the higher self stage, he will believe in the God that is within him – the God that he is. He will deal with other humans in his life using a wiser outlook, regardless of the data that is within him or the result that will come out of the situation. He will handle others with happiness because he will always believe in himself. This level of loving the self will lead a human to do everything he does being himself, without feeling any obligation; always coming from the heart, where there is no place for judgment or blame for himself or others.

Believe me when I tell you that a human is born with the knowledge of how to deal with other humans. Dealing with a love partner or a spouse is a part of this knowledge. A human's expression of his action or reaction comes from the knowledge he was born with, combined with what he has learned through his experiences in this life. In a relationship, there are always new creations in the way a human expresses himself using pure love, which can only happen if a human is in his higher self. When creating new ideas, he will be adding a little bit more to what he already knows. His Subconscious will help him by borrowing some information from his Conscious, to let him go as wide as he wants in his creation.

Now, when a love relationship ends, it is usually because it was not based on pure love. This means that if a human always looks for what he is gaining from a relationship, he will end it when he figures that he is no longer gaining anything. A relationship that depends on wants and needs usually will not last for long. But let me also tell you this: every relationship between two humans always starts with a need because need is what gives a human the push to seek what he is seeking.

When a love relationship starts between two humans, they both expect a lot from each other. For a while, both of them will always do their best to keep the other happy. If, for whatever reason, one of them does not keep up with expectations, the relationship will begin to fade. This is when problems start between the two humans. Both partners will begin to see changes in the other that they do not like and this will create an uneasy relationship. Each partner will have the feeling that the other is not completing him anymore. Suddenly each partner will focus more on his own needs, rather than trying to please the other; so they will both make changes to please themselves first. These changes will cause problems in the relationship because each human will see the other differently than expected.

Issues like this are usual when a human allows his hopes and dreams, his happiness or misery, to depend on another human; which is a perfect condition for a failed relationship. This human will stop having a need for others to satisfy him only when he starts depending on himself; and not until he starts loving himself with no conditions. In fact, the most important relationship is always with the self; so when he loves him, any problem that he faces in life – especially in a love relationship – will have a very easy solution, without any complications, and the experience will always be perfect for the purpose of his own satisfaction. He will also understand that to have a good relationship, he must concentrate on the way he is treating the other human instead of how he is being treated.

A part of mastering the self is for a human to recognize and understand the way he is behaving toward others; and not only to notice how others are behaving toward him. This does not mean that the human has to give of himself to please others. He always has to love and please himself first – and when he does, no experience will cause him harm, regardless if it is good or bad.

I will always remind you that when a human is created, the main purpose of his being is to experience and create. The relationship experience is a very important one in a human lifetime. When the soul makes its plans for a relationship experience, it does not depend on any other human in particular to finish the experiences with – in fact, souls decide to work together, but they do not choose the shape of each other's shell. The relationship experience is not any different in procedure than every other experience; the human's Subconscious and his Conscious provide all the tools a human will need to create the circumstances and reactions that are meant to occur. Both will be engaged by the human's free will, to make the experience what the human wants it to be; which could end up being different than what the soul planned. If a human allows his emotions to run the experience, they will only show the human how to judge and blame and to believe that he is always right and all others are wrong; that happiness or sadness is not a choice, but a sentence, and so on. But I tell you, if a human can stop these feelings for a moment, he will be able to choose and achieve new feelings that will start creating a *new* him – a wiser him who will know how to move through a relationship experience, or any other, without getting stuck.

When it comes to a cheating spouse or partner, the human should ask himself why he is allowing this action to hurt his feelings. He should understand that whatever his partner did was not done for the purpose of causing him hurt and pain. It happened for the satisfaction of both souls to finish an experience, no matter if this experience was planned or not. So, if this human feels angry and starts looking for revenge to physically or emotionally hurt the other, what would he be gaining? I can tell you what he would be losing – his balance, control and self-love. If he controls his ego, he will recognize that what occurred is done, and it cannot be erased; but he has a wide choice of how he wants to react. He can act lost; he can think he is a victim; or he can plan his future, including or not including the partner who cheated. This is very easy to do but it can seem very hard to accomplish. The more a human connects to his higher self the easier it will be for a human to have this kind of control over his emotions.

You can be sure that one of the toughest experiences a human could go through in this life is to change himself to be in his higher self. He could start by pausing to think a little bit of his past in his current life. He should see what and who he was and what kind of relationships he already had. He should look at all the experiences that he has gone through – from good to bad – to recognize and understand all the creations that he has accomplished so far. He can evaluate how he is taking care of himself by letting himself grow with each experience and by allowing love to conquer his eyes and his heart. He will see how he is creating a new him. With this love, he can get rid of any fear, anger, doubt or judgment of himself or others. He will never think of what he is gaining or losing from doing something because he will be doing it from the purity of his heart. He will be in his higher self, loving himself exactly the way he is, feeling his best, and creating better experiences for himself.

Remember again, loving the self does not mean letting the self do what it wishes. There is a big difference between loving the self and being selfish. Loving the self means that a human is satisfied with all of him, which will let him look at others and give them what he wishes for himself. Being selfish is when the human looks at others and always seeks to find what he can benefit from. A selfish human will not give unless he is getting.

So going back to the relationship experience, if a human loves his partner as he loves himself, he will be full of love. When a human is full of love, he will never allow hurt or judgment or blame to affect him. But even if this human allows his emotions to control him, he could always catch himself by asking himself this question: why am I doing this to me? Asking himself this question will help him find his way back to using his heart; then with a full understanding and belief in himself, he can decide if he wants to turn the other cheek or walk away. If he turns the other cheek, it means that he is letting his partner experience more through him, without judging. If he walks away, it means that the partner will no longer experience through him anymore. His partner will be finishing the experience, but with some other human. A human is always free to choose which way he wants to go.

Now let's talk about how two humans could live together, as partners, without guilt if cheating is involved. First, I will tell you that most humans who cheat will try their best to hide the fact, without considering any other option. But if you think about it, there is no need for a human to have a relationship with someone other than his partner – to satisfy the need of the body – before discussing the reason with his partner. The way a human deals with a love relationship should always come from the heart. These two humans should open up to each other and say what is bothering them and whatever is on their mind. They should tell each other if they are unhappy or dissatisfied with their sexual relationship. If the situation is not solved and satisfaction is denied, then the need could be satisfied with a human other than the main partner. There is no need for anger or frustration in this process. When a request is made and it is refused by the other, they both should listen to each other very carefully and act accordingly. These humans should not feel negative about it; they should be calm and always let their words come from the heart. If they do not reach an agreement that will satisfy both of them, it does not mean that it is a bad outcome.

If one partner is not content in providing sex to the other partner, and is refusing without any logical explanation that will satisfy both, nothing should come by force. I say that if the human failed to convince his partner to have sex, then he can share his pleasure with another human that is willing, without breaking that relationship with the spouse or the partner at that time. A human should never accept anything in his life just to satisfy another human, and make himself miserable. Treating the self with love will help a human understand that he can only hurt himself mentally and emotionally, by allowing his ego to make him feel that he is the boss, or the victim, in a relationship. The kind of balanced reaction I am talking about can only happen if both partners are in their higher self, and if they have the same feelings and love toward each other. Most of the time, one or both partners are not in their higher self so they live in anger and resentment instead.

Remember what we talked about before. Human traditions and beliefs tell the human that he is born with sin and that having sex, if not married to the sex partner, and if the spouse is not of the opposite gender, is also a sin. But let me tell you the truth: "sin" is defined by man and I especially assure you that sex is not a sin. Sex is all about pleasure and relief for the physical body, which a human needs to satisfy his physical health.

Would you tell me if there is anything worse than taking advantage of somebody else through love? Help me to better understand what "taking advantage" is in this case.

On Earth there are a lot of traditions and rules, and all of them are manmade. From generation to generation, through the passing of time, most of these rules become traditions and beliefs. Humans follow these blindly because it is how they were raised and what they were taught since they were born. It is the same when people read any holy book. They usually understand the words but not the meaning of what the book is saying. They believe what they think it is saying, according to what they were taught from day one. One of these rules that have been passed down from one generation to another is that a human should not take advantage of another human when they are in love.

Let me go a little deeper. When a human falls in love following his heart, without any needs or expectations, the other human will feel protected and secure with this love. But when a human falls in love without following his heart, and when he treats love as a business deal, the other human will feel confused. He will not understand what is really going on in this love story, and the protection and security that he once felt will turn into fear. The trust between them will start to dissolve, leading to chaos and loss of confidence in a love that is no longer understandable.

A human should love, value, take care of himself, and be free before he can love another human. When a human does not appreciate himself, he will always need another human to depend on. This is when he will allow his partner to run his life. He will be scared to leave his master, so he will stay even if he knows that he is being taken advantage of. Sometimes he will accept all kinds of abuse, knowingly or unknowingly, because he fears being alone. This will not happen if a human finds himself and seeks happiness within himself first, before looking for an external tool to make him happy.

Love is never blind, but it causes blindness through emotions. When a human is in love, he will follow his emotions and feelings without question. A human's ears will be deaf and his eyes closed so that all he sees and hears is what he wishes for from the partner that he is in love with. Because these emotions control every feeling in the body and heart, it will be very hard and painful to leave this love relationship. But I tell you again, if a human has love for himself then it will be very easy for him to let go of the other human, with the understanding that this love is one–sided, not mutual. This experience will then provide useful data to a human's Subconscious that he will apply to later love experiences; which will make him wiser next time.

Believe me when I tell you that a love experience might end but it does not vanish from a human's memory. Even when a human does his best to forget over a long period of time, it always comes back to his memory. Even if there were a lot of bad times with the ex–lover, and even if love turned to hate, a human will always remember a beautiful moment that will be remembered and wished for. The only way for a human to get over the experience is to find his higher self and believe for real that it was an experience that passed – it's gone. It is now time to move on to another experience for him to learn from. This will be harder to do if a human leaves this kind of relationship without being sure. He will convince himself to forget the bad, and to only remember the good in that relationship. In fact, he will be doing this to get back the love and respect of the partner that took advantage of him. This happens only because this human is refusing to let go, remembering only the faith he had in what he *thought* this love was. He will lie to himself every time he hears a voice in his head telling him the truth. He will create all kinds of negative stories to convince himself to ignore the voice of truth that he is hearing. He will keep lying to himself about the facts only to get back what he had, so that he does not have to face the unknown factor of his future.

Humans are stubborn, and they tell themselves that their belief is always right. A lot of times a human will get stuck and not see an exit from a relationship, only because he is refusing to see. Other times, a human will leave but only after he learned a hard lesson from experiencing misery, sadness, and sometimes abuse. Even if other humans try to open his eyes and advise him to leave the relationship, he will refuse, until he is ready to open his own eyes. When he does, he will see and realize that he is hurting himself and that it is time to leave. This can only occur when this human uses the power within him to give himself the confidence to start healing himself. He will then believe and know that he left by his own choice and for his own good, not because someone forced him to leave. Trust me when I tell you that this belief will come only when a human follows his heart; not his emotions and feelings anymore.

You promised you would tell me more about unconditional love. What is the beauty of unconditional love, and how does it affect a human being?

Every human experiences some kind of love in their life – through family, relationships, jobs, religion, music, and even through the beauty of nature. When some humans feel this kind of love, they might falsely believe that they are in their higher self when they really are not. The difference will start to show if any of these situations or relationships does not go the way he feels it should. His emotions will change to create negative feelings towards the situation. This human will reach a point of confusion where he will blame the situation or the other human involved for not being able to give love as he believes they should. His solution will be to look for different humans to share love with but he will always remain unsatisfied. He will go from one partner to another, from one situation to another, trying in the same way to recreate what he thought was unconditional love – but he will always fail. Humans like this have not yet come to the stage of loving the self for real.

Unconditional love is God, which is the real source of love. Unconditional love starts when a human being loves himself and can love other humans without any conditions, promises or expectations. It is not the easiest thing to achieve, but when a human can for real get there, he will feel like a free bird – like a butterfly following the happiness of his heart; peaceful in mind and body. Unconditional love can only happen when a human allows it to flow from the purity of his heart; which can only be accomplished if he is in his higher self every minute of his days and nights. It is like the beautiful love between a mother and her child; it is the love between two lovers that only shows them the best their heart can see; and it is the greatest love that could ever be. This love is unselfish, gorgeous, and heavenly.

Unconditional love is when a human is willing to be with another human without the necessity of sex; where the two like to share a lot of time with each other regardless of the conditions and circumstances of their lives. Two humans that have unconditional love for each other will never judge how the other runs his life; it will not matter if one is rich and the other is poor; if one is educated and the other is not…and so on. The only condition of unconditional love is for the human to love himself unconditionally. Only then can he love another human without any expectations or needs attached to his love.

Unconditional love is a limitless method of the human form of life. A human does not have any limits to the way he thinks and feels, and he can create any reality he chooses to focus on. The possibilities that come out of these thoughts and feelings are with no limits; and this will permit a human's freedom to go beyond any distinguished restrictions. If a human can dream, he can build. Life, from start to finish, with unconditional love, is an incredible journey that brightens the human's trail with happiness. It is a very powerful energy that helps humans face all problems and challenges with happiness and satisfaction. This love is always available to a human, and it has no limits to what it can accomplish! It is very easy for a human to experience it – but it requires nurturing and practice for it to flood every moment of his life.

If a human does not love himself, he will be missing the *real* meaning of love. When he does love himself, he will realize the need for love in all his doings; and he will apply it to every minute of his living; believing in himself and expressing his unconditional love to all others that he encounters in his life, without exception. He will be in complete peace and happiness, and he will see other humans reacting toward him in peace – only because they, also, will be experiencing that human's love themselves. In fact, these other humans may provide him with an even greater love than what he gave them.

Unconditional love is very natural, and it comes from the heart. It comes with tears of joy; it comes through looking and seeing. It comes through the high self; from inner depth, showing a human how to evaluate but not judge himself. It shows a human to love others through loving the self. When a human feels this love, he will instantly know the difference between love and unconditional love; he will accept that this unconditional love is coming from the heart, which is full of faith and belief that such love does exist. When he accepts this fact, it will be easy for him to live in unconditional love. It is when he will see and hear his angels cheering him and hymning a love song. He will feel the sacredness of his existence; feeling his guardian angels, and his angels and soul mates celebrating the joy of life.

When a human reaches this beautiful stage in his life, he will start questioning the way he has been running his life. Questions will pop up in his mind that will help him to choose the way he wants to live from then on. What does he wish for his future? Will he have an easier, smoother life? Will he be kinder, forgiving, gentler and more loving? Is he going to give his power over to his fears and doubts? This will be a powerful opportunity for the human to choose the answers to his questions by looking deep inside himself.

Inside every human resides a lot of love, and it is up to the human to release this love. He can choose to release love, or he can release anger and fear instead. If he chooses to release love, he has to start practicing on himself first. He has to control all his thoughts and feelings to be all positive. It does not matter how big or small the problems that he faces are; forgiving himself first will always assist him in overcoming negative thoughts. Then he will start to understand that a lot of the situations that he considers problems are not worthy of his time anymore.

Love is the most powerful energy that exists, and it is in every human every second of his existence. The most wonderful quality of pure love is that it is accessible by the human's Conscious; so when a human chooses to love another human unconditionally, this love will go beyond the human's lower awareness, rising to a higher reality. It will have no conditions; no rules or favors to be expected. Unconditional love only sees the beauty of the moment; it does not wait for a result; it is given only for the will of giving. Give love, and you will experience love itself. By experiencing this love and giving it to the world, it will return to you full of energy and power. This love resides within, and it is the human's choice to express it the way he chooses.

There are special ways for a human to practice existing in unconditional most of the time. Forgiveness is the most important one. Forgiveness is a beautiful method for letting go of the past, and loving with no conditions. Forgiveness is freedom; and it will put a human on a limitless, peaceful path in his life. But, even the most aware humans will have moments of doubt. This can be very easily changed by taking a few deep breaths, focusing his attention only on the breath and nothing else, which will help reset the direction of his thinking. A human can also stand in front of a mirror, see himself without any judgment; hug himself and remind himself that he loves him unconditionally. Focused breathing and remembering his self–love will help him clear his mind, so he can see the best solutions for his worries. When he takes care of himself like this every day, he will be able to share a very beautiful love connection with others, which is like a superpower when shared.

I want you to remember that life on Earth is full of choices to be experienced and it is up to each human to create a life full of joy, happiness, forgiveness and love. Every second is a new beginning. Every second of time opens an opportunity for a new way of living, giving a human the chance to create without any limits. With every breath he takes, comes an opportunity for him to drop any old data that taught him to feel guilt or that forgiveness is very hard to give; that love should depend on needs. Believing in the self will make every day a new day of self-discovery, and a fresh new beginning on a path of forgiveness and love.

The actions of this new awareness should be carried through everything a human does, being alert to notice any negative messages that might come his way. To help himself live his life without any fears and doubts, he should ask himself very sharp questions about any messages that he receives, either from his own thoughts or from other humans. If his heart tells him that he is receiving a message of love, he can accept it, live by it, and nurture it to grow. If his heart tells him that a message is not of love, then he can let it go, so that he can return to his peace.

You and your soul mate are angels, and you both exist in a beautiful reality of unconditional love. You share this love with every human on a daily basis. You do this with the belief that you are free and happy. You love…and you are loved. By doing this, you are creating peace and happiness for all the humans that you touch; and you are putting yourselves in the best stage that a human can be in to finish a lifetime on this Earth.

I want to know more about life and love. Go deeper to help me understand better.

Let's take a trip so that you can see what life and love are all about. I want you both to drop any emotions that might allow you to feel fear, and follow your hearts. Understand all that you see, not only parts of what you are going to see. Now let's go.

We entered a big hall. There was a very bright light filling the room. There was a semi–round table with a bunch of old people sitting behind it. They had white robes on and all of them had white hair. Some of them were short, some were tall; some had beards, some had none; some were men, some were women; some had a beautiful, innocent look in their eyes; some had mean looks on their faces. James, my soul mate and I went into the room. We approached the table to notice that all these people were judges. Each of the judges started announcing himself: they were the judges of Fear, Judgment, Panic, Guilt, Blame, Lying, Dishonesty, Hurt, Upset, Stress, Anger, Sadness, Unhappiness, Grief, Pressure, Cheating, Wrong, Theft, Ego, Right, Honesty, Happiness, and Love. Each of them started asking us questions about whatever subject they represented. My soul mate and I took turns answering their questions about things that happened in our current lifetime. After we finished answering each question, each judge taught us how to get rid of the fear and confusion that their subject is causing us. They each also taught us the best way for a human to live happy in relation to the subject they each represented.

A bunch of judges then left the room and only six stayed. We were left with the judges of Fear, Hurt, Stress, Judging, Ego, and Love. Each one of these judges asked us new questions…and we answered. They told us how fear and hurt prevent a human from fully loving himself by changing the capacity of the human to love the aspects of the self. They explained that the Subconscious mind keeps bringing fear back to a human to try to protect him, by providing what is familiar to him – until the human becomes at peace with himself. They told us to expect the transition of the self from fear to peace to sometimes make us feel like resisting at first. This stress and judging of the self will cause a human to create negative stories based on his own imagination, and he might convince himself that the stories he created are his truth; even though the human's heart will be telling him something different.

Then four out of the six judges left. The Ego and Love judges stayed. The Ego judge said, "I am the worst enemy a human could have, but without me, a human cannot survive in this life." The Love judge said, "I am the best friend that a human can have. Without me, a human cannot survive in this life." Then both judges left the room. As they were leaving, an older man with long white hair all the way down to his shoulders came into the room. He had a pure, innocent look on his face, and he was wearing a white and golden robe. As he walked toward us, a beautiful golden halo surrounded him. He looked at the three of us and introduced himself as the Judge of Unconditional Love. He paused for a minute, looking at us. We could see love pouring out of his eyes. He said, "Each one of these judges you just met is part of your life. They are with you every day. They decide for you how to *run your life. You humans are like small kids who do not know better than what you know. You feel want and need to know everything, which makes you listen to everything these judges say. You follow their lead, only because you do not know better than that.*

"The last two angels you met were the judges of Ego and Love. Let me tell you some more about them. Ego and Love are like white and black angels that are always hugging and surrounding a human. Each one of them is doing his best to grab the human's attention. They blind the human's eyes and deafen his ears so he can see and hear nothing, except what they tell him and show him. The black angels win most of the time. This is because they use every trick they can to provide the human with a life that the ego in a human loves to live. Ego, or the black angel, wants a human to have desires and needs that will keep him attached to his earthly existence, which will prevent him from moving toward completing what his soul planned. The ego wants the human to suffer more and more in trying to accomplish his soul's plan. It wants him to have the need and the urge to come back again and again to this world, to relive the same experiences that he could not finish only because his ego kept him stuck in them. Accomplishing this makes the black angel happy because it means he has won in convincing a human to live on the dark side of life.

"Love, or his white angel, is here to help the human finish what his soul planned on. It will help him to finish all the experiences that he came to do, without pushing him to do what is 'right' or what is 'wrong'. The white angel will always be with the human through all the choices he makes, without judging or blaming him. It will help him to leave this life happy, so he can come back to finish more, different, experiences that his soul will plan on.

"Through these judges, every human will have his experiences in an earthly lifetime. These judges usually work together — even though they can also work one at a time — to provide the human with knowledge and

wisdom from his experiences. A human does not know where they come from, how to control them, or what the end will be; but without them there is no human to be.

"Every human starts his life doing what he came to do on Earth. He will begin experiencing what is meant for him, which will provide him with knowledge. As he grows in knowledge, the human will realize that he has choices in the way he runs his life. Very often, a human will decide to make a change, but this choice will make him struggle to find the truth of who he is for real, and what the real purpose of his life on Earth is. This struggle will be caused by the conflict between the data that is in him from the way he was raised, and the new data he has chosen to follow. He will start having different thoughts and experiences in his adult life that will not represent the ideas he was raised with. In some cases, this human will be able to conquer his old beliefs and training, and he will figure out who he is. This might take more than one lifetime to be accomplished. Humans seek and find the answers they are looking for, but they mostly refuse them, because they are not in agreement with what their old beliefs tell them. Sometimes a soul will need millions of Earth years to reside in a human that figures out what the Earth—life experience is all about."

Now that you have heard all this, I want you both to remember one thing: it is very important for both of you to realize that you are not doing what you know all the time. Knowing and not doing is the worst thing a human can do to himself; but knowing and doing will let you conquer the world. You both know and believe a lot of things that you have discovered lately and you both love every word and incident that has taught you to be wise; but you are still letting small things control you between now and then. You two are lucky to have each other so you can catch each other when you forget to be wise.

Chapter 16

HIGHER SELF

You always talk to me about the higher self. Can you tell me more about the procedure for staying in my highest self?

The first step is very easy. Think of an incident that made you feel great about yourself and put you in a happy mood. When you wake up every morning keep thinking about this very beautiful incident or thought. Think about it all the time when you are awake. Now imagine always being happy because all you are seeing and imagining is that happy moment! Just think about how you would respond and react toward others – no matter what they tell you – when you are in a great mood. Whatever they say will not bother you, hurt you, or upset you. They might try to hit your ego or your pride, but you will be in a great mood so nothing will have the effect of changing the way you feel.

Now think of a situation or incident that put you in a bad mood. If you have this thought in your mind from the minute you wake up until you go back to sleep, how do you think you will be feeling? You will be sad, mad and depressed. When you are depressed, what do you think your reaction will be to every word you hear? I will tell you: you will be pissed and mad. You will want to hit something or someone to avenge your ego – to hurt the human firing you up or adding gas to your fire. Your ego and pride will boil and feel hurt. Look at both thoughts and see the difference between them. Now that you know the wide range of your possible reactions, you can choose which thought you want.

Keep practicing and promise yourself that you will do your best to be in a good mood. You should also watch what you say. Pay attention to every word that comes out of your mouth. Make sure your communication with others comes from the heart, not from your ego. Do this for yourself first, because anything that comes out of your mouth will affect *you* more than the other human. At first, choosing your words and thoughts and believing that you can, will start a certain denial inside you. You might feel exhausted physically because it will feel like two different powers are fighting within you. Do not worry about it, just keep going. If here and there you lose control of yourself, do not judge you; know that judging will only lead to worry and guilt. Just promise yourself that you will pay more attention next time…and move on; keeping in mind that feeling hurt – or happy – is your own doing.

I hope that by now you understand that every action and reaction is determined by a human's free will. All thoughts with a reference to a human's past reside in his Subconscious; and new data from his daily thoughts and creations are also added to his Subconscious every second of a human's existence. Because every human has free will, he can choose which Subconscious thought is going to control him. Allowing a negative thought to control the way he feels, will be followed by drama and stress; but it does not have to last. It is also up to the human to choose to change this bad thought to a happy one. It is never too late for a human to catch himself and change his choice of action and feeling, even if he already allowed himself to react in a negative way. He can regain control of his ego by redirecting his full attention to the incident that made him the happiest. He will then be able to follow his heart. It needs a lot of practice; but when a human can do this, he will be coming from his higher self, loving himself so he can love the world.

I tell you, every master who came to this world to teach humanity also went through this experience. As humans, they, too, had good and bad thoughts. These masters took abuse from many people, but they faced the abuse with happiness, only because they had mastered the self. A lot of humans laughed at them, judged them and condemned them, even though a lot of others followed them just to hear the pure words coming from their hearts. With all this, these masters only preached love, because their intention was from the heart.

I will tell you again and again – if a human wants to stay in his higher self, all he has to do is change his thoughts. The sooner he does this, the more wisdom he will gain from the calmness he is creating for himself. Loving the self will always keep the human in the happiness of his higher self. That is when any thought, emotional feeling or physical task that a human faces will be an instrument for learning a better way to finish his earthly journey.

I feel that now I am in my higher self, but sometimes I am failing myself. A few days ago, I got mad and released my anger on one of my friends. How can I prevent this from happening again?

You are doing a great job staying in your higher self, but you are still human with feelings and emotions; so every now and then you become weak. Now let me explain for you, in a different way, what your higher self is and what it does for you. Your higher self is the ideal figure of you. It will lead you to finish your trip as it was planned by your soul for this lifetime. It will point you in the direction of your soul's purpose.

It is like an angel voice whispering in your ear all the time. It will show you how to deal with yourself and others and it will help you control any negative feelings you may have toward you or others. It will provide you with wisdom and knowledge for you to use while going through your experiences in this life, as it did in all the other lifetimes that you already went through.

Your higher self will never, ever love or care for any other human more than you. Your higher self, itself, will help you stay connected to your higher self – so that you can finish all the physical, emotional, and mental experiences the right way. It will provide you with all that you need to finish your experiences happy and content, which will keep you in full freedom and peace with yourself. I remind you that in this life not all your experiences will be blissful and enjoyable. A lot of them will be painful and pressuring; but do not forget that you can also learn from hurt and pain. The trick is to go through these experiences without becoming depressed or lost. This is where your higher self will help you choose the easiest path, by showing you any and all possibilities that are available to you. So, when you choose to always hear and listen to me, I will lead you to hear and listen to yourself before attempting any experience.

Your higher self is your best trainer because it remembers all the experiences that you went through in this lifetime and in previous lifetimes. Never forget that all your experiences were planned by your soul in advance, before you came to this life; and because your higher self knows this, it will help you to choose the best way to finish each experience. It will show you the best that you have been in your past lives and the best of what you have accomplished in this life. Your higher self loves you and knows you better than you know yourself. It is always here for you, to show you the easiest way to master yourself and how to stay in that love, which is coming from your heart. The most important thing is to always love yourself with unconditional love, which will keep you connected.

As a hint for loving yourself, let me tell you that you should feel self–sufficient and free. You must believe in your self–sufficiency and freedom and you have to be independent of any affection from any other human. This means that your feelings should not be hurt by their opinions or judgments of you; it does not mean that you should not talk to anyone, or that you should break your relationships with others. It only means that if you are in your higher self, nothing should affect you in a negative way mentally or emotionally. All you need to do is to depend on you, without feeling any need from others.

I do not ever tell you what to do, but I will suggest that if you are in a love relationship where your love is based on need, and the other person's love toward you is based on a need, you should directly end the relationship because it will prevent you from existing in a higher state of consciousness, meaning your higher self. When love has needs, it means: if I do what you want then you will give, or if you do what I want, I will give. When love is full of conditions, it is better to cut it off and start again, looking for unconditional love somewhere else.

In some cases, like immediate family, you might want to think twice. I say you should not get rid of them like any other relationship, but you should understand that each of them also has their journey of experiences to go through. All you have to do is treat them the same way you treat yourself, without any blame or judgment; then you will not feel hurt or pissed if they judge you. You will accept what they say and evaluate it yourself to decide if it is right or wrong for you. Always keep in mind that in this life, there is no absolute right or wrong. There are only the choices a human makes and the results of his choices. Remember to never take anything personally. Just listen, evaluate and then ask yourself, how should I react to what has been said? There will always be a positive and a negative answer to this question. You choose. I tell you, when you evaluate, see the situation using your heart. Do not see with your eyes because your eyes might show you the wrong thing, but your heart will never fail you.

I want to hear more about the higher self. The more I hear, the better I understand how to stay there and how to teach others if they seek my help.

Now that you are what you are, I want you to know that your higher self knows and always sees you. Your higher self and you are one, only because you have discovered that part of you. All the experiences that you went through in this life, you finished in the way that was best for you at the time. You did not know where your choices were coming from or what was causing you to make the decisions you made, but let me tell you, in whatever you did all your life, you always followed your heart. Every time, you chose the best reaction for the experience according to what your heart was telling you then. You would be wise to really understand that all this power that you have recently discovered in you has always been with you since day one, and it will stay with you until your soul decides to end this life. It will always be your choice to acknowledge and have faith in this connection.

With all this talking about how to stay in your higher self, I should also tell you what will keep you from being there. As a human, when you judge, blame, or hate; when you talk about others; when you show off; when you are not being straight with yourself and others; or when you are angry, jealous, greedy, sad, moody, depressed or selfish, you will find a quick answer to cover why any of the above is occurring. You will blame it on whatever you were taught when you were growing up, or you will compare yourself to other human beings, showing yourself to be better. You might justify your insecurity by convincing yourself that you have smaller problems than others, and so on; but you will be unaware of the fact that you are feeling this way only because you are in your lower self. Every human faces incidents in his daily life that will pull him away from the higher self, which is what brings joy and contentment. Let me show you some examples so you can understand what I mean and let us discuss them.

Let's start with a human that lives with a partner or a spouse. If a spouse is an overambitious person, the other human will be living like a slave or doormat to his spouse. His or her job will be to please and satisfy the needs of the spouse. This will keep both of the spouses or partners living in their lower self because one of them will not have the freedom to live the way he wants, and the other will not know any better than to make a slave of his partner.

We can look to a human's daily work life for another example. If a human is bossy and always gives grief to others, threatening them that they might lose their job if his own needs are not met, he will be a sad, miserable human. He will be using the power that he has over others in a way that makes him blind. Someone like this needs a lot of help to reach his higher self.

Then there are humans that always doubt and never trust any other human. This kind of human will always be confused, and he will hesitate to conquer his mind and feelings. Whatever is said or done to this human – good or bad – will have a different meaning to him from what was meant, and his reaction will be according to the way *he* sees it. These kinds of humans are far, far away from being in their higher self and it will be very hard for them to get there.

There are also humans who are mostly mad, upset and angry, and who take out all their frustrations on others. These humans are short–tempered people who are always stressed, and they wait for a minor incident to occur to have an excuse to jump on others. These humans will yell and scream, while inside of them they feel sad and miserable to the point where they might think of ending their life. When a human reaches this point in his life, he will never, by himself, know or figure out why he feels or reacts the way he does. All his reactions will lead him deeper and deeper into self-pity, which will be a major obstacle to reaching the higher self.

Then there are the humans who are selfish. Being selfish is one hundred percent different from loving the self. Being selfish always depends on wants and needs to satisfy the self. A selfish human will do anything in his power to satisfy himself, even if it means hurting himself and others physically and mentally. He will always relate whatever he hears, sees and thinks to money. All his thoughts and decisions will be directed to earthly needs that money can buy. He will convince himself that he does not have enough money to spend to socialize with friends, usually because he will be competing to be the richest among them. He will also convince himself that anybody that he does socialize with is after his money, because they have needs and wants like he does. A human like this will make exceptions to socialize only with people who can make him more money. He might refer to this kind of interaction as "business". He will believe that the best word that can come out of his mouth is "mine." This is the lowest stage of the lower stage that a human can exist in.

You also have some humans who are not honest with themselves or others. All they do is lie. They start a lie and live it to a point of confusion where they forget how it started and/or how to end it. They believe their lie as if it is the truth. If they are caught in the lie, they deny it only because deep inside, they really believe that the lie *is* the truth. They sometimes become embarrassed with themselves because living their lie stops them from knowing what is up and what is down anymore. These kinds of humans will often create a new personality according to a person or people they are imitating. They will try their best to live their life up to a different standard than what their life is providing for them, only because they believe in the lie they have created. Pretty soon, fear rises up inside them – fear of going on with the lie – but by this time, they are stuck in it, so their ego will keep pushing them to do the impossible to continue to live that lie. They will come to a point that they will not remember how their life used to be and what the purpose of their being on this Earth is. They will be lost and not able to make decisions, coming from their heart, by themselves. Their self–esteem will drop very low, causing terrible feelings and stress for the rest of their life. Their ego will refuse to let them open their eyes to see the fact of who they are.

Then there are a lot of humans that are labeled lazy and quitters by earthly society. They never start a new event or project or experience because they are scared that they will get very tired of it and not finish it. Deep inside, they do not have the self–confidence that whatever experience they go through will be accomplished. These humans will feel depressed and maybe even suicidal. They stay in their lower self until another human comes into the picture to open their eyes to the reality of life. Sometimes they will be lucky, according to earthly terms, to find that other human to open their eyes; and other times they will not be lucky enough in this lifetime for their soul to accomplish what it planned on doing.

You see, all these experiences are real and they happen on this Earth on a daily basis. If a human adopts one or more of these experiences or other similar ones, if he begins to live them, and if he believes in what he is living, it will be very hard for him to discover his higher self. In this case, if some other human does not get involved in the human's life to open his eyes to the real light, he will always stay stuck in his darkness. I assure you that humans who choose this way will leave this life term, but their souls will come back in a different body to finish the same experiences in a different lifetime.

Basically, only humans who are always happy – regardless of the experience they are facing or creating – will be in their higher self. They feel less threatened, and they know and believe that there is no need on this Earth to judge or blame themselves or others. Always being in the high self requires a strong belief and a lot of practice. With belief and practice, and by his free will, a human can create and enjoy a life of satisfaction and gratitude.

Chapter 17

PRIDE

———————

Talk to me about pride. What is it? Where does it come from? How does it affect a human?

Pride is a tool in the human experience that can be helpful or hurtful, depending on how a human chooses to use it. Pride can force a human to refuse what his intelligence and intellect is telling him to do, and it is also why a human will believe that he could do the impossible. On Earth, many humans have their moments of pride that makes them overconfident in what they accomplished through the successful completion of a mental, physical or spiritual task. Their pride might be so excessive that they even believe that their truth is the only truth.

It is also pride that allows humans to view humanity as the supreme creation on Earth – above all other creation. So, what makes humans a better species when a human is nothing other than dust? The simple answer is because a human is capable of changing experiences that occur in his life from moment to moment using his pride! Humans are way more intelligent than animals because they use common sense;

and because they have feelings and ego, which makes them feel either ashamed or proud of everything they accomplish. Humans also know that they have free will to choose how they feel, act and react. Pride is the tool that lets a human understand the meaning and context of the experiences that he is facing, and allows a human to change these experiences, by re–creating the thought of how they should be. The purpose of this re–creation is only to make it easy for the human to fulfill his needs of happiness and contentment.

Now, even though humans have this great knowledge and ability to re–create experiences they face, how many of them still feel confused by their existence? How many humans feel safe with changing and improving things around them for real? Why do humans continue to deal with their experiences the way they know how – because it is what it is – without even understanding what they need to accomplish? The surprising answer is because pride is at work either way. Remember what I said before – pride is the tool for happiness or misery, as a human chooses, and it is active in a human no matter what he chooses! It is a human's pride that makes him accept his choice and live with it. No matter how stuck a human is in an experience, he will always have hope, which will give him a feeling of pride for what he has achieved within the experience.

We cannot discuss pride without talking about selfishness, which is also in every human. Pride is to be high–minded; raising the human to think of himself as unique, a superhero – as more than ordinary. Selfishness is when a human pays attention only to himself, satisfying his own wants and needs and not caring for any other's wants and needs. Pride will let a human feel grand, because pride is measured by what was intended by the action first, and then by the achievement of this intention. Selfishness depends on acquiring what is aimed for, to fulfill itself. Again, these two work together, but there is a fine line between pride and selfishness. It is up to the human to balance himself along this line, or to go one way or the other.

To be balanced, a human has to be aware of the enormous creation that he is. He has to have an idea about his own power and free will, and of the unseen help that keeps him going. Let's consider that all humans breathe, eat and digest food without even thinking of how and why these functions are happening. This procedure is accomplished through the Conscious. If a human's Conscious had him think of how to perform the functions of the body, he would consciously be aware of how these functions are performed but he would have no time for anything else. This is important to consider for a human to understand for real that he is more than he thinks he is. Through the Conscious–brain relationship, a human brain knows what needs to be done in an action or experience at least ten seconds before the human does, which is basically the body manifesting the unseen. This is the miracle of a human on Earth. The human body cannot function without the brain, and the brain is fed by the Conscious in all actions – the actions he is aware of and those he is not aware of – and through his free will, he can affect both.

When a human completes anything to his own satisfaction, he is proud of what he accomplished. But when the idea that he is working on does not work for him, he will feel that he has failed, and this will affect his pride. His unhappiness about this failure will turn into fear or worry. Humans have a tendency of finding something to worry about if they are not proud of what they have accomplished.

Let me say it this way: a human understands certain facts about the universe. He knows that there are forces out there that keep all the planets in line and working together, just as he understands what a physical body is made of and the functions of its parts. He might also understand that he has a brain and a Conscious that lead the body. He knows that every human deals with different conditions and experiences, and that he acts according to what his brain and feelings tell him and lead him to do. A human understands that hope, by itself, cannot create his reality; he knows that he will have to follow a certain fact that is introduced by his common sense, toward that reality, and this is what will make his hope a success or failure. According to this result, a human will be proud of himself, or he will not be. Even though a human understands all this – and knows it as a fact – he does not make the connection to his own creative power, including his pride, in making his reality what he wants it to be.

Now let's ask the big questions. How much pride can a human handle and how should he use it? Does a human's pride limit him from doing the right thing to achieve what he wants? I say, all of this depends on the human's perspective – how he understood what he got out of the experience – which will be a result of how well he satisfied his pride through that experience, according to what he had wished to accomplish. There is no right or wrong perspective. Every human will get out of an experience his own understanding. As long as the human gets satisfaction out of the experience, then his understanding is right for him. Now let's keep in mind that because a human is a student of his environment and his society from the time he is a baby, he has beliefs that he goes by and rules that he follows. The defining properties of his pride will reflect whatever has been dictated to him by the society that he lives in, even though sometimes these rules and beliefs will make him feel miserable and hurt.

Let me give you a few examples. Let's say that a human gets into a fight with another human and he wins the fight. Even though the winner may feel deep inside that he caused pain for the other human, his pride will not let him apologize for what he did. A lot of humans do not apologize because they believe that apologizing is weakness.

This judgment is too much for some humans' ego so they rather see the other person face to face to reaffirm their action, rather than apologize. This is how these kinds of humans protect their pride from being hurt. On the other side of this example, there are people who feel insulted over what is said to them and their pride does not let them tolerate the insult. But think about this for a minute. What makes a human feel insulted? It is the human's pride that has been touched by his ego, which led his emotions to control his feelings. This human's pride will make him fear being humiliated in front of others or being laughed at or mocked but it is up to the human himself to control his pride. If that same human takes the insult with a smile on his face and walks away, and if he believes that the insult is just a bunch of words that have nothing to do with the truth, then he will create a different experience for himself. He will not be ruled by his fear so he will not care about being laughed at. Knowing that no insult can really hurt a human, he will feel free to do or say whatever he wants. Understand that an insult will hurt a human only because of the way the human accepts the words that are said to him. So yes, unbalanced pride can hold back a human from accomplishing and finishing what his idea or experience was supposed to be.

A human can always sit and reflect on how he handled an experience to learn by it. He can evaluate how his pride affected his emotions and feelings, and how he can control the way his pride directs him. As a human, a lot of incidents and actions affect your emotions, but there are tools you can use to cool yourself down, to balance your emotions and to help you think about how *you* can affect your impression of any experience. Music is one of these tools. It does not matter what kind of music it is, as long as you listen to a joyful sound that moves your feelings in a positive way. Just imagine how you will feel when you hear a song which has a big effect on your emotions, and is tied to an experience you went through in your life. Looking back at these memories with the help of this tune will allow you to relive the experience and fill in the gaps; it will give you the chance to make what *you* choose the experience to be for you, regardless of how good or bad the memories are. This will let you make up for a lot of things that you feel you had lost the opportunity to finish. Listening to the right music that flows with your emotions will make you very proud and happy, and it will affect your mood and your pride positively, which will create healthy physical reactions in the body. Improved blood circulation will create a very strong connection between your body and mind to a point that will raise the heart and the soul to its highest connection.

Balanced pride will make a human humble and happy. Being humble means that you are in your higher self, which creates unconditional love for you, and you will never blame or judge yourself. As a human, the challenging part is to be in your higher self all the time. I am not saying that it cannot be done. I am saying that it *could* be done. It is hard to reach there, but once a human does, it will be very easy for him to stay there if he wishes. A humble human will always be proud to have eyes that show him the beauty that exists in life and ears that let him listen to, and hear, the music of the universe. He will always believe that he has the great comfort of his angels to lead him in the confusing world that he lives in.

Chapter 18

FAITH

Tell me about faith. What is faith? How does it start? Does it have any effect on the way a human lives his life?

Faith is one of the most beautiful subjects that we can discuss. Faith is a real and true belief in values, in an idea, in a person, or in a truth; without any proof or evidence to support the belief. Faith can supply the human with the wisdom needed for his continual actions, loyalty and self–leading. Faith always looks for what is coming through trust and wishes. Faith engages humans with a high stage of confidence that is not based on the intellect, to shift a human to a knowledge based on self–evidence that is very powerful in becoming a confirmation. Feelings and sensations are the main leaders of faith.

Faith is the substance of things that were hoped for that are not touched or seen. I do not mean that faith is wishful thinking. I mean it is a certainty for the human who has faith, to act with his best ability from what is in his heart. Faith is feelings and confidence supported by a beautiful, great relationship with the self that grows with the way it is experienced and practiced. With faith, a human will see with eyes full of obedience to his beliefs and in the human experience, which will give that human the assurance to carry on with his life.

Every human has this wisdom of power within him. It is up to the human to choose the way he uses this power, so that he could create a strong bond with himself. This bond of trust will free him of any fear so that he can focus on life in a new way – to enjoy living – and to finish his life as it was planned to end. When a human trusts himself, he will be on top of everything in his life. This will leave him open to handle new experiences without hurt, blame, or judgment. Without faith, it is very hard to please the self and resist self–judgment. Without faith, it is very hard for a human to believe that he is a powerful entity that can act and react in a way to notice and appreciate the creation around him.

Faith came with the birth of humanity, which means that faith started with the fact of the human experience. It is awareness, where the clarity of living is in real wisdom, without any terms and conditions. Faith will change a human who is tough and mean to being calm and lean; only because of the pure love that he will exist in. Human faith is not a magical tool that makes all wishes come true; it only leads to an assured attitude that motivates the Conscious to direct the human to act according to what he wishes for. Faith is a school for honesty, truth, and freedom that touches the Conscious to connect to the heart.

For a human to live a better and happier life, he should look at the way that all the real masters who came to this world lived their lives. These masters lived in faith; and by doing so, they motivated other humans to have the belief and the self–confidence to love the self. Even though these masters did not set out to teach, by living according to their beliefs, people followed them. Their faith was more than acceptance and belief. It was what elevated them to be the "Gods" and "prophets" that led people to believe in them. But these masters never believed themselves to be Gods for other humans to follow. They believed that they were masters only of their own self, and not leaders to motivate other humans. Instead, it was the humans attracted to these masters' faith that made leaders of humanity out of masters of the self.

Having faith is the same as believing that the universe exists, without the need to see it or touch it. This faith will let a human live in happiness and with hope; and it will let him look forward to a great future to come. Having faith makes the human understand that even though he is a small object in the endless universe, he is very powerful in comforting himself. But, saying that you have faith and saying that you believe, is not enough. You have to start changing the way you run your life with the real belief and faith that you can. The ancient Greeks had a belief that Atlas held the world on his shoulders. When a human does not have faith, he will feel like Atlas, trying to hold the world on his shoulders all by himself, which will only bring misery.

Living in faith requires a lot of work and dedication. Living in faith requires cherishing knowing and loving you. Living in faith is to understand that on this Earth there is nothing called "next." Life is living in the exact moment you are in, and believing that the way your life is running is the way it is supposed to be. To live in faith, you have to understand that looking high will make a dream come true, in the way it is supposed to happen. It is only human to have doubts and fear about a big step you are thinking of taking, but if you follow your heart and your dream, it will come true through your faith.

In this world, humans lock themselves into fear and worry; they lack the wisdom of trust and self–belief, which prevents faith from conquering their hearts. Through the ages, humans have always asked: how do I get faith, or how can I make my faith stronger? I tell you that faith is something that could be built up through a human's free will;

it needs a human to believe that he can trust himself...and he will. He needs to have confidence that he can accomplish...and he will.

The world that you exist in right now has a lot of troubles, difficulties, dilemmas and crisis. Humans have a lot of hate, sadness and judgment for themselves and others. This is one of the many reasons why faith is missing from their hearts. But, when these humans start to believe that there is a God within them, which is a God of love that sees nothing except love, all the headaches they face on a daily basis will stop existing; and real faith will conquer their minds, emotions and hearts. Remember that the soul – which is part of Spirit – is all love, happiness, harmony, kindness, integrity and self–control. Every soul has these qualities of faith, which come from Spirit itself, and are available to every human, only if he believes that faith is within him.

Most humans believe that faith is only a constructive thought. They believe it is a beautiful feeling that a human creates for himself if he has a cheerful outlook – if he stays positive about every incident that happens in his life. But I tell you this is not enough for a human to have real faith in his heart. A lot of humans believe that faith is only expectation of an outcome and self–belief. I say that expectation is very important for a human to build his future, self–belief is very important and valuable for survival on this Earth – but both combined are not enough to build real faith in a human's heart.

Humans also believe that going to a church, a temple or a mosque – or any other holy or religious place – is enough. They believe that hearing a holy man preach will put faith in their hearts. Again, let me tell you, there are thousands of different holy places on Earth and with every holy man preaching about faith in his own way, this world has many thousands of different ideas of faith to be believed in. I say, a human's faith cannot be found through any other human, or in a physical location where religious or spiritual events take place. A human's faith is much deeper than that. It is a spiritual thing – it does not deal with the physical. It is a certain oath that comes from the soul. A human could pray and put all his effort and power into praying to the unknown, thinking he is practicing faith. Humans do and say things that they were told to say since they opened their eyes to this world, and they wonder why their prayers are not coming true. A human does not understand that this is because he is lacking awareness of his faith. He is just repeating what another human told him to say, in the hope that his dreams will come true.

Faith is an indescribable sense – it cannot be explained. It is special, it is puzzling, and only one of a kind for every human. It has no real description, no real formation, or any understandable reason to exist – yet every human is born with it. Faith is similar to a promise that a human makes to himself, with the hope that this promise will occur. When a promise is hoped for, it means that it has not been received yet and faith is the guarantee that it will be received – so faith is proof of things that are not visible. It is whatever a human thinks and wants it to be. In simple words, faith has a different definition and meaning for every human depending on how the human's soul directs his faith, to help itself fulfill its plan; so faith is what each human feels about it… but it is built on a universal confidence. So, with faith, proof cannot be looked for – because every human already has it! All that a human has to do is notice that he does.

Faith is misunderstood and confused with feelings and emotions, but faith has nothing to do with these. It is part of the human experience to help every human to create and face feelings and emotions, but these come from the mind. The mind practices what it has received, by engaging a human's feelings and emotions, to come up with answers about a situation. But this is not faith. Faith rises above feelings and emotions and is truly understood only when a human masters himself, and his feelings and emotions, to create a reality based on an absolute understanding of himself. If this human has faith in his heart and believes in himself, his faith will lead him as it is meant – then all his dreams will come true – regardless of if he prayed or not.

Faith is in every human not only to be turned on in his time of need and turned off when he feels great. Faith cannot be turned on and off any time a human wishes. Either a human is aware of his faith, or not. Faith cannot be considered; it is what it is, and it will always be there when a human follows his heart, not his mind. A human who does not have an understanding of real faith will be very confused about everything in his life. He will not recognize what is fact, so he will not be able to finish his experiences the way he is supposed to.

One thing I want you to always remember is that faith is a power that is created within the human, to help him function according to what his soul planned on doing before coming to this Earth. Faith is...a human believing in himself. Now you believe – and have real faith – that I exist in your life. Now you are finding the real happiness that you were looking for your whole life. You also have a soul mate with whom you share unconditional love, which rarely exists in other humans these days. But I tell you, if it was not for faith itself, you both could not have reached where you are today. If it was not for faith, you could not have written what you are writing, and your soul mate would not have had the wisdom to help you in what you are accomplishing today. These beliefs, and your faith, are now a part of both of you, and they will stay with you until the end of the journey that you both planned on for this life.

Chapter 19

HEALING

I know that my life is changing and I am seeing the real me. What is left for me to do now with the rest of my days on Earth?

First let me tell you that you have a lot of days left. The final experiences that your soul planned on doing in this lifetime are to give and heal. You were born as a giver, and you now discovered you are also a healer. It took you all these years to see and feel all the power you have within you; but now, with the help of your soul mate, you will achieve what your soul wanted you to do. The time has come for you to start teaching yourself how to explore this power that is in you even more. It is time to learn from all the sources around you how to calm humans, how to heal humans, how to help them finish their journey on Earth, and how to touch humans with your energy to change their lives.

Now that you have learned how to hypnotize yourself, use self–hypnosis to really understand who you are and to get rid of the remaining fear that you still have inside you. Hypnosis will help you understand that what happened in your life were all experiences that your soul chose to have. You have, so far, done a great job healing yourself through hypnosis, and it has made a big difference in your life. As we have discussed before, now you know that nightmares are nothing but scenery showing you what has happened so far in your life. Your thoughts and feelings, which come from your Subconscious and ego, add salt and pepper to the script of the movie nightmare you see. This nightmare seems real as you are seeing it while you sleep, even though you are not living it on the physical and nothing can hurt you. Keep going, do not give up. You are almost there. Finish taking care of you and then you can begin to heal others.

Now I want you to look at me and hear me well. See my white robe, the one I have on all the time? This is *your* robe, waiting for you to wear. See my white beard? This is the beard that you will wear to finish what is written for you. This beard will be the symbol of the last experience your soul planned on, which you are looking forward to accomplishing. See my wrinkled hands that you love to look at and touch? These hands that you have told so many people about are *your* healing hands, and you are going to wear them whenever you are ready for them. Your last experience of being a great healer is the main reason you came to this earthly life, and now you will start this last part of your beautiful journey.

When you say I am a giver, I am a healer, what does this mean? How is this going to change my life?

In your current lifetime, you went through a lot of experiences that were good and others that were bad, as humans define them. When you say good or bad, good is defined as positive and bad as negative. Good is something great to aim for and accomplish in happiness; bad is something that is accomplished with fear and sadness. I tell you, every experience you went through in this life, from good to bad, were already planned by your soul before it came down to inhabit your shell on this Earth.

Your soul, for this life, chose to be born in the Middle East to a middle-class family. Your soul decided on experiencing war as a young man – to see how a war condition affects a human being while he is in a war, and after he leaves the war condition. During this period, you laughed and you cried. You went through tough times that were considered bad; and you went through easier times that were considered good. You saw people dying in the fighting; you saw people being born into that life. To change your life, you came to America and started a new life that had nothing to do with the war.

It only took a short while before you decided to go back home to the Middle East because there was a long pause in the war. At that time, you got married. Soon after, the war started up again so you decided to immigrate to America to start a family and live in peace, away from the problems and troubles that were occurring in the Middle East. You suffered a lot trying to make a living and raise a family in your new home. At the same time, you enjoyed your life and the freedom that you gained from this new life. For you, this meant a new life, a new society, new understandings and new beliefs. You did what you had to do to survive, and with all this, you built a family. Then you decided to move from one state to another. You moved your whole family to a new home in another state. Also in this state, you saw the good and the bad. Again, you suffered, but you also enjoyed your life. You worked very hard to give what you could for your family to live in peace, which always gave you pleasure, but this also came with the burdens of stress and pressure.

One of the experiences that your soul had planned was for this pressure to cause you to become depressed and feel physical pain. Doctors decided to put you on legal drugs to take care of the pain and stress which made you become a zombie, overusing all these medications that your doctors prescribed. After a while, you had enough of the way you were running your life, depending on medications to get through your day. At the time, your brother had a healing and learning center close to where you lived. You opened his door and went in one day to see what his center was all about. You took some classes that he was offering, and you learned. You became a Reiki Master Teacher; but even with this, you were always, always on the cautious side. You did not trust anyone; you kept your back to the wall and your eyes wide open. You were like this because you were not ready yet to see and feel the real you. Then – out of nowhere – your soul mate came into your life at your brother's center.

Meeting your soul mate marked the end of your old experiences and the beginning of the new ones that your soul had planned on going through. Since you met her, a different human started acting inside you. You can be sure that your soul mate's soul and your soul met and decided on helping each other before coming to this lifetime. It took a while for both of you to meet, and that was also planned. When you finally met was when the first part of your earthly journey ended, and the last part began. Your soul had decided that through this body, it would help heal a lot of humans, with a trusting partner. Your soul mate's soul did almost the same thing. It decided to occupy her body to come here to help you in accomplishing what your soul decided on doing, which also makes her a healer human.

Since day one in your life, you have always felt that you wanted to help others. During the war in your birth country, and later in America, you donated your blood to people you knew and also to strangers. You helped a lot of seniors and orphans mentally and physically; you helped single moms by raising money and providing them with food for themselves and their kids. You did all this because you wanted to help. Your soul mate also helped and gave to other humans directly and indirectly, but this was not enough for her to finish her journey. Let me say it again – when you and your soul mate met, that is when the last part of your journey started for both of you. Your souls had planned on this, and all these years you were each trying to accomplish it without each other's help. You both did a lot for others and gave a lot, but that was not enough for you to finish what was planned. Now, after the two souls that are occupying your physical bodies have united, you both are starting to get ready to give whatever you can to finish this journey.

I want you to look in the mirror. Have your soul mate look in the mirror with you. See the halo that is around you two? This halo is the symbol of the beginning of your last journey. This is where this part of your journey is starting, and it will be a while until it ends. Believe me when I tell you, it is going to be a beautiful journey full of love, healing and giving. Cry as much as you can to release anything that is heavy in your heart. This will be very important if you are going to help others. Let your tears come down; you both keep on crying as much as you can. These tears are going to clean your eyes from all the dirt they have in them, and from now on you will see very clearly. These tears will be cleaning your eyes to purify your heart from any hate or mistrust that you had or have in your life. Crying is going to make you a new human. Crying will make you the *you* that you have been looking for all your life. Now, you found *you*.

I assure you that your giving and your healing are going to help a great number of humans. Men and women of all ages and races will feel the love that is coming from your hearts. All you have to do is believe that through your healing touch, which you call Reiki, a lot of love is going to be received from heart to heart; and a lot of healing is going to be accomplished – only when the humans that receive your love believe in the power that is in them to heal. When all this is accomplished, it will be the end of this beautiful journey that your souls planned on.

Now that I know I have some time left, I want to be healthy. What is the best way for a human to keep his physical body healthy?

Good question. Let me first say that there are different reasons why people get sick. There are some humans who get sick and stay sick because they love the attention they are getting from the others around them, and they love when others feel sorry for them. These kinds of humans are sick because they want to be sick. If this kind of human loses the pity, he will at first pity himself but as time goes on, he will heal quicker without the attention of others. The important thing to know is that this kind of human gets himself sick indirectly, without even being aware of his desire to get sick in order to get attention. He may even be surprised when he gets sick, and start to wonder why. Humans also get sick because they become stressed to a point where their physical body cannot function as it is supposed to. Stress is the number one enemy of human beings. It corrupts the balance within the human body and causes changes that create disease.

Think of the human body as a machine. This machine needs maintenance. It needs perfection to function right, and it needs someone to take care of it, so it can give what it was made to give. For example, if you add water instead of gas to your car, the car will stop running. If you use juice instead of motor oil, the motor will blow up. It is a similar situation with the human body. If you feed it unhealthy food, if you are worried, stressed, and sad or mad, you are causing your body harm. You could cause yourself to have a heart attack, a stroke, or any disease you can think of. Most humans will take their car to a mechanic or fix it themselves if they hear a strange noise coming from the engine; but they will not go to a doctor or try their best to find a solution for their own health problem. If you feel there is something wrong with your body and you do not get help or look for a solution yourself, then you are allowing whatever is wrong to get worse and more serious.

As a human, when something goes wrong with your body, you will be surprised, and you will ask yourself what happened to your body. You will ask yourself why you are feeling sick; but in fact, you are the one who created this sickness. You did it indirectly – not on purpose. You did not plan on and decide to get sick. Unconsciously, thoughts that were based on a belief you had, helped in making your body sick. For example, a human will eat unhealthy food for his pleasure, without thinking that eventually it might cause harm to his arteries. He will believe that he can keep eating this way and still stay healthy. When he gets sick, he will have a hard time understanding how this happened. He will not consider that if a human does not maintain his body, his body will become fragile.

Another example is when a human smokes cigarettes for years. He does it because he saw some other human enjoying smoking. This human will try it, and convince himself that he loves it, because it gives him a feeling of pleasure – physical or emotional. This same human might decide to quit smoking when he sees a different human who got very sick because of smoking. He will then convince himself that smoking is hurting and ruining his body; but the damage he did to his body will already be done, so quitting will be useful only for preventing more damage to the body. The same happens with drinking too much alcohol. A human will start drinking for pleasure, but if he sees something that scares him, he might change his belief and stop drinking. Again, by the time a human decides to stop drinking, the damage to his body will already be done; he will only be preventing the damage from getting worse. It is always a human's belief that will run his experience, but he always has free will to change his belief if he wants to.

Now let's go a little deeper. Your physical body was made to have a lot of experiences, without the consideration of any physical damage occurring to it. The soul plans experiences that it will have through the physical shell, without planning what tool will bring the soul the experience it desires. The soul expects that the shell will be healthy to go through them all. The soul also plans to drop its shell when it is done experiencing in it, or when that body can no longer provide it with the experiences it is looking for. So, if a human destroys his health and cannot provide the soul with what it wants, the soul will drop this shell and go through the process of creating another one for the same purpose.

On the human level, when you are acting in an experience, you use your feelings, your thoughts, and the programming of your traditions to convince yourself that you are fine for the time being; and whatever happens in the future, happens. Let me use the same examples again. You might smoke a few packs of cigarettes a day because it gives you pleasure, not believing that this will cause emphysema, cancer or other disease to your lungs, heart, or other body parts. You will only worry about it when and if it occurs. This is the excuse that a human will give himself to ruin his body, even though it is done indirectly. So, you want to eat junk food because you love the taste, you want to smoke because it gives you pleasure, you want to drink alcohol so that you can forget your stress for the moment; and only when you notice real damage to your health, will you start taking care of the body that you abused. Do not let this happen. Take care of your body the same way you take care of your car; do not wait until you are sick and then ask yourself, "Now what do I do?"

Now let me remind you of something very important. Thoughts have power and vibrations. A human can go a long way in healing his physical body, to the best of that body's ability, by directing his own thoughts. Thought power can go anywhere on this Earth in a split second, and nothing can stop it. Thoughts always control your mind, and they are full of vibrating energy. Negative thoughts and positive thoughts each carry a different kind of energy. When the body and the mind are full of positive energy, it means that the human is full of unconditional love for himself. This will make him live longer and stay healthier, and it will keep him joyful and happy. But when this same body and mind are full of negative energy, a human will be mad, sad, upset, and worried about what tomorrow will bring. This human is hurting himself. He is choosing to live in whatever sickness negative energy is providing him with.

Always know and understand that every human is built to handle every experience that is meant for him; and healing will also have an individual meaning and context for every human, according to what is planned by his soul. Within this fact of what is meant for each human, there is always a place for healing that is accomplished through the human's free will of positive thoughts and strong beliefs. "Healing" is a word that is defined by each human as it relates to his own experience, which makes it a word with countless considerations and expressions. It is the power of perspective and belief that runs each human's healing experience.

The physical body could be controlled and healed to its best potential by the human himself, only when he elevates himself to his highest possibility. Your thoughts, feelings, and faith could heal your body as much as your human experience will allow. Just listen to your higher self, feel what it is telling you, and act accordingly. Watch what you eat, watch what you drink, and do not abuse your body with things that you *think* it needs. Always think twice about what you are doing. If you do, you will be a lot healthier. If any part of the body is already damaged and needs to be healed, this could be done through the combined power of the mind and the body, to the body's highest ability. The combined power of the mind and body will direct the energy of the universe to pass through the human's body to best heal any disease that the body carries. The secret is for the human to believe in that energy, and to believe that he could create this miracle for himself. He has to have great faith that vibrating universal energy could heal him.

The best healing exercise is to reach the higher self through meditation or self–hypnosis. The power of the mind can do anything the human desires. The more a human concentrates, the deeper his faith will be that he can do it. He will be better able to send the energy of the universe to the part of his body that needs to be healed. Believe me when I tell you, when a human connects to his higher self, miracles will start happening in his life, directly and indirectly.

To begin, lie down or sit comfortably and concentrate on your breathing. For the first minute, do nothing but listen to yourself breathe. Then, inhale for a few seconds until your lungs are full; hold your breath for a few seconds; and then exhale slowly until your lungs are empty. Close your eyes and keep breathing this way until you are very relaxed. With your eyes closed, see a figure of you inside your eyelids. Keep looking at you for a few seconds, and then start looking beyond you, at the whole picture. Keep concentrating and looking for a little bit longer. Make sure to keep paying attention to your breath. Start feeling and seeing the part of your body that needs to be healed. Let healing energy flow in and out of your body, with your thoughts leading it to the part of your body that needs it the most. Feel the energy and control it. Let it go smoothly back and forth through your body, until you feel the pressure of the energy affecting the spot that you want to heal. You can do this as much as you want and as often as you would like; but I will tell you, the more you do it the better you can heal yourself.

Another way to heal you is to do Reiki on the body itself. When you give yourself Reiki, you are connecting to the highest energy. This higher energy will combine with your own energy through the palms of your hands. With your palms, you can direct it to any part of your body, especially to the part that you want to heal. When you focus this beautiful energy on any part of your body, you are unblocking the chakra located in that area; and you are feeding your entire body with its healing power. Wherever you direct this healing energy, you will be able to stop whatever ache or pain exists in that part of your body.

Even better than doing Reiki on yourself is to have another human who you trust and who believes in the power of this energy, to perform Reiki on your body. The combination of your own energy, the giver's energy, and the higher energy, will balance all your chakras. I tell you, positive energy will do miracles; but if you do not believe and have faith that it will, then do not waste any effort or time working with it. No healing will occur without your belief and faith.

After a deep meditation or Reiki session, whether it is self–Reiki or Reiki given by another human, the receiver might feel light–headed, or he might have a feeling that he cannot explain. This will be due to the increased amount of pure energy that is flowing through him, which he is not used to. This could happen because when you meditate deeply or receive Reiki with an open heart, you reach a stage of unconditional love for you, where your consciousness level rises and expands. The energy flowing through you at that time will be very strong. When you come out of this high stage, it is always better to have the excess energy leave your body by grounding it. Grounding means to let all excess energy drain out of your body without affecting your own energy. The energy left will be only what your physical body needs to be balanced.

Cutting excess energy is very simple. It could be done by grounding yourself before the procedure[10] or by breaking the loop of excess energy after the procedure is finished. To break the energy, all you have to do is sit up and place your right hand over your left knee and your left hand over your right knee, forming an "X". This will slow down the flow of energy that is going through your body, and you will no longer feel light–headed. If another person is giving you Reiki, sit facing that person with your palms up, and let him hold your right wrist with his left hand and your left wrist with his right hand, and then cross your hands, together forming an "X" with your arms. The same result can be accomplished by crossing the hands on the knees and/or crossing the ankles. As long as the flow of energy is being broken, it is up to the giver to break the energy the way he prefers. The grounding procedure should be done for a couple of minutes, or until you are feeling balanced and can stand up on your feet without any help.

How can I live my life in balance with my spiritual being?

I am glad that you came to me today with this question, asking for my help and the archangels' help directly. We are always here to help you; but if you do not ask for a specific kind of help, we will not impose it on you. The more you ask, the more you are going to get. The more you get…the more relaxed and stress–free you will feel; and the more you are going to clear yourself from any wants and needs.

Now let me answer your question. The body and the mind cannot live without the Conscious and the soul. The Conscious itself functions like a program that is all over the universe. The mind and the body are tools for the Conscious to manifest this program. The Conscious can

---

[10]. Self–grounding is done by visualizing two imaginary tubes – with the excess energy flowing through them – going from your palms, up your arms to your shoulders; coming down your back, down your legs, and out the bottom of your feet, going deep into the ground.

live without the body and the mind, but it cannot live without the soul. The body could be healthy or sick, but not the soul. The soul is always healthy because it could be free from the body without any needs. The body without the soul is lifeless; and there is no treatment to revive the body when the soul leaves it. So...life and Conscious–ness are equal, and their main concern is to heal the shell that they reside in.

The best healing for the body is spirituality; the best remedy for healing through spirituality is meditation. Meditation energizes the body so it can handle sickness and discomfort – if it is physical, mental or emotional. While the body itself may stay sick, meditation will change sadness to happiness. The human mind is very powerful, and it controls everything in a human every second of his life. As long as the mind is healthy, the body can still heal. But, if the mind is sick, it will affect how the body functions, so the body will not be able to heal. In this case, the meditation should first focus on healing the mind.

I want you to understand that meditation is not only a tool for spiritual and physical healing – it is also the key to love in a human being. If a human's mind is sick and he does nothing to heal himself, then he will completely miss the understanding of love. So, what is the secret that meditation holds that it can heal any corruption or illness on the physical, mental or emotional levels of a human? I say, it is because meditation is a total rest for the body, the mind and the soul. It is where a human can connect and be in his higher self without any thinking at all. To better understand meditation, I want you to really understand that the mind is part of a human's Subconscious; so the mind can be on pause while the Subconscious does all the work. During meditation, the Subconscious will provide a happy experience with no physical material involved; so happiness will be the normal condition of consciousness. By creating this situation for yourself through meditation, you will be bringing the same consciousness to everything you experience.

Happiness could not be brought to a human from the outside; it can only be created within a human, if the human chooses to allow this creation. When a human can free his Subconscious of any thoughts by resting the mind – regardless if the thoughts are good or bad, white or dark – the Subconscious could then function properly to help the soul finish what it had planned on.

Remember what we said before. Up or down, good or bad, white or dark energy; however you say it; both are needed for the body to be balanced. Notice something: look and see how beautiful a rose is. It has a scent that tickles the feelings, but its root is in the dirt. Without the dirt, there is no beautiful aroma; so the dirt and the rose balance each other. The same thing is true when it comes to the human experience on Earth. When a human accepts and embraces this partnership of energies, he will be in balance. That is when the human will be beyond the limitations of functioning only by using white and dark energies. Even though these energies will still be providing the experience they are meant to offer for the purpose of his soul's completion, the human will be in control of his emotions and feelings, so he will move from one experience to another in contentment and peace.

Make sure that you do understand what kind of happiness we are talking about. I did not mention material happiness. A lot of humans have so much money that they do not know how to spend it all in their lifetime, yet they feel very sad. Then there are some humans that do not have a coin in their pocket, but are very happy with the way their life is going. It is all up to each human to choose to run his life in contentment, or not; because there is nothing else to stop him. As a human, you have the power to choose. You are free to choose to blame and to judge; you also have the freedom to love. These are things that no other human can take from you. You are the one who decides which to keep and which to give away.

From now on, it will be very important for you to really understand, deep inside, that any feeling you have or feel is your own doing. The dark entities that want you back are going to play on your emotions and feelings in mysterious ways. They will try to make you feel helpless and weak; to confuse you in a way that you will not know how to get rid of these feelings by yourself without the help of your angels. A part of their job is to put pressure on a human to somehow affect the way he runs his life, to make him hate himself and others. These dark entities want nothing more than to stop a human from being on the right path, and to corrupt what a human's soul planned on. But I tell you, as long as you follow your heart, with the help of the archangels and me, nothing will have power over you.

I will repeat this again. Meditation is the best medication. Meditation will keep any human in his highest power, and it will prevent a loop of emotional and mental confusion that causes chaos in a human's life. Meditation will stop you from allowing your ego, and his close friend, fear, from controlling your outlook. A balanced you will not allow dark entities the opportunity they are waiting for, which is to corrupt your peace. Believe me when I tell you, through meditation humans are able to feel and hear the archangels and guardian angels that are always with them. These angels are here to help so keep on asking for their help; make your request very specific and I promise you that the help will always be provided.

My soul mate and I have reached that stage where we are able to help others heal just by offering our touch and by sharing a few wise words with them. How could we deal with the experience of helping others without getting emotionally involved?

I can only suggest what I think is the right way to do this. I can give you straight answers and sometimes hints of what I think will work well for you, but I will never dictate to you what you should do. I can never force you to follow my suggestion; it is all up to you to choose to follow what I say, or not.

Now let's talk about your soul mate's experience with the young client that came to see her yesterday, which is the real reason why you are asking me this question. After spending some time with this young girl, your soul mate suggested to her that she come back to speak with both of you next time. At the end of her visit, the girl came up with a lot of excuses not to come and see the two of you again. During the girl's visit, your soul mate became very emotionally involved when the girl told her that she is going to see a doctor that will give her strong medications to relieve her physical symptoms and her stress. Your soul mate started to worry about the girl because she believed that there is a better and safer way for this girl to heal, without using medications with serious side effects. Your soul mate thought that it is better for the girl to make herself strong by finding balance within her, and by taking care of her physical body. But the girl was refusing to hear this option.

Now I want you to hear me very clearly. The first thing you have to always believe when you are dealing with others is that whatever situation they are in, it is an experience that they have to go through. If you feel good or bad, it is not going to change the fact of your client's experience – or that your feeling is only coming from your ego. Your ego will make you adopt others' feelings to make you feel sad when they are sad and happy when they are happy. I will tell you that adding your worries and fears to a situation will only lead to confusion. When you work with any human, always think of the human as a project for you. The project is to help this human get over whatever he is troubled with, without living his life for him. Just clear your mind, follow your heart, and then all that comes out of your mouth will be wisdom. When you do this, you will have conquered all of your own emotions that might get you involved in the emotions of the person that you are trying to help.

When we talked a few days ago I asked both of you, what is the worst enemy of a human? You answered that all problems created within a human come from fear. And you were right. Every human has fear in his heart, and every human has another human or a tool to anchor in to relieve himself of the emotional pressure created by his fear. The best way for you to help this young client is to find that human whom she anchors in and ask him to work with you to help the girl. The girl will listen to her anchor way more than you, and this will be a good start for her. The important thing for you is to not have an expectation for a specific result.

Now let me explain a little bit better to make sure that you understand. If a person has fear that is causing him problems, the best thing to do is to find the reason that is causing the fear. You and I can go back and see this girl's past to discover where her fear is coming from, which will help you understand where she is headed. Once you have all this information, you can sit down with the girl and her human anchor. Talk to her about her fear, and tell her a little bit about how it can control and ruin the body. This girl is smart and she has common sense. She uses her senses and her free will to think freely, so it is up to her to decide how she will hear and understand your words. When you talk to the girl, give a little and absorb a lot. I say, let her say whatever she feels like saying. Let her words flow freely so she can release the stress that is in her. Listen to what she has to say very carefully, and answer her accordingly – to help her understand that taking dangerous drugs is not the only solution to choose from. Tell her that in her case, these medications will temporarily stop the symptoms, but they will never cure her. Make sure that the human she anchors in is also talking to her, not only you. This might put her at ease to open her ears to hear what you are saying. Tell her what you and I know she is meant to hear, and then let it go. She found you because was she was meant to hear your words, but not for you to have an expectation of action. That part is not up to you.

Follow what I am telling you only if you believe this is the right way, not because I am suggesting it. Stop worrying right now – and remember that you and your soul mate are healers that are trying to help heal others. I know this is not easy to do, but with practice, you will be great.

Chapter 20

DEATH

What happens to the human body when we die? What happens to the human's mind and awareness during the last minutes of life, and after the body dies?

The reason for understanding the way death happens is to understand for real the way life moves on a daily basis. A human examines the procedure of nature to observe the endless chain of life, happening again and again, and to understand that change is the heart of life. What human beings label "life" and "death" arise out of each other, and cross into each other in the in–between stages.

Death is the only definite thing that a human cannot run away from. Life on Earth has an end, and time brings a human closer and closer to dying; but no human can predict how long he is staying. He might die when he is still in the womb, or sometimes age to over one hundred years – but every death on Earth has a cause. No human dies without an incident, disease or disaster to make his life end. Most of the time, it comes suddenly when a human is not expecting it; and no money, no wealth, no health and no human can prevent death from happening.

On Earth, the words "die", "died" or "death" are very fearful words because suffering and pain are always associated with death; and because no human knows where they are going after they die. Some humans believe that if they were good – having done well with others, if they worshipped in a holy place, if they listened to a holy man preaching to them, and if they followed the teachings of the holy book – then they will end up in heaven, even though they do not know for real what heaven is. They believe that if they were not good by neglecting to do all of the above, they will go to hell, which is their greatest fear. If you think about this for a little bit, you will come to understand that "heaven" and "hell" reside only in a human's mind and nowhere else. There is no actual physical place that a human goes to after he dies. If you go a bit deeper with your thoughts, you will realize that humans are living in "heaven" and "hell" here on Earth, during this lifetime.

Now let me explain to you how physical death works. Every human consists of four different bodies: the physical body, the emotional body, the mind body and the soul body; and they exist in this order. None of these four bodies can work alone – all four have to work together to keep a human going. The physical body is the one that you can see, touch and feel and where all the physical experiences are felt. The emotional body, also called the astral body, is a template representative, or copy, of the physical body. When a human is asleep and dreaming, he experiences his dreams through his astral body. When a human is sleeping, the physical cannot see and hear as when a human is awake, so the emotional body takes over to help the physical see all the dreams and experiences that occur within the dreams. In some humans, the physical and emotional bodies can separate easily even when they are awake. You are one of these humans. You can leave your body any time you want, to experience whatever you choose that is not in your physical environment at that time. You visit places and other humans – if they are alive or already dead – by which you gain knowledge and understanding to help you be the healer that you were born to be.

Sometimes when humans die and are revived within seconds, they will remember what they saw while they were dead. They talk about having seen their body lying down, sleeping, while they floated above it. In reality, the emotional body was the floating body that saw the experience. Even when a human body is dead, the emotional body has its job to do, which is to provide data to the soul for the time immediately following physical death. This information will help the soul finish its experience of transitioning to not having a physical body any more. Keep in mind that when a human dies and is not revived, the three bodies will separate from the physical, and the after–physical–death experience will begin.

There is a procedure in the death process beyond what we typically think death is. Death of the physical body is only the first stage of death. In the second stage, the emotional body starts vanishing. It will take a while for this body to fade and vanish. In the third stage, the mind body will recollect all that it had seen and done, and it will add all this information to the Conscious, so the mind body will survive without the physical body, only until it unloads all the information it holds into the Conscious. When the mind body dies, it is dead for good. When the soul decides to come back, it will come back with a new mind body. The fourth stage of death will be the movement of the soul body to its Source, where it will wait until it comes back to Earth to experience in a different shell. Again, it will be a combination of physical, emotional, mind and soul bodies; which will create a new human for the purpose of experiencing within a new physical shell again.

Death is not a moment; it is a process. When a human dies, the first thing that happens is the lungs stop working and no oxygen goes into the body or blood anymore. The face and front side of the body turn pale because blood is not flowing anymore. The feet and back side of the body will turn black due to the draining of blood from the human's veins, which settles on the back side of the body. The brain cells die a few minutes after the body dies. Now, the heart is known as the ticking organ of the body, and it is said that when it stops ticking, the body is dead. This is a very true statement, but the heart and most of the other organs and cells in the body remain viable for a few hours after the death occurs. Bone cells stay alive and active for a few days before they decay and die. The bones are very solid objects that stay solid on the outside, but decay on the inside. The body will eventually break down and turn into ashes. Hot weather will cause the body to decompose faster. Sometimes the decomposition will take a year, and sometimes it will take less time, depending on the temperature of the environment. This procedure is only the physical part of death.

Death, in reality is a very peaceful experience. At the moment of physical death, the human feels very relaxed, and then he feels the separation of the physical body. After a human dies on the physical, his mind and Conscious continue to function for some time. His soul will remain attached to his physical body through the silver cord,[11] but it will be able to fly around and experience something new that it never did as a living human. If other humans revive that person, it means that his soul was not ready to leave yet. His soul was experiencing a brief departure, and learning from the experience of departing briefly

---

11. The silver cord is energy that attaches the physical body to the three other bodies: the emotional, the mind, and the soul bodies. When a human goes into a deep sleep, these three bodies leave the physical body, but they remain attached to the physical body by this cord. There are some humans who can leave their physical body when they go into deep meditation and their other three bodies can travel all over the universe.

but not letting go of the physical body. It means that this soul came back to continue finishing more experiences on Earth in the same shell. As a human, he will realize that he was floating in the room. He will remember that he was flying over his body where he could see, hear, and feel everybody and everything that was in the room, without being in his physical body. If the human is not revived, in his mind he will start seeing white light; then this light will change to red and then black. When darkness covers the whole scene, this will be the last scene of death, and it is when the Subconscious combines with the Conscious. After they become one, the Conscious starts to leave the body. When the Conscious leaves the body, it will go through seven stages that will let the soul go back successfully to its Source.

Let me explain each stage in detail for you to understand.

Stage 1:

A human's life experience and knowledge gained plays a very important role for the soul in its after–death experience, but the human is unaware of this. A human's life should have a very well–built base; it takes a human almost a lifetime for this base to be built. If and when a human follows a path of knowledge in his life, he will be creating a strong base for his life. Whatever is created in a lifetime is as strong or as weak as the base that it is built on. Humans are not always aware of what they have accomplished through their creation ability during their life. They do not know how strong the power of their mind is in gaining wisdom from the experiences it creates for itself, or that it will matter after they die.

Humans' power of experience leads to building a strong base of knowledge, which includes the wisdom gained from this knowledge, added to their existing life experience. But humans are not aware that all this happens for the purpose of making them strong enough to become a *tool* for knowledge. In the first stage, this knowledge will be added, by the Conscious, to the soul's bank of knowledge, to create more wisdom; which the soul will carry with it when it goes back to its Source.

Stage 2:

Buddha, who was a great master that came to this Earth, once said, "A human cannot travel the path until he becomes the path."

When the soul comes to Earth, it occupies a human body for a while in order to experience within it. The soul already planned on what it wants to experience with this shell. A basic part of a soul's journey on Earth is for the human it occupies to be given free will to choose his path in whatever he faces. Most humans choose their path of knowledge according to what their holy book dictates to them, believing that it is the only right way. These humans have to understand that *they* are the power, and that *they,* themselves, are God. Only by believing this will they realize that no other human, or book, or power should control their choice of the path they want to follow. They also have to know that the soul itself cannot control the human's choice! If or when the human decides to go a different route than what his soul planned on, the soul will go with the human's decision to experience differently. The soul will still experience and gain knowledge, even though the plan is different from what it had planned on following.

In the second stage of the Conscious after death, if the soul did not get to finish its experiences as it had planned, the Conscious, with the help of the soul, will start to research the best way for the soul to follow for it to gain the experience it needs to control the next human it is going to occupy, in the next life, so that it can accomplish what it had planned.

Stage 3:

After the Conscious goes through the first two stages, it then has to review and absorb the knowledge from all the experiences it went through so far. To do this, the Conscious will go into meditation to calm itself down so it can comprehend what it went through. After this meditation, the Conscious will have cleared all thoughts and absorbed all knowledge, which will then be added to a clean and balanced mind. The Conscious will do this only so it could help the soul to come back and finish its mission successfully in its next lifetime on Earth.

Stage 4:

The soul, with the Conscious, will now start looking beyond what the human physical is all about, and together they will look at the mental and emotional dimensions of the formula the soul was in. The Conscious and the soul know that a human suffers mentally, and this tortures the soul, which leads to a serious malfunctioning of the body and mind. With this understanding, the soul and the Conscious will look to past lifetimes of the soul to learn from and absorb from the incidents the soul had experienced. Then the soul will start to create a balanced growth using this information, so it can be at full alertness to have the body and mind work in a helpful cycle when the soul comes back to its next lifetime.

Stage 5:

A human is a part of something that is greater than him. As you know through your own experience, life is within humans but also way beyond, in the universe. A soul exists within a human, but it is way larger than any individual. It floats in the infinite universe, which means that a human is part of something that is alive on Earth, yet also exists far beyond. When creating a new human, lifetime after lifetime in earthly terms, this connection is in full consideration by the soul and the Conscious. The soul knows it is endless and limitless, and that it is a part of Spirit itself; which is the force that shapes and guides the whole universe with forces known and unknown to humans.

In the fifth stage, the Conscious will start looking into helping the soul to create itself within a new human – keeping its link to the spiritual realm, without having an attachment to its past experiences. When this process has taken place, the soul will try once again, through the new human, to finish its original plan.

Stage 6:

On Earth, there is a relationship between consideration and wisdom, which is a basic part of humanity. This relationship is under pressure rather than in agreement. In plain English, this means that there are always an infinite number of choices for a human to make in leading his life, and no matter the choice the human makes, the soul will still gain wisdom from it. Sometimes, when a human makes a choice that is not in agreement with the path that this human's soul had planned to follow, there is tension between the soul's desire and the human's choice. But again, the soul will go along with this, and it will gain wisdom from the experience. Even though there is tension between consideration and wisdom, they are like two wings on a bird, where the achievement of one makes the other possible. Keep in mind that wisdom will teach a human how to be calm, which will make possible full access to the power of the mind; and this will affect the way a human chooses to lead his life. Basically, this is how wisdom affects consideration. I want you to understand that if this power is not used by the human, the mind will become weak and lost. When the mind is weak and lost, the human will suffer – on the physical – with the first experience that hits him. This kind of weakness and confusion will be a lesson to be considered by the soul when it creates a new human.

The funny thing about wisdom is that it always has a role to play as a tool for the human and for the soul. For the human, his wisdom will help him endure any suffering – even if he does not realize it – so that his experience could have a useful meaning for him. For the soul, human wisdom is a necessity for it to get the job done within the human it created, so that it can continue to come back in different humans for the purpose of its own completion.

During the sixth stage of death, the Conscious will do its best to provide the soul with an endless, wonderful understanding of any confusion that the soul put itself in during the lifetime. The Conscious will help the soul understand that what happened in this past life was intended for it, for it to experience and gain knowledge, even though it was not what the plan was. The Conscious will lead the soul to believe that it should go back to its Source to start again in a different, wonderful human being, to again get more knowledge and wisdom to add to what it gained in the past life; regardless of what the considerations and results will be.

Stage 7:

For the soul to reach this final stage, it is important for it to master itself; to finally be able to drop any feelings and thoughts that it might still have. It will even drop the final moments that the human went through before his death, even though these final moments were full of thoughts and feelings. Thoughts come from the mind, and feelings come from the intellect, but both of them are influenced by the soul.

At this point, the soul is ready to go back to its Source, but it still needs a push to understand that whatever it decides on experiencing, will happen – regardless of what the human that it occupies feels or thinks. The soul will now believe that there is no limit to the experiences that it wants to go through, and it will find the right shell to help it go through them. As soon as this last stage passes, the soul will come back to a physical life within a new human.

We can simply say that death is the end of the unity between the mind and the body. It is the mark of the soul's decision that it has accomplished all it could in a body, and it is time for it to leave and go find another body to finish the rest. These seven stages can take a very short time – or ages – to be accomplished.

If you go deep in your thoughts, you will realize that in reality, there is no real death. The death of the body is not something to be scared of. With death, all of a human's pain, suffering, sadness and stress end immediately. When a human believes in reincarnation and in the cycle of life, he should be happy knowing that comfort is waiting for him, and that the soul will come back again and again, to play a role on this Earth.

On a chosen earthly journey, the soul plans on using a physical body to experience through, but it is accomplished by using the non–physical mind. The mind and the physical body always work together to create the necessary attachment to the earthbound experience, challenging the soul's desire, through the human's free will. The soul will work through the mind and the body to finish what it wants without being attached to the procedure. This means that the after–death attachment of the soul is not to the human experiences it had, but to the *form* in which it experienced through.

Even though the soul will exist again in another physical body, it will come with a new emotional body and a new mind body – so it is the Conscious of the universe into which the soul is born. This period of coming back will occur until the soul has finished all the experiences that are needed. This is when the soul will reach total purity and no longer needs to come back in a human body. The truth is...there will be no reason for it to come back to this world or to this universe. In fact, this will be a conversion from the consciousness of experiencing in physical bodies to the consciousness of the All–Knowing.

As a quick review, when the soul wants to leave, nothing can stop it. When it does leave, the Subconscious will dump all its information into the Conscious and it will die with the physical body. Then, the Conscious stops working with the consideration of the physical body. It stays for a while with the soul to help it go through the stages of death, and then the Conscious itself dumps all the data that it has into the Superconscious. The Superconscious holds all this information until the soul decides to come back and reside in a new shell. The Conscious will then take the information from the Superconscious, and that is when the same soul with the same Conscious, will create a new Subconscious to work together with a new body, to start a new beginning in a new life. Now you have the same Conscious that is still attached to the Superconscious, with the same soul, in a different physical body. So, all the experiences that happened in the past human lifetimes of that soul are still stored in the Conscious. You already know that this information could be accessed through hypnosis. But, to make it easy on you to understand the procedure better, think of the physical body as a hotel, and the soul and the Conscious as visitors in it. When the visitors are done with their mission, they will vacate that hotel. When a new mission comes up, they will start looking for another hotel to occupy, suitable for completing the new project.

Now I know there is no real death on Earth or in the universe. Would you tell me more about the way death is understood on Earth?

Death is fairly simple and clearly defined, by humans, as the end of the physical body's life. It ends when a human stops breathing and his heart stops beating. All humans believe that one day they are going to die, but they hate to think about that day because no one for real knows where they are going. They are confused due to all the wrong information and scary things that they have heard from their first day on Earth; either from their holy man or from other humans.

All humans live their lives as if tomorrow is coming as another physical day; and it always looks, to them, like they are staying on this Earth indefinitely. The pleasure of having and demanding more and more in this life, dedicating all their power to the enjoyment of earthly values, tricks them into believing that they are here to stay for as far as they can predict. By convincing themselves of this idea, humans are unprepared for when the time comes for their soul to drop the physical body.

On Earth, there are some cultures that celebrate death because they understand and believe that the soul will come back to live on Earth again. They mourn the departure of the physical body because they will miss being with that human, and because they feel bad for the dead person's family; but they salute the soul, knowing that it will be a new life to come.

In other cultures, people will be sad and very scared of death because they believe that they do not know where their loved one is going. For them, death is the feared unknown. The only understanding they have is that the brain is not getting any more oxygen to function and the heart is not getting any more blood to flow; so, for them, death is a physical procedure. They will be in a state of confusion because their beliefs tell them that if you are good you go to heaven, and if you are bad you go to hell. In fact, I tell you again, there is no heaven or hell; they are only ideas of humans' making.

All of these cultures have different traditions that tell them what should be done with the physical body. Some of them will bury it because they believe that it comes from dust and goes back to dust. Some will burn it and spread the ashes to fly with the wind. Others will freeze the physical body hoping that, when the world comes to an end, there will be another life for the same human to live. Some cultures used to bury the body before it died, to purify the soul. Some used to dismember the head or stab the heart, only to make sure that the person actually died before they buried him. The important thing is that it does not matter what humans do. No one is right and no one is wrong. They all do what they do because that is what they know, and because it is what they were told and raised to believe.

You are now above all these things, and this you understands that there is only a physical death; you believe that the soul will reside again in a new physical body, and that life will always go on. There are a lot of humans who do not understand that life was meant to be eternal. It is very tough for a human who does not know and understand, to believe that the physical body dies but the soul does not; and especially that the soul will come to Earth again in a new physical body.

The older a human gets, the more his fear of death will conquer his emotions. Many will have an experience that will make them stop and think, briefly, about life and death on Earth. These humans will examine the way they were raised and the beliefs and traditions that they were taught about their spiritual needs. Some of these humans discover and adopt a new way of thinking, which will become a tool for them to understand what they are doing here and what comes next. This will replace their fear with an appreciation of the beauty of life. This kind of human will make choices that will make him finish differently from what his traditions and beliefs taught him. He will finish his life with love and happiness instead of fear. The idea of knowing the truth about this life will make him understand that the body itself is a shell for the soul, and that this physical body is disposable. This human will look at birth as a starting point for a new life in a new body, and he will see death as the end of this life for his physical body, not for the real him. When he reaches this point of understanding – that the soul is here to stay – he will believe that life on Earth is a bunch of experiences for the soul, and that the soul will use a physical body as a vehicle for these experiences as many times as it chooses to.

For the human who is scared, the more he experiences pain, the more his Subconscious will be loaded with negative references, which will make it very hard for him to find love and peace within him, because he is refusing it. It is very important to remember that the role of the Subconscious is to protect a human from being hurt by always presenting him with what he is familiar with – but there are an unlimited number of references, or wisdom, for any experience the human faces. Eventually, it is also with the help of his Subconscious emotions that a human will start to convince himself that he does not need this life anymore, and by dying he will find peace. These emotions are also controlled by the soul, to help the human begin to accept the fact of his approaching departure. This is when aging and sickness start ruling the emotions of the body, telling the human that death is the solution to relieve him of his pain and misery. The more awful the pain becomes, the more the human will want to let go, even though this idea will be against what his traditions and beliefs have taught him. Even though he is scared, he will start seeing death as more favorable than suffering.

But think with me for a minute: we both know that if a human is given the choice between health and death, and between aging and youth, he will always choose to stay healthy and young because this is what he thinks will keep him happy. As a human, he will not recognize that he is still going to live after his physical death, and that he has the choice to be at peace even if he is aging and unhealthy. This is because from the time they are born humans are taught and convinced that a human will never live forever. So as a human grows in age, his fear of death, of the unknown, will also grow. The minute fear controls a human, the physical and emotional pain begins, which will make it very tough for that body to stay healthy and to function forever…and this, too, is meant to be part of the human experience.

Today I wished a human happy birthday, and he answered, "A birthday is one year closer to death." Tell me a little bit about birthdays and death.

"Birthday" is an earthly word that was labeled by humans to define the day when a human leaves the womb and starts breathing on his own. Physical birth is the beginning of the soul's experience in a fresh, new body. For humans, "death" is a simple word that has been understood as the end of life, and it is known as when a human's heart stops beating. We talked about death before and some of the traditions that humans have followed. Now, let's discuss birthday traditions that have been used since humans were created on this Earth.

There are many societies on this planet, and a lot of them celebrate the day when a human is born. It is celebrated every year on the same date of the physical birth, to rejoice the event that occurred on that same date years ago, and to remind the human that he is a year older and wiser. But this celebration is not a must in all societies. Some societies do not celebrate the birth day because they believe that every day that shines on them is going to be the last day for them on Earth. Some people would rather name their kids after a saint's name when they are born, to celebrate only the name day. Some wait until the infant reaches thirteen years of age, and then celebrate his maturity. Others will only celebrate their prophets' birth dates, and so on. All these man–made traditions are passed on from generation to generation.

Some of these societies celebrate birthdays with a cake. They put candles on it, each candle representing a year of life. The idea of the cake and candles started with Greek society to honor their gods, especially the god of the moon. The round cake represented the moon, and the lit candles represented the glow of the moon. Then humans started changing the shapes of the cakes to come up with their own ideas, which later on became traditions. Some people believed that before blowing out candles, a human whose birthday is being celebrated should make a wish. If he blows out all the candles in one puff, then his wish will come true. Some societies use one big candle in the middle of the cake to represent the light of life. Some add gold coins inside the cake, and they believe that the person who finds it will become wealthy. Others believe that every candle on the cake is a symbol of something that God created in a human, and the brightest candle of all is the love of God that shines in that human's heart. A lot of humans will also celebrate birthdays by giving gifts to the human who is being celebrated. In other societies, the one who is celebrating his birthday will give gifts to others. Some will sing songs to celebrate. Over time and through the ages, every generation from every society adapts and changes these traditions to fit their new thinking. But again, understand that all these traditions are man—made.

Every human should understand that physical birth onto Earth represents the beauty of the soul that embraces all the experiences of life in the human's heart. Understanding this will give joy and happiness to a human, and it will help him realize the meaning of his life and the lives of other humans around him. Life holds so many features – and Earth is, and has always been, one of these features.

This morning, around eleven o'clock, James said to me:

Listen to what I am saying. Get into your car, and follow my directions. I will lead you.

I wondered where we were going, and I asked him to tell me.

Go into your car and follow my lead.

I ignored what he said and I did not go right away. Then I started to feel a lot of pressure and confusion. I felt guilty because I thought that I should have followed his instructions. I told my soul mate about what happened and then I let it go. In the afternoon, I heard James again. He was asking me to go in my car and drive, the same as he had in the morning. He asked me to drop everything now, go into my car and follow his lead! It took me half an hour, but I finally got into my car and started driving. James was my eyes. He led my way. I turned right and then right again, then another right and then a left. I reached a rehab center where elderly people usually recuperate from their ailments. I reached the parking lot and James told me to park the car in a spot where I could see the whole building. He asked me to look on the roof above the building.

You are a little bit late. You will still see and learn from what you are seeing, but it is not everything that I wanted you to see. You missed a big part of this knowledge. If you were here earlier, you would have witnessed the death of an elderly human, and the last minutes and seconds of how the soul leaves the body. You could have experienced the death part when the soul drops the body. The soul has already left, but I want you to see and experience a little bit of what happens to that soul when it leaves the body. Look at the roof. See that soul in the middle that has a silver cord attached to it? This silver cord is a little bit different shade, and there is different energy around it from the silver cord that you see when you meditate and leave your body. Look at the energy that is surrounding the roof of the building. Look at the colors that are in different shapes – from gold to white to blue, green and even black. The colors look more like colored clouds, covering the area directly above the building. Look at all the floating figures and entities that are making a circle around the soul of the elderly human that just died. Look at that soul, how scared and confused it is.

The beautiful part is that all these entities, figures, and angels that surrounded the soul were happily dancing, clapping and singing. All of these figures, even the dark entities, were happy for the soul they were surrounding. They were cheering him, and energy was floating all over the place in the form of different kinds of symbols, and a cloudlike form covering the area. What I saw was scenery that I have never, ever seen before. I paused to appreciate what I was seeing, but I also felt a little bit guilty because I felt that I should have come the first time James told me to.

I wanted you to be here to see and witness what the soul does and what it goes through when it drops the body. I do not want you to worry and feel any guilt for not witnessing the whole incident at this time. I assure you, there will be many times when you will see and experience similar incidents. What you saw, for now, is that when a human dies his soul is not alone. You saw that there are different souls, entities and angels waiting for that soul; to cheer it on and to help it get used to the emptiness that it feels after it drops the body. Do understand that every angel, entity, and other soul that is available at that time, will show up to help that fresh soul. They will combine their effort to help that soul get used to the after–death; and they will help guide it in the direction that will help it be ready to go back to its Source.

One afternoon, my soul mate called to tell me about a car accident that had just occurred. She told me that she had just seen a car accident and it looked like the cars were in very bad shape. She thought I would like to go to discover and experience new things. She told me the location of the accident so I meditated, spoke to James, and then left my body and went where the accident was. The cars were still there but no humans were in them anymore so James and I went to the emergency room of the nearest hospital. I saw a light blue figure of a young girl standing above her own body, crying her heart out. Surrounding her were angels and other souls. Some were talking to her and some were there for support. I got close to her and asked her if she was in pain, and she said, "no". I asked her why she was crying. She said that she was thinking of going back into her body because she did not want to die yet, but she was scared to go back to the bloody and broken body down there. I asked her why she wanted to go back, and exactly what she was feeling at that moment. She said, "I feel happiness inside me, and I feel free like a bird. I can fly, and I can move without any rules or conditions." So I asked her why she was crying if she felt so happy and free. She answered, "I do not want to be away from my friend. I love her very much and we were going to get married soon. I cannot survive without her." This seemed like a strange comment to me, so I asked her, survive what? I told her that she is already dead, so there is no more survival for her in this life. I asked her if she would really leave the freedom she had at this moment and go back to her body, just to be with her friend. She said, "Yes and no. I would rather have her come to me, but if I cannot have that, then I will go back to her."

I looked at James and asked him what was going on. He told me that it was time to leave and that we would talk in the morning, after I had enough time to think about and absorb what I saw.

Around one o'clock in the morning, James and I took another trip to the hospital for me to learn more from seeing these two girls again. Neither of the two girls that were in the car accident yesterday was in the emergency room anymore. We found the soul of the dead girl in the basement of the hospital next to her body, which I did not see because it was hidden in a cold draw where bodies are stored. All kinds of angels and souls were in that room.

Everyone was busy taking care of the girl's soul, preaching and educating her how to let go of her body. I asked the girl's soul how she was feeling and she said, "Good, very relaxed. No pain or pressure. I am waiting next to my body to say the last good—bye to the container that held me all my life." I asked her what happened to her friend, and she said, "They moved her to another place where she has a big chance of surviving." I asked her what she was going to do about that and she said, "I will hang around my body for a few days, then I will go stay around my friend until the time comes for me to leave this atmosphere and go back where I came from." I asked her why she wanted to stay with her friend and if she thought she could communicate with her, and if it would bother her if the communication was only from one side. She said, "I have nowhere to be for now except to say good—bye to my body. Then, I will stay with my friend and I know that she will feel, hear and see me sometimes, because I know she wants to. I do not have fear that she will not communicate with me. I know that I will see her and talk to her, and if she also sees or hears me that will be great; and if she does not, that will be o.k. also. I will know that I did my best, and I will keep on trying until the time comes for me to take my last trip back to where I belong. Then, I will wait for her until she is ready to come back to me. I believe, after we reunite, we will come back again to experience the same experience that we were going through, only next time it will be a little bit different. In this past life, we were together for a long period of time, and I know that after we reunite, we will be ready to come back and redo what we did not finish." I looked at James very surprised to see the difference in the soul's behavior from the afternoon until now. He told me that it was time for us to go back and talk a little bit about it.

When we returned, my soul mate was waiting for us. She said, "How come I was not invited to be with you this time? What happened? Tell me in full detail!"

I assure you, there will be many other times that you will come along and see and feel a lot. The good thing is that you know for sure that you will know in full detail what went on.

Now let me explain to both of you a little bit about what happened today. Today is a beautiful experience that I was hoping for you to see and experience so that you can gain more knowledge and wisdom. I promise you, there will be way more experiences that are similar to what you have seen lately; similar experiences with different reasons for the death and different after–death reactions from the souls. Every physical death has its own way to be dealt with; it depends on the age of the human, on the sex and on the reason for the death.

A lot of times death is expected and the human will have enough time to consciously prepare himself for his last moments. For a human, death is still a fearful thing even if he prepares himself. For the soul, this kind of death situation and separation of the soul from the body will be much less confusing than a sudden death. This is what happened in the first incident with the elderly person at the rehab center. Other times, death comes very suddenly and it is not accepted. In this case, the human and the soul will not have enough time to prepare for the death, which will cause surprise and shock for the soul when it leaves the body. This is what happened in the second incident with the young girl. It took the soul a little while to realize what happened to the shell that it was residing in, and to accept what was going on, with the help of all the angels and entities surrounding it. The soul had to figure out how to deal with this new experience.

The young girl was not expecting death at all for now. In fact, she did not even think about death when the accident occurred. So, when you saw her soul this afternoon a few minutes after it left her body, the soul was confused over what happened and it did not want to leave. The confusion was not because it wanted to stay in the physical body;

it was because the soul was not prepared to see itself this way. When you saw the soul at night, it had had enough time to begin to accept the reality of what had occurred; it saw itself floating all over the room and over the friend that was in the accident with her. Earlier, the emotions of losing the friend were still fresh and this made her stop and think of how hard it was to be separated from her friend. These emotions weakened a little bit with the help of her guardian angels, angels and entities that surrounded her, helping her to adjust. They helped her start to understand that what happened was for real; that it was not a dream that she would wake up from.

As a human, this girl did not ask for this. She was not expecting any of this to happen to her for the time being. She had earthly plans, looking forward to a beautiful future. Suddenly, in a split second everything that she had planned was destroyed and became history. For her soul, it will take a while to completely accept the fact of her physical death, especially if her friend's soul decides to stay to finish more experiences. I assure you that this soul will stay for a while around her friend trying to get back with her. It will give her friend all kinds of signals to let her know that she is still around but her friend will not hear or feel her; except there might be a few incidents where her friend might see her and talk to her in a dream, or in a meditation session, or by a sign she might notice.

For now, the dead girl's soul still has a part of her earthly emotions attached to it. Her soul still has some hope left and it is not sure if it should stay a little longer or leave. But I tell you, the girl's guardian angel is now her biggest support and leader, followed by other angels and souls who will also help her. They are all working together to help her soul follow the right path of return. They will keep talking to her and guiding her until she goes back to her Source. When she eventually reaches her Source again – by absorbing and understanding what her guides are telling her – this will all seem like a joke to her. She will laugh at herself for having refused to let go.

When she finally goes back to her Source, where time does not exist, her friend will follow her very quickly; but on Earth it might be years and years later. When they meet again as souls, they will laugh about all that happened and they will want to take another adventure together like they did before. The main thing you should be aware of is that for these two girls, everything they did and everything that happened was all planned for before they decided to come to this life. They had planned how they were going to come, how they were going to experience alone and together, and the time they would leave and go back to meet each other again at their Source. But the part that is not planned is the period after the soul decides to leave the body up until the point when it realizes that it is time to go back to its Source. All the confusion that you saw in the girl's soul after the death – the panic that she was in after leaving her body – up until the soul reaches its Source, was not planned on.

In the stage after death, before the soul reaches Source, there are no more earthly traditions; no more rules to go by, no more pain, no more needs or wants, no difference between the sexes or races, no more desires. Whatever the human was before death will not matter anymore. The soul will feel free, but it will hesitate to accept its new freedom because it will still worry about leaving the human it was attached to. Soon after, it will accept its new condition and it will be like other floating souls, trying to go through the process of reaching the Source it came from.

I am happy for the way you are handling yourself now. I am very happy that you are not feeling a lot of fear when you see bloody, broken or dead bodies. I know you still have fear and questions about why this is happening to you, but by now you know that you asked for it. Trust me when I tell you that you are leading yourself on the path that your soul planned on. I know that you saw and understood a lot of new things today. I promise you that there will be a lot of similar experiences to go through in the near future. Just listen to me when I ask you to do something. Next time your soul mate will also come along with us. She needs to see and experience also, and I assure you that she is ready. She is very ready to feel what you are feeling. She can meditate and clear her mind whenever she wants. Now she can hear us and she can see some of our figures a little bit better than before. Pretty soon she will feel us, hear us, and see the real us, and then she will be able to do what you do and more.

One of my soul mate's friends died a few days ago. She asked me if I would like to experience this death to learn from it. Later that day I left my body and went to the funeral service for a quick visit. I knew that the man's funeral would be at twelve o'clock at one of the nearby churches, so I went back to the funeral home before twelve o'clock and followed the body to the church. I returned again later when the body was being taken to the cemetery to be buried. James was with me as usual. I did not see anything that was any more special than the other two times I had visited death experiences.

I approached the dead man's soul to ask him about what was going on. He was surrounded by all kinds of help. He had beautiful angels next to him, and even though he looked a little bit confused, he was not worried about what was happening to his body. By talking to his soul, I discovered that he was more than happy to die. His pain, stress and fear were gone now. He was not sorry for leaving his body, but he felt emotionally disturbed for the humans that he left behind. I asked James to enlighten me about what I had just experienced. I asked him to explain to us what the reaction of the soul is when it is attending its body's funeral.

When writing your book, I want you to mention here that you did not know this human and that you have never seen him before. Also mention to your readers that you did not see his physical body at the funeral home, the church or the cemetery because every time you saw him the coffin was closed. I want every reader to understand that souls always talk to each other without any limitations; and at the stage that you are in right now you can talk to any souls or angels any time you choose to. This incident was the third dead person that you experienced recently within hours of the death. All three had different experiences for you to see and understand.

I hope that by now you are sure that, on Earth, there are reasons for a birth and reasons for a death, and the soul plans it all and acts accordingly. For the soul, it does not make a difference how old the human is when he dies; nor do race, sex, age or the reason for the death matter in any way. There is no young or old soul. There is no male or female soul. All souls will follow the same procedure from the time of physical death to the time they go back to their Source. The transition part of going back to Source will always be the most difficult stage, even when it is ready to depart. Even though the soul will never be alone, and it will have all the help it needs to move on, it is always up to the soul to listen or not. Usually, the faster the body is buried or cremated the easier it will be for the soul to accept the fact.

When a human's life ends, his job is done and over. Even though the silver cord will take three days to completely disappear, the soul could never go back into that same body; but there is knowledge to be gained by the other humans affected by the death. They will gain knowledge and understanding about life on Earth, each in his own way, which might cause them to change how they see their own life. There is no right or wrong way to understand death. It is about what each human's soul is seeking to experience at that time, which will make the experience understood in different ways by different humans.

Each community has its own traditions and beliefs on how a dead human's body should be handled and what religious or spiritual ritual will be held. Whatever the tradition or belief is, all of them end up with a ceremony to mourn or celebrate the dead. All of these traditions have the same purpose, which is to guide the soul of the dead person to its eternal world – to reunite the soul with its Creator, regardless of who the Creator is. Humans believe that by doing all this, they could prevent any delays that the soul might face in reaching its end. Keep in mind that the soul is there attending the funeral of its body, so these rituals might also help the soul in accepting that it does not belong to this earthly life anymore, and to look forward to its last journey back to where it belongs.

Most earthly religions believe that ceremonies and preparations for the funeral should last at least three days before the burial. They believe that this gives the soul enough time to say good–bye to its body – and if the soul chooses, to somehow come back to reside in it. Their religious leaders chant, pray and perform rituals according to their religion. They might use all kinds of tools and instruments like bells, drums, oil, incense, and burning sage. Family members attend at special times within the three days for prayers; friends might burn candles, pray, or give offerings. In fact, these actions are basically for the comfort of those who are still here, not for the dead person.

On this night, James came to me earlier than usual and told me to hurry up and follow him. There was a new experience that he wanted me to see, learn, and benefit from.

Come on, we have to go now. Both of you – follow me. I want you to see and experience something new.

My soul mate, James and I went to a highway somewhere in our state. We reached a car accident that looked like it had just happened. A big, fancy car was bent around an electric pole with two people still inside the car – a man in his fifties and a kid in his late teens who I thought looked like the man's son. They looked badly hurt. Blood was all over the inside of the car and even on the smashed windshield. Next to both of them were a lot of entities and angels, talking to them, trying to relax them – maybe until help comes. Suddenly, I saw a huge black figure with eyes full of fire and all kinds of energy surrounding his body. Energy was flowing in and out of this figure's palms. It was the same figure that I had seen and visited a few weeks ago when we took the trip to the chalice and ended up at the river, where he and I met. I asked James to tell me why this entity was here with these two humans now.

On Earth, people believe there is a devil. In fact, this devil is the same dark entity, dark energy or dark angel that every human has around him, just as each human has white angels and guardian angels around him. This entity's job is to keep humans content in their physical experience on Earth, so that they stay attached to their earthly existence, and want more and more. In this incident, this entity is here to talk to these humans and see if their souls are still willing to reside in these human bodies; if not, he will help their souls make the decision to drop these humans. His job is to discuss, judge, blame and make the humans feel fear in their hearts. He will make them feel miserable and sorry for themselves for what, under his lead, they did and did not finish in their lives. The devil is not satisfied with these two humans because at some point both of them had decided to rebel against him. They did not do all of what the devil wanted them to do, but they also did not allow their souls to accomplish what it had planned on finishing.

The devil approached the older man first, who was the dad. He looked at him and touched his head. The older man looked at him with fear controlling his eyes and his whole body. He asked the black figure, "Who are you? Why are you here and what do you want from me?" The figure said, "I am here to take you with me." The older man asked, "Why me? I am not ready for this. I am a rich man who has power and money. I am not done making and collecting money yet. I worked all my life to build the empire that I have. I did not have time to enjoy it yet. You do not want to take me yet. You can take whatever you choose from what I own. You name what you desire and want, and I will make sure to give it to you with no questions asked." The dark entity said, "I do not want your money or anything you own. I gave you all that you have and whatever you own. I worked on you all your life until I made you what you are now. I gave you all the power that you have. I led you step by step. I held your hand and walked with you all the way to where you are now. But lately, you started rebelling against me. You thought that you became greater and bigger than me. You stopped listening to me and you started doing a lot of other things that I had been stopping you from doing. So now, I am here to take you and replace you with another human who will obey me." The older man said, "But I am not ready to go. I refuse to leave with you. Take my son instead of me. He is handicapped and good for nothing, so take him and spare me. I promise you I will do and obey everything you ask me to do. You order me, and I will do whatever you say without questioning anything." The devil said, "I gave you so many chances but every time, you went back to your way of life. I am sure you will disobey me again. What is going to change in you this time so that I should spare you again? You are coming with me. No more debate." Suddenly the older man's soul left his body. All the angels and entities next to him welcomed this. They surrounded his soul and were leading it a little bit away from the body as they whispered to it.

Then the dark entity turned and looked at the teenage boy. He touched the boy's head and said to him, "I am here to take you with me." The boy looked at him and said, "What took you so long? I have been looking forward to this moment, and I have been asking you for this all my life, since I opened my eyes to this world. I always wanted to die and leave this miserable life that I have been living. I always wanted to die and end this, only to take this burden off my shoulders. I am here now, ready to go and I welcome you with open arms. But before we leave, I have a small request from you. Take me, but spare my dad. He always treated me well. He took very good care of me and always did his best to make me happy. He tried whatever he could to keep me going – so please take me and let him stay here. He still has a lot of things to finish, but I was done and finished years ago." The dark entity said, "I am taking you to help you from your misery; I am taking your dad to help the world from him." Then the boy's soul also left his body. His angels and the entities around him did not have to do too much in leading and relaxing his soul because he was expecting to die so he was very ready for all this.

Life on this Earth is very valuable to a human when this human has a lot of wants and needs to accomplish and fulfill. At the same time, life stops having true meaning when there are no more needs and wants; this kind of human will look for all means to end it. The interesting thing about what you saw in this incident is that death happened when one of the humans was not prepared for it, while the other had been waiting for it all his life. All that you saw occurred only on the physical. One human wanted to stay and the other one was ready to die, but both souls were ready to go. The soul of the older man had had enough with the human choosing his own experiences rather than choosing what his soul had planned on. As for the kid, his soul was experiencing what it came to experience, and it reached a point where it finished its experience as a handicapped human, so it was time for it to leave.

The older man was a powerful human. All his life, he built wealth and accomplished a lot. Until the last second, he was still building an empire for himself. All he ever did was to follow the dollar and, unknowingly, he sold his soul to the devil. He loved the earthly needs he was being led by. His life was only about making money and gaining power, but he did all this without ever being happy. He told the dark angel that he spent his life building an empire and that now it was time to start enjoying it. For his whole life he was being led by dark entities who kept him hungry for more and more. The job of dark entities is to make the human love earthly material things, and to make him become a slave for them; without finding happiness, satisfaction or contentment in what he is doing. The dark entities made this man believe that he will never die, and that nothing can hurt him because he is very rich and powerful. There is nothing wrong with having money, but the soul's purpose on Earth is not to reside in a human to only experience the power of collecting dollars. This man was following the way of dark entities, not allowing the soul to experience what it had planned. At the same time, he was also beginning to find himself, little by little, by rebelling against the dark entities from time to time. This is what the dark entity meant when he said that he is taking the older man to save the world from him. Understand that the dark entity believes that he rules the world. By taking the older man, he was saving the world from a human who was beginning to follow something other than dark entities.

Death came unexpectedly to the older man but it came with anticipation to the kid that was waiting for it. The kid was handicapped, weak and powerless physically. Since he was born, all he wanted was to stop his pain and misery. He sometimes convinced himself that this was a beautiful life, but most of the time he hated his life. So for him, death was expected and accepted.

During the recent war in the Middle East my soul mate, James and I took a trip to Israel to see the war up close. It was four thirty in the morning sharp. We decided to fly to the Middle East to check out what the effect of war is on humans when they die. My soul mate and I, with James leading the way, reached Israel/Palestine, and it was a little bit before noontime over there. The closer we got, the louder we heard explosions and roaring bombs. From far away we saw rising smoke reaching the clouds. Then suddenly we heard people screaming and crying either from fear, pain or agony.

We got closer to a town that was being bombarded from all over: by air, by land, and by sea. We heard the mosques screaming with prayers; and we heard individuals gathering in a shelter or house, praying to their god for help. We got very close to the ground where we saw clouds of black and white smoke rising up to the sky, which made visibility very poor. We saw fire everywhere. Houses and cars were burning; people were running out of a shelter right after the shelter was blown away. We saw people holding other injured people, running with them, trying to find a safe place to bring them. People were sitting in corners afraid, shivering and scared of the bombs and all the loud sounds.

Men and women of all ages were worried about where the next bomb was going to land. When they heard a bomb explode a few yards away from them, they felt blessed that a miracle happened to let them survive without any injuries. Another group felt very unlucky because they got hurt from that bomb. They were bleeding badly; and the sad part was that nobody could reach them for a while to help them stop bleeding. They knew that they were still alive, but they were wondering why they had not died yet. Some of the unlucky ones got lucky and help reached them, even though it was with great difficulty. For the others that could not be reached, it was a terrifying scene of blood draining out of their bodies because of their serious injuries. That was when the souls gave up on these shells and left those bodies.

All over we saw souls leaving in a big hurry, without a trace, after the bodies that they had been occupying were blown up to a thousand pieces. Then we saw souls that were around dead bodies that were still in one piece. These souls were floating around, wondering when to leave. Looking up and down and all around all we could see was a bunch of souls everywhere. Some were flying out of the area; some were trying to go back to their Source; others next to their bodies, waiting for the right time to leave.

We saw a wide range of energy colors covering the whole area. We saw white and black energy or white and dark angels, if you will. We saw them all over the humans that were fighting, all over others that were too scared to move, and on the ones that were in shelters or in their homes. We heard these angels, the black ones and white ones, talking and whispering into these humans' ears, giving them the courage they needed to keep them going on and fighting; or giving them the comfort to handle their fear; or giving them the wisdom to let go of their bodies and leave in peace. We saw bodies with missing parts; we saw blood and body parts all over. It was scenery that a human cannot see every day and still stay in his higher self, because his emotions will be too strong. We felt sorry for all these people. We felt very strongly that we wanted to help, but there was nothing we could do. It was out of our hands.

Through all this, we knew that we were very safe and that no harm would come to us. We were there among them, seeing and hearing everything that was happening around us, but we felt no fear. The only thing that affected us very deeply was the fact that we could do nothing to help. The sad part for us was to see the way some of these souls had to depart Earth.

James, tell me what just happened. How does a war start? What happens to all these souls during war?

First, I have a question for you both. Why were you feeling sorry for all these people? Usually, on the physical, you will feel sorry for them and be scared for them, and feel that you want to help them. It looks like you used your earthly emotions for a few seconds, and that is what made you have these feelings. Nothing wrong with this, but following your emotions in a situation like this will prevent you from learning about and fully accepting Life, which is a requirement for the healing work you came here to do. I am not saying that you should learn not to care about other humans who will come to you for help. Compassion does not have to come with judgment of their experience or yours. Compassion will help you to help them, judgment will stop you.

But I tell you, when you are in the higher stage, you will understand that all these people asked to experience this before they were born to an earthly life. Whatever is happening was planned on, and it was meant to happen. They chose to go through this experience before their physical birth, and they are living it according to their souls' plans. Feeling sorry for them only helped your ego and your pride by helping your emotions to accept what you saw; which means that, for a second, you chose to make this experience more physical and less spiritual.

When you are in the higher stage, nothing like this should bother you; no feelings or emotions should affect you this way. The only reason you let it happen for a split-second today is because you felt confused and lost seeing all these souls who did not know what to do next. Any human that allows himself to be controlled by his earthly emotions while he is in his higher stage will quickly drop down from the stage of heightened awareness. When this happens, he will be stopping himself from accomplishing what he is supposed to be doing. Humans like you can be out of your higher self and back in instantly. This allows you to basically stay in that higher stage, even though for a split second you might judge and doubt. Remember all this when you are helping others. Feeling sorry for them is going to confuse you and make you useless for their progress toward healing and happiness. As I said before, compassion is way different than pity. You can help people change their life through compassion, and you can help them stay miserable through pity. I think you know what your job is.

Now let us talk a little bit about war, and especially about religious war. War has existed since the beginning of time. The reason for war is to reach a firm aim or goal using a particular power and force to accomplish it. There are all kinds of reasons for wars: religion, which is killing in the name of God or prophets; wealth, which will make a human want to have other humans' gold, jewels, diamonds, land or other wealth; to gain power over the weak; ego, to prove that one is better than the other; greed, because one wants what is his and also what belongs to the other; and sometimes the hate of other humans who are a different color or race. Always, when harm is done to a human, as in war, revenge automatically kicks in. But revenge will wait and it will appear at the right moment. When it appears, it is worse than the original act.

The worst wars happen when leaders get angry with each other and convince their people that war is a matter of pride. They tell their people that their honor has been attacked and that they have been insulted by the opposing nation or group. War starts and soldiers are sworn in to defend their nations, taking the burden and suffering the casualties of their leaders offended pride. The sad part is that after soldiers are killed, injured or handicapped, the leaders often decide to end the war by somehow agreeing to certain terms. Nations or groups will declare themselves friends again, as if nothing happened. But remember – the souls of the humans that are hurt in a war, that declare war, or observe war have all asked for this experience.

All religions teach that war is wrong, and that war should happen only if it is the last option to resolve a disagreement. Holy war comes about only because different groups of people or nations do not have the same religious beliefs or the same prophets. There are too many nations and communities whose holy men translate their holy books in a way that will start a holy war in the name of their religion. Even though their holy book teaches them that violence and killing is wrong, killing in the name of justice is acceptable, as long as war is fought within certain rules. In the Middle East, where you were born, there are three major religions that rule: Judaism, Christianity and Islam. Since these three religions were founded, people have been killing each other in the name of their prophet.

Judaism teaches that a nation shall not lift a sword or a spear against another nation; neither shall a nation teach war. So peace is the main teaching of their holy book. Their holy book even speaks against the idea of revenge. The Jewish nation, however, is surrounded by Muslims who want to fight them in the name of their prophet. So according to the Torah, which is the Jewish holy book, for the Jewish nation to survive, it then has the right to go to war to defend itself.

Christianity also teaches nonviolence. Jesus told his followers, "Blessed are the peacemakers, for they shall be called the children of God." On another occasion, he told his followers to "turn the other cheek." But Christianity itself went through three major religious wars in the name of Jesus. Politics played a big role in convincing the people to fight in the name of Jesus. Most Christians these days believe that it is shameful to start a war, but if it is unavoidable, then it must be fought under certain rules and conditions.

Islam, itself, means to give in. This religion was taught through a prophet called Mohammed. In Islam, a Muslim's obligation is to give himself to God's needs. They believe in jihad, which means to try hard in the way of God. Islam is a nonviolent religion, but some holy men preach that Allah, which means God, dictated rules for human beings to follow on this Earth and if they disobey these rules, they deserve to be killed.

Differences in religion can cause arguments even between very close friends. Since a human is born, he is programmed by his parents and by his society to follow and believe certain religious ideas. It is very, very hard to change this human to make him believe something different from what he has been programmed to believe. It does not matter what part of the world a human resides in. Humans are taught, through the holy books they follow, that faith in God is something that humans need to work on all the time. They are taught that a human's main job is to work hard and strive to gain the love of his God, in the way his religion dictates.

There are some humans that do not accept what their holy men are teaching, and they begin to question their religion. They start to look for different ways to satisfy their spiritual needs, which leads them to create their own beliefs. These beliefs arise from their own opinions and experiences rather than the interpretation of God by a religion or religious leader. These are the humans that start on a journey to find themselves, instead of believing blindly in what someone else is telling them. This does not mean that they will have to completely give up their religion to find satisfaction. It only means that their relationship with all their beliefs – and their understanding of their beliefs – will start to change, if they choose to keep their religion or not.

During self–hypnosis I saw one of my past lives where I died by a natural disaster. Can you explain the importance of this experience for me?

What you saw in hypnosis the other day, where you died in a tsunami, was something I was waiting for you to ask me about. You were ten years old, living with your family in a village in Indonesia. You were a kid, playing outside in front of a straw hut a few miles away from the sea. It was a few hours before noon – the sun was not high in the sky yet. Suddenly a roaring, loud noise was heard. You looked toward the sea and saw from far away a huge black wall standing high in the sea, approaching the shore. It was an enormous wave coming toward land. A very loud, terrifying noise was getting closer; every second the noise was getting louder and louder. Humans were screaming and yelling from fear, running inland toward higher ground – and you were one of these humans who were running, not knowing where to go.

All the humans were terrified and panicked. They were running right and left, bumping into each other; some losing their balance and falling down. Some of them got up again and ran for their life. Some were overpowered by their fear and could not get back up, so they stayed down and gave up. The noise was loud – very loud – as you heard the water reaching land. You heard the rush of the water breaking trees and swallowing up all the huts. You heard water moving and rushing, carrying large debris with it. You heard humans screaming and yelling for help. Suddenly, the screaming stopped...then you heard sounds of pain and agony, and a great panic took over. It was a matter of seconds before the panic stopped. Many, many humans vanished with the speed of the water that hit the area.

While you were running to higher ground, you found a hut that was made of wood and straw and you followed the other humans who went in for shelter. The hut filled with humans and there was no more space left. You felt like you were all squished together like sardines in a can. It became very dark in the hut, and you could hear screams of horror; humans panicking and pleading for help. Then suddenly, there was no more yelling. All you could hear was silence. You felt heavy pressure on your chest, and you felt very weak. There was no more air to breathe. You felt a very hot, sharp, tingling feeling all over your body. You touched your body, and your skin was peeling off very easily. You realized that you were drowning and burning at the same time. This lasted for a minute before you gave up.

While you were in hypnosis, you saw your soul embracing the other souls of the humans that were in the hut. You saw all the silver cords dangling and hooked together because the room was so crowded. You saw the silver cords beginning to fade very quickly because all of their human bodies melted — nothing was left of them anymore. Then you saw souls floating all over; some searching for the melted bodies they had been attached to. Some bodies had not completely melted so you saw their souls next to them. Other souls were floating above the water, over the spot where the body had drowned.

I am happy that you did not panic after all that you saw during your hypnosis. Instead, you experienced everything as if you were seeing a movie. You now know that you have been here on Earth many times before, and you are here now; and you know that you will be back again and again. Now hear me well. Open your ears and listen carefully to what I am going to tell you. Knowing all of this should make you understand that in this life, if you worry about anything, if it is something silly or something that you think is serious, you are gaining nothing and going nowhere. You will only cause yourself confusion and sadness that will conquer your life, and stop you from finishing your healing journey. Humans will come to you for help who have lived through similar events to the ones you just experienced, maybe worse. You cannot be their human angel if you do not live in your higher self.

A human lives in a God–centered space, where God is within him. When he discovers that space, it is like a personal connection that a human has with God himself. When he finds his high self – which is the God within him – and as long as he accepts himself, he will not care anymore if other humans accept him or not, if they agree with him or not. I say this to you because you might face resistance from humans who do not understand your kind of help. Your help will not include pity; it will be all about helping a human to see and feel the power that is within him; and to find peace by understanding the cycle of life, the basis of human existence, and the great happiness of following their heart. You will help humans reach this stage and to stay in that peace always. You will help them to never accept or believe that there is any other tool to keep them happy and peaceful. If a human tricks himself not to accept this way, he will be confused and lost until the end of his life. Think of what I am telling you. Make it a rule that you follow and finish your life accordingly. When you do this, no worry whatsoever will bother you or conquer your thoughts and your feelings and this will make you a rock of hope and faith for others to learn from.

You have found the God that is within you; now do your best to keep yourself there, and to always stay connected. Again, I know that for now, with all that you have seen and gone through so far in this life, and all the lives that you have lived as a human, you believe that your being on this Earth is just a visit. You know that you are here to finish what your soul has planned, again. You also know that when you leave, you will come back to do more and more. The best rule to follow is to never look at what was; always look at what is. It does not matter what yesterday brought, or what tomorrow will bring; because yesterday is gone and tomorrow might never come.

My mom is having a heart problem and she has to have surgery to replace two arteries and a valve. Should we convince her to go through it so that she can live longer, or shall we let her make the decision herself without any interference from us?

We know that your mom is in her early eighties and she just had a heart attack. According to her doctors, she needs arteries and a heart valve changed to keep her alive, and you are wondering how you can help her. First, let me tell you a few very important things to help you understand. Your mom is a strong woman. She has great power that lets her know how she could control herself and her future very easily.

Believe me when I tell you, deep inside, she knows and believes that her end is near. She has her beliefs, and she prays every day to the god that she has always believed in, according to the teachings that she was raised with. She believes that her god will take care of her when she dies. There is nothing wrong with that. You should not think that she is wrong if she does not believe what you believe. There is no right or wrong. She is happy with her faith and she is not going to change now.

Your mom's soul has been leading her and taking care of her all her life and she always lived according to what her soul planned for her. She went through many good and many bad experiences, not knowing or understanding why things happened the way they did. She laughed and cried; she felt joy and sorrow; and now she knows and believes that the end of her trip is getting closer. She is very confused, like every other human that does not know where they are going after they die. She is scared and wants to know what is going to happen to her. Is she going to die now and end her suffering, or will she stay for a while longer and suffer a little longer?

Your family members talked to her, each one in their own way, trying to help her be at peace. They all told her basically the same thing. All she said was that she is leaving her burden in the hands of God and the only thing that worries her is pain and suffering. She is thinking, deep inside, that she does not want to go through the surgery. She would rather die, but she is also very scared of death.

When you spoke to her, you mostly used words that were familiar to her; you told her that there is life after death in heaven. You tried to explain to her a little bit about reincarnation but she refused to hear what you were saying; only because since she opened her eyes to this life, she has been taught that there is God and there is heaven and hell. She was told that after she dies, she will go to heaven and be with God as long as she was a good human being. She believes that when she goes to heaven, she will be reunited with your dad, where together they will have a new life with no sorrow or pain. Do not try to change what she believes in. It's too late now. All you have to do now is agree with everything that she says. Do not make it any harder on her than it already is. When she is ready to leave, do not force her to stay one minute longer than she wants to. Trying to keep her longer than her soul desires to stay will not hurt the soul, but it will confuse your mother. So I am telling you, when she is ready to go, do not try to convince her any other way. If you do, it will be only for your own satisfaction. You can help her by sharing your wisdom and knowledge with her on her terms, only to help you not judge yourself for not trying enough. Keep in mind that whatever is meant to be is going to be – no human can change the way the soul has planned to finish the journey.

Are you telling me to convince her not to do the surgery and tell her that it is o.k. to die?

I am not saying anything close to that. Listen to me with your heart and not with your ears and mind. I am saying that you and your close family are her tools for relaxation. Do whatever you can to provide her with relaxation for the rest of her life, and for a safe departure. If she refuses any procedures, do not force her to go through with them. She will know exactly when it is her time to leave this Earth. So do not try to add to, or change, anything of what her soul already planned. Comfort her without trying to change any of her beliefs. Just agree with whatever she says, and show her all the love you can.

So is she leaving now, or is she staying for a while?

I have already told you that angels are not psychics or miracle-makers. I cannot change what is planned and I cannot tell you if she is staying longer or leaving. She is the one who knows how long to stay and when to go. With all that the doctors are predicting, it is a guessing game. Just to protect themselves from being judged, they will always tell you the worst possible scenario that could happen based on their experience. If the worst – which they believe is death – does not happen, they will feel that they accomplished something by keeping her alive. What they might not be aware of is that no human knows, decides, predicts or controls when another human's time is over.

Your mom has reached the end of her journey, but that does not mean she will die today, tomorrow or the day after. It only means that she wants to go, and it is up to her soul to let go when it is ready.

Chapter 21
LIFE AFTER DEATH

I know that humans believe in heaven and hell. Can you tell me more about real life after death?

The majority of humans refuse to think of the day when the end of their life will come. A lot of them believe that humans live only once, and that after they die they will be judged, and they will either go to heaven or hell. If they believe this theory as a fact, then there is no reason for them to think differently; they will accept what they are told. Yet the same humans have a lot of questions that contradict this theory. They will always, deep inside, ask themselves questions like, where did we come from and where are we going? Humans have been asking these questions since their first day on Earth. There were no other answers for them, so they had to believe what they were told. But now, technology has proven to humans, through the exploration of the universe, that there is no physical heaven or hell; so it is a struggle for them to stay satisfied with their old beliefs.

If you think about it, you will agree that everything in this life comes in opposite pairs. Up and down, day and night, love and hate; happiness and stress, good and bad, life and death, etc. What you might not know is that all these pairs have a conversion structure. They run opposite each other and can, at a point, meet and/or switch turns. If we take life and death, we could say they are opposite of each other. But life comes to existence through humans via physical birth; death comes to be through humans via physical death. So, no human dies unless he has lived, and by conclusion, no human lives unless he has died. Life and death go together, and neither can exist without the other. If you do not live, you cannot die; if you do not die, you cannot live. This is the cycle of life.

For a human who does believe in life after death, the big question will be: who is he going to be in the next life? Is he going to be the same sex? Will he have the same family or will he come to a different one? What personality is he going to have? I tell you, the way a human runs his present life will have a big effect on what his next life is going to be. This human should know that the Conscious in a human is carried by the soul. The heart of the Conscious is the ego, and a human's personality is the heart of the human's ego. This means that the experiences that the human goes through in a life term make a difference for the other life to come. If he finishes all the experiences that his soul planned to go through in this lifetime, then the soul will come back to finish different ones. If the human gets stuck and does not finish what was planned by the soul, then his soul will come back to repeat and finish what he did not accomplish.

If a human lives his life taking care of himself, always following his heart, he will not fear what is going to happen next because he will be in his higher-self consciousness. This human will focus on his own affairs, and direct his mind to his spiritual energy. The higher the human can think of himself, the better his understanding of life will be. He will then train his Subconscious to live the way that his soul planned on. This is when the human understands the method of life and death. He runs his life on a day–to–day basis knowing that today is the most important day, until the today is done; then tomorrow will be his today.

Humans always ask about what occurs near the last part of life on Earth, only because they are aware of the pull to non–physical life. They want to finish what they came to do perfectly; and when they accomplish being in their higher self, they will be alert to the truth. But life is still very tough to deal with, and it will always distract humans from seeing the truth. Very slowly, humans can lose their interest in believing in the non–physical life. They start to get confused between this life and non–physical life that they want to know about. Then, very soon, the body starts to get old, where weakness makes it give up at the end and die, similar to an oil lantern. The first time it is lit, the light is very bright, and then, by and by, when the oil starts to reach its end, the light will fade until it dies. Remember that the last two hours of the human's life are very important. These two hours reveal to the human a summary of all the experiences that he went through in this earthly lifetime; and it is a very important part of the transition. It is when the Subconscious starts to dump all the information it collected through the years, into the Conscious.

After the physical death where the soul separates from the body, the physical body begins to decompose, and the soul will send signals to Spirit that it is ready to go back. The ego will still be attached to the emotional body but soon after it will free itself from earthly energy and needs. How long the ego takes to free itself always depends on how a human ran his life. If he lived a spiritual life, then it will take the ego a very short time to release itself. If the human lived his life full of blame and judgment, then it will take the ego longer to release itself. When the release of the ego occurs, that is when the second death happens that marks the end of the personal ego, at which time it enters a new condition of consciousness. Basically, death is when the connection between the human's personal ego and his higher–self ego ruptures, where the old thinking is no longer needed and new data replaces it. After this stage, preparation for reincarnation begins.

Humans often ask why they cannot remember their past lives. This happens because when a soul comes back to another lifetime, it has a new body with all new organs, including a new brain. This new brain does not hold the memories from an old life. It is the Conscious that holds all these memories. However, every human can see his past lives by meditating and hypnotizing himself. By doing this, he will be using the power of the Conscious that holds every past life that his soul has lived. But, there is a big difference between visiting past lives and fantasizing. A lot of humans will see things and believe that what they see is really what happened to them in earlier lives but, in fact, these could just be scenarios they created through fantasizing.

My soul mate and I went through hypnosis together, and we saw a past life we shared in Italy. Let's talk more about after–death life. I want to understand as much as I can.

This question has been asked since the beginning of life on Earth but no straight answers, based on human facts, have ever been given. There have been a lot of predictions and guesses, but unless a human can connect to his higher self and talk to the angels that are involved in his life, and to his guardian angel that is protecting him, he will not get a straight answer.

Let me make it clearer for you and your readers to understand. Since the beginning of humanity on Earth, humans have always been asking, when a human dies will he ever live again? Is there exact proof for life after death? Believers and non–believers came up with all kinds of methods to try to find an answer to these questions. Reincarnation theories became normal from generation to generation in specific cultures and communities. Many humans became comfortable with the idea of returning to Earth to live again, so they could finish what they could not finish before; or to improve the situation of their life. Others still believe that death is the final end.

For humans, there is a very fine line between belief and un–belief. But when it comes to spirituality and beliefs, a human either believes there is an afterlife, or not. Depending on their religion and beliefs, the words they use to describe the period after a body dies, whether it be afterlife, next life, passed on, etc., is a reflection of how these humans see themselves, how they see other humans; and how they relate to the god they believe in.

Usually, when a human reaches fifty years or more of life on Earth, his thinking starts to change. He starts thinking of all the experiences that he has gone through to try to reevaluate his life. He will judge every detail of his life according to his beliefs; labeling each experience as either good or bad, or even as a miracle. This is also when a human will for real start to seriously believe in an afterlife and the idea of heaven and hell. He will begin to change the way he runs his life so, according to his beliefs, he could end up in heaven when he dies. Some humans think that heaven and hell are actual places. They think that heaven is a place where every day is beautiful and sunny, with gorgeous landscapes, in a peaceful, relaxing environment. They believe that hell is a gloomy and dark place with disturbing sights and stressing scenery. Other humans think that the afterlife is a state of being where a human is always happy; where no stress, sadness, or danger exists that can affect them on the physical. Others accept the idea of reincarnation as the truth, which they believe to be a return trip to life on Earth. They believe that this trip will be repeated again and again until the human knows how to live and finish life as he is supposed to. Some believe that when they die, it will be the end, so why worry about what is next? If there is another life, then let it be.

Real confusion comes when questions are asked that cannot be answered using physical evidence. Does an afterlife really exist? Does afterlife or life after death mean the survival of physical death? Does it mean that the body will come back as it was? Will the personality come back as it exists now? Does this existence keep on coming back forever? If life after death exists for real, is there any logic or scientific proof that says so? Does the belief that death is the end, lead some humans to refuse any idea of the continued existence after death? Throughout human history, scientists and philosophers have come up with predictions and a great variety of different answers. These predictions and answers make sense to a normal human that does not know any better than to believe what he is told. He believes these answers because he does not have any way of disproving what was said. One of these scientific guesses has been that when a human dies he will never exist again. Or, after this life, a human will come back to another life but not on Earth; he will go to another place in the universe where there is no suffering. Another answer says that when a human dies, the body and everything he was made of also dies but his memory lives on. Others guessed that a human will come back with another body, but it will be a duplicate of his present body, either in shape or personality.

The troubling part for humans is finding proof that an afterlife exists. The existence of an afterlife cannot be proven scientifically, and it cannot be proven logically or practically either. Even if a human hears of a theory that he might consider to be logical or practical to prove the existence of an afterlife, it will be true only for that human, coming from his own point of view. Logical and/or practical do not equal real... but... they also do not equal un–real!

Usually, it is the experience and belief of humanity that miracles and experiences always occur before death, but some humans might challenge their mind to think beyond this belief. You see, logically and practically speaking, a human might convince himself to believe, because there is no reason *not* to believe. Do you see the beauty in this? There is no reverse proof either! A human cannot prove that it is for real, and he cannot prove that it is not for real. So as a comforting, hopeful thought with no evidence to support it or deny it, the human will choose to believe. This is the same as humans believing in God or not believing in God. There is no scientific, logical or practical proof that God exists. It is a human's belief that makes God exist in his life. On this Earth, belief in something that exists outside of a method cannot be disproved by observing the physical performance of the method.

Let me give you an example that will be easily understood. Go back and think of Source. The soul, which is part of Source, needs to experience. It needs to grab as much knowledge as it can. The soul comes to Earth where it finds a womb, and it starts working on creating a shell to grow in it. Just think about the way a ship is built. First, the plan for building the ship is created. When it starts to be built, it starts as wood on dry land – a ship is never built in the middle of the ocean. Then, the ship will float for years and years doing its job but, one day, that ship will have to be retired. It will have finished its mission and a new one will be built to replace the old one, to satisfy the job and needs of whatever source planned for its existence in the first place. This theory is exactly how the soul uses a human body to exist through and experience. First, it creates the plan. Then it builds that body on a solid base. It uses that body to finish all the experiences it needs to go through and when the body cannot function according to the plan, the soul will drop it, and it will start planning on building another one.

The soul needs to experience – the physical body is the experiencing tool. The soul does not care too much about the shape of its shell as long as it will serve its needs. Color and sex do not matter, except to satisfy the soul's desire for knowledge. The soul will find itself a shell to help it in whatever its experiences are meant to be, but when it creates itself in a shell or body it wants that body to be the best that it could be, for the purpose of satisfying the experience that was planned. Now pay attention. This does not mean that the body has to always be healthy. It means that the body has to satisfy the experience. Sometimes this does not work out as the soul desired. The soul will then use that body as much as it can, then it will drop it and build another one to finish with. I assure you and your readers that this is the process of life, which means that life after death exists.

Life itself is not matter – it cannot be seen – but the organs of the body need Life to function. The soul cannot be seen, but it also needs Life to function. The organs die when Life leaves them – but the soul does not die when the organs or the body die. Life will leave the body but not the soul, and when the soul is ready to reside in a new body, Life will reside again in that new body using new organs. Because the soul does not have parts – it cannot decay. You can cut out body parts into organs and organs into cells; and all these parts will decompose in time; but you cannot cut out a part of a soul. So Life exists, and it will repeat itself again and again in a different human each time, using the same Conscious with a new Subconscious, with each different body every time.

I tell you, your soul and your soul mate's soul have changed shells many times, and your souls always find each other in different lifetimes, to fulfill the plans that were chosen for you. You have a very beautiful job to do together in this lifetime. Your soul mate is improving her communication with us all the time, which is going to be a great help in the mission. Now she is capable of communicating and hearing us better than before – she is doing great. Believe me when I tell you, both of you are going to do miracles in this life. Stay bonded and always be a team. You both have gone through many challenges and tough experiences so far; and believe me when I tell you this life is not the end of your souls' journeys.

EPILOGUE

My hope is that those who read this book will take from it what is needed for them to open their eyes, to make them understand the reason for their being on Earth, and what their next step will be when they leave this life.

Every person goes through many, many experiences in a lifetime. Whoever understands the meaning of this book will know that in this life there is actually nothing that is in fact good or bad. Good and bad alike are simply experiences that were planned by the soul to experience in a life term, which have been labeled and judged by humanity. When a person believes this, then every experience that he goes through will be acted upon from the heart. He will have deep faith that this is what is meant to be, and his goal will be to live all of his experiences in peace.

I hope that by now every reader understands and believes that a human life starts with a cry from the womb and ends with a smile at the tomb —without fear of the unknown… because now it is known. Always follow your heart to finish the beautiful journey you are living, so it can be finished as it was planned by your soul.

Printed in the United States
by Baker & Taylor Publisher Services